Reference only not to be taken out of the library

CHILDREN'S CONCISE NATURE ENCYCLOPEDIA

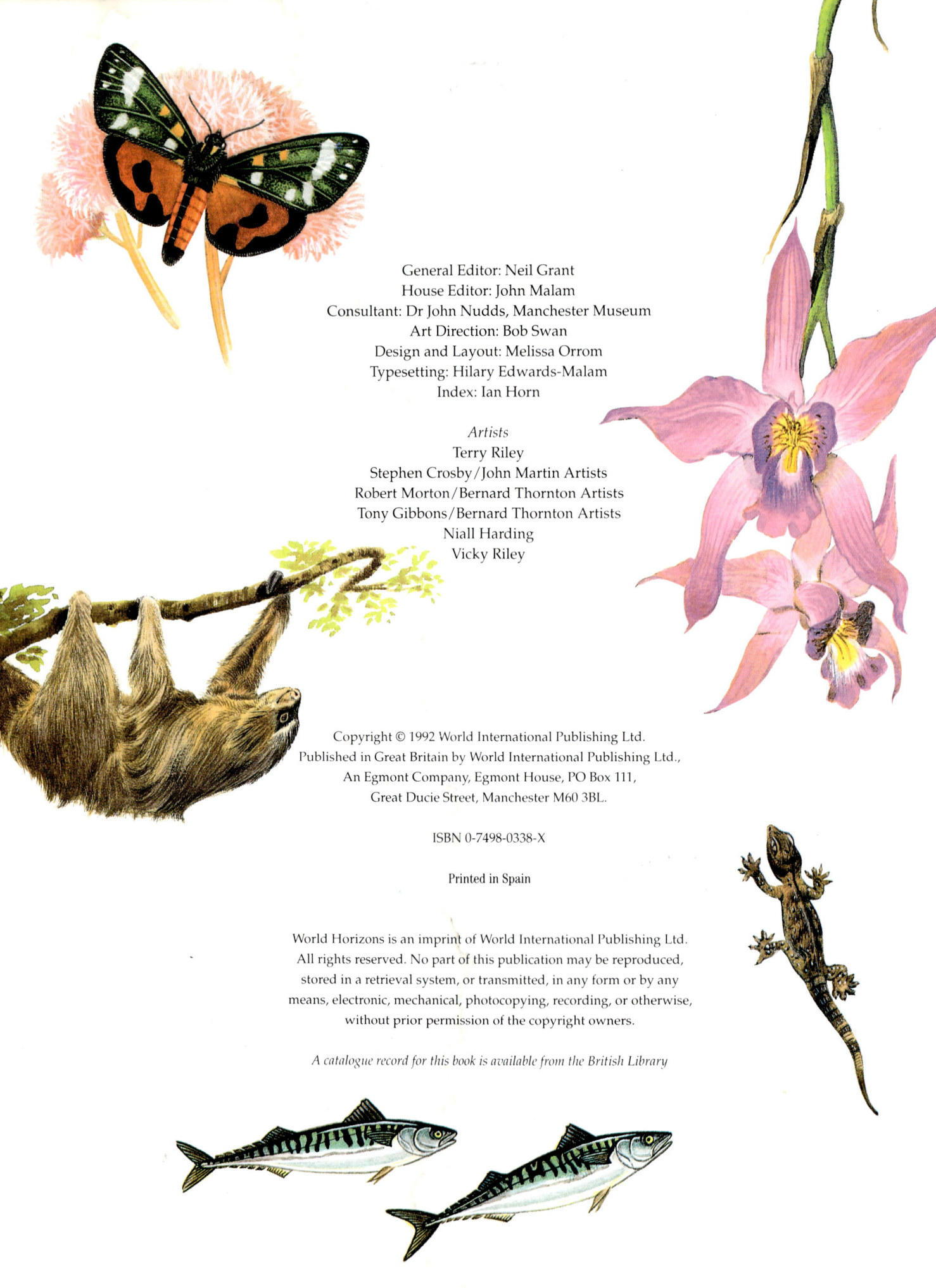

General Editor: Neil Grant
House Editor: John Malam
Consultant: Dr John Nudds, Manchester Museum
Art Direction: Bob Swan
Design and Layout: Melissa Orrom
Typesetting: Hilary Edwards-Malam
Index: Ian Horn

Artists
Terry Riley
Stephen Crosby/John Martin Artists
Robert Morton/Bernard Thornton Artists
Tony Gibbons/Bernard Thornton Artists
Niall Harding
Vicky Riley

Copyright © 1992 World International Publishing Ltd.
Published in Great Britain by World International Publishing Ltd.,
An Egmont Company, Egmont House, PO Box 111,
Great Ducie Street, Manchester M60 3BL.

ISBN 0-7498-0338-X

Printed in Spain

World Horizons is an imprint of World International Publishing Ltd.
All rights reserved. No part of this publication may be reproduced,
stored in a retrieval system, or transmitted, in any form or by any
means, electronic, mechanical, photocopying, recording, or otherwise,
without prior permission of the copyright owners.

A catalogue record for this book is available from the British Library

World
HORIZONS

CHILDREN'S CONCISE NATURE ENCYCLOPEDIA

MARK LAMBERT

Contents

Introduction — 6

Simple Life

What is Life? — 8
Cells and Life — 10
Many-Celled Life — 12
Fungi — 14
References — 16

Animals Without Backbones

Corals and Jellyfish — 18
The Many Kinds of Worm — 20
Animals with Shells — 22
Animals with Outer Skeletons — 24
The World of Insects — 26
Scorpions and Spiders — 30
Spiny-Skinned Animals — 32
References — 34

Animals With Backbones

Sea Squirts, Lancelets and Lampreys — 36
Sharks and Rays — 38
Bony Fishes — 40
Amphibians — 42
Reptiles — 44
Birds — 46
Mammals — 50
Monotremes and Marsupials — 52
Hedgehogs, Moles and Vampires — 54
Primates — 56
Rodents and Rabbits — 58
Aardvarks and Elephants — 60
Hooved Mammals — 62
Carnivores — 64
Sea Cows, Whales and Dolphins — 66
References — 68

The Plant Kingdom

Algae — 70
Mosses and Liverworts — 72
Ferns — 74
Seeds in Cones — 76
Flowering Plants — 78
Pollination — 80
Fruits and Seeds — 82
References — 84

Prehistoric Life

Fossils	86
Evolution	88
Ancient Life	90
The Age of Reptiles	92
The Age of Mammals	94
References	96

Survival

Food and Energy	98
Movement and Senses	102
Attack and Defence	108
Partnerships	112
Migration	116
References	118

Ecology and the Environment

Biomes and Ecosystems	120
Geographical Distribution	122
Polar Life	124
Tundra and Mountains	126
Coniferous Forest	128
Deciduous Woodland	130
Grasslands	132
Deserts	134
Tropical Rainforest	136
Life in Freshwater	138
Oceans	140
Islands	142
Life on the Seashore	144
Wildlife in Towns and Gardens	146
References	148

Wildlife in the Future

Nature and Human Beings	150
Conservation	154
References	156

Index	157

Introduction

The natural world is a vital part of all our lives. We ourselves are just one of the many species of animal that inhabit the Earth, and every day our very existence depends on a range of other living organisms. We live our lives surrounded by millions of tiny bacteria. We eat other animals and plants, all of which have natural origins. And wherever we live, in cities or towns, amidst farmland or in wild remote places, we coexist with many other different species. Without these animals and plants our planet would be a barren place, impossible for us to live on. So it is vitally important that we understand the natural world that surrounds us. If we understand it, we can take steps to protect it when it is threatened.

In order to help us understand the natural world scientists have, over many years, developed a system of classifying living organisms into groups. At the bottom of the scale, each individual type of animal or plant is known as a species; members of the same species can breed with each other, but generally cannot breed successfully with members of another species. Different but similar species are grouped together in a genus and each species is given a two-part scientific name which is in Latin. The first part describes the genus, the second describes the species.

The human species, for example, is known as *Homo sapiens*; that is, we form the species *sapiens* ('wise') that belongs to the genus *Homo* ('man'). In our case we are the only living species that belongs to this genus. Other genera (the plural of genus) may include two or more species; for example the genus *Panthera* includes *Panthera leo* (lion), *Panthera tigris* (tiger), *Panthera pardus* (leopard) and *Panthera onca* (jaguar).

The modern system of classification groups genera together in families. Several families form an order and orders are grouped into a class. A number of animal classes together make up a phylum, whereas plant classes are grouped together in divisions. At the upper end of the classification system animal phyla and plant divisions form the animal and plant kingdoms.

This encyclopedia begins by looking at living organisms group by group, which is the easiest way of describing what kinds of creatures and plants exist. However, organisms do not exist by themselves. They live in communities, both large and small, in which their relationships with each other are very important. Thus, in addition, there is a section that describes the world's wide variety of plant and animal communities.

Another section looks at what kinds of creatures have existed in the past and how the animals and plants of today have evolved from prehistoric organisms. Yet another section looks at the ways in which plants and animals ensure their survival in a highly competitive and sometimes hostile world. Finally, the natural world is under threat, largely due to the activities of we humans. The last section of this encyclopedia takes a look at how human beings affect nature and how we can help to conserve rather than destroy it.

Simple Life

SIMPLE LIFE

What is Life?

A tree or a cat is obviously very different from a rock or a piece of plastic. But what is it that makes living things different from non-living things? It is, in fact, very easy to tell them apart. All living things have seven characteristics that distinguish them from all non-living objects. These are feeding, growth, respiration, excretion, movement, sensitivity and reproduction.

The seven characteristics of living things
Feeding is simply the process of taking in materials from the outside. Food is needed for energy and in growth – the formation of new body tissues. Energy is obtained from food materials during the process known as respiration, in which oxygen is used to help break down the food chemicals. This and other chemical processes that go on inside a living organism inevitably produce waste materials, which are got rid of by processes known collectively as excretion.

Animals move in order to find or gather food, and a limited amount of movement can also be seen in most plants. Similarly, animals have senses and nervous systems that enable them to find their way about and detect their food. Plants, too, show a certain amount of sensitivity.

However, the most important characteristic of living things is reproduction. Every organism tries to perpetuate itself by producing offspring. All the other characteristics of living things aim to make this possible.

WHAT IS LIFE? 9

The origins of life

The living organisms in the world today have evolved over a long period of time. The first living things on Earth probably developed from chemicals present in the warm, mineral-rich seas that existed some 3,500 million years ago. These chemicals may themselves have developed on Earth. But there is also some evidence that certain vital chemicals may have been brought in by meteorites.

Scientists believe that the molecules of these chemicals began to join up to form larger molecules. In this way molecules of DNA, the hereditary chemical in every living organism, appeared. Other chemicals formed membranes, which became wrapped around molecules of DNA, and thus the first living cells were formed.

The first living organisms were probably bacteria of a type that survived without the need for oxygen. They, in turn, probably gave rise to bacteria that acquired the ability to make their own food, using the vital food-making process we know as photosynthesis. These organisms began producing oxygen and as the amount of oxygen in the atmosphere increased, other animals and plants began to appear.

The first plants were of a type known as blue-green algae. The first animals were probably very similar to the tiny, single-celled creatures of today that we know as protozoans.

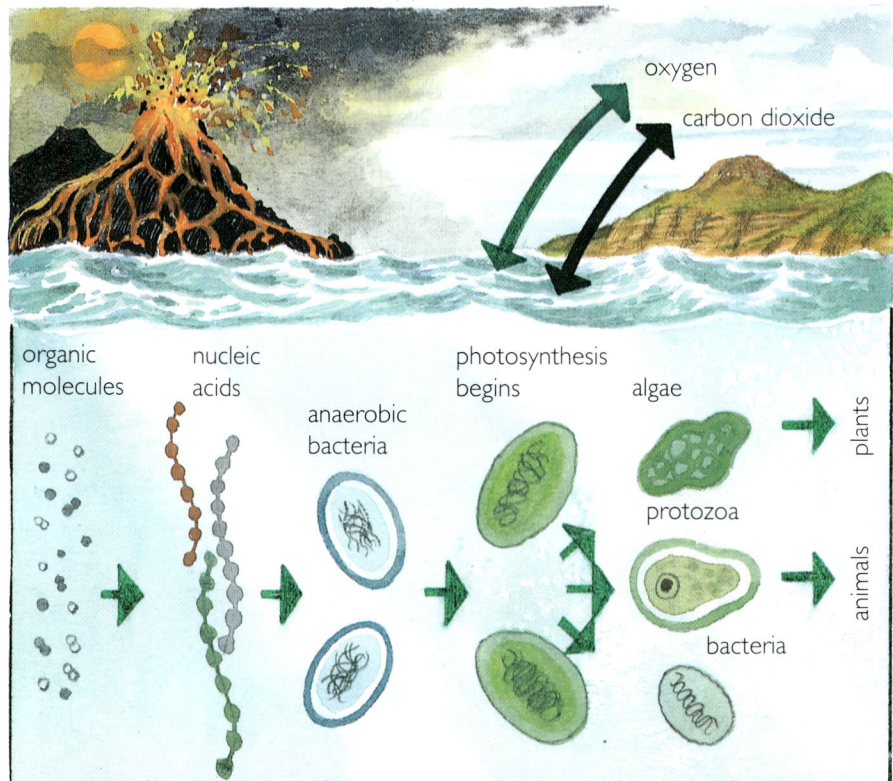

Life on Earth began in the sea. Over millions of years chemicals evolved into cells – the basic units of life. When cells acquired the ability to make food by photosynthesis, the way was opened for the evolution of plants and animals.

THE EARLIEST EVIDENCE OF LIFE

Over a very long time, a colony of blue-green algae produces a mound of calcium carbonate, laid down in layers, which is called a stromatolite. Rocks at Warrawoona in Australia contain fossil stromatolites that are about 3,500 million years old. That is close to the time when, scientists believe, life on Earth began, and these fossils are the earliest evidence of life on our planet that has been found so far.

layers inside a stromatolite

stromatolites in Australia

Cells and Life

> The body of nearly every living organism is composed of one or more units called cells. Each cell has its own special function, but its activities are often co-ordinated with the cells around it.

What is a cell?

A cell consists of a membrane surrounding a jelly-like material known as cytoplasm. Inside the cytoplasm lie a number of small organelles that carry out the work of the cell. The most important is the nucleus. It contains coded genetic instructions, in the form of the chemical DNA, (deoxyribonucleic acid) which control what happens in the cell.

Other important organelles are the mitochondria. These are the cell's power houses, where energy is produced from food materials. Another structure, known as the endoplasmic reticulum, is used as a site for manufacturing proteins, chemicals vital for growth. Plant cells contain green chloroplasts, where photosynthesis occurs. Around the cell membrane is a stiff wall made of cellulose.

This drawing shows the structure of an animal cell. The nucleus controls the activities of all the other organelles.

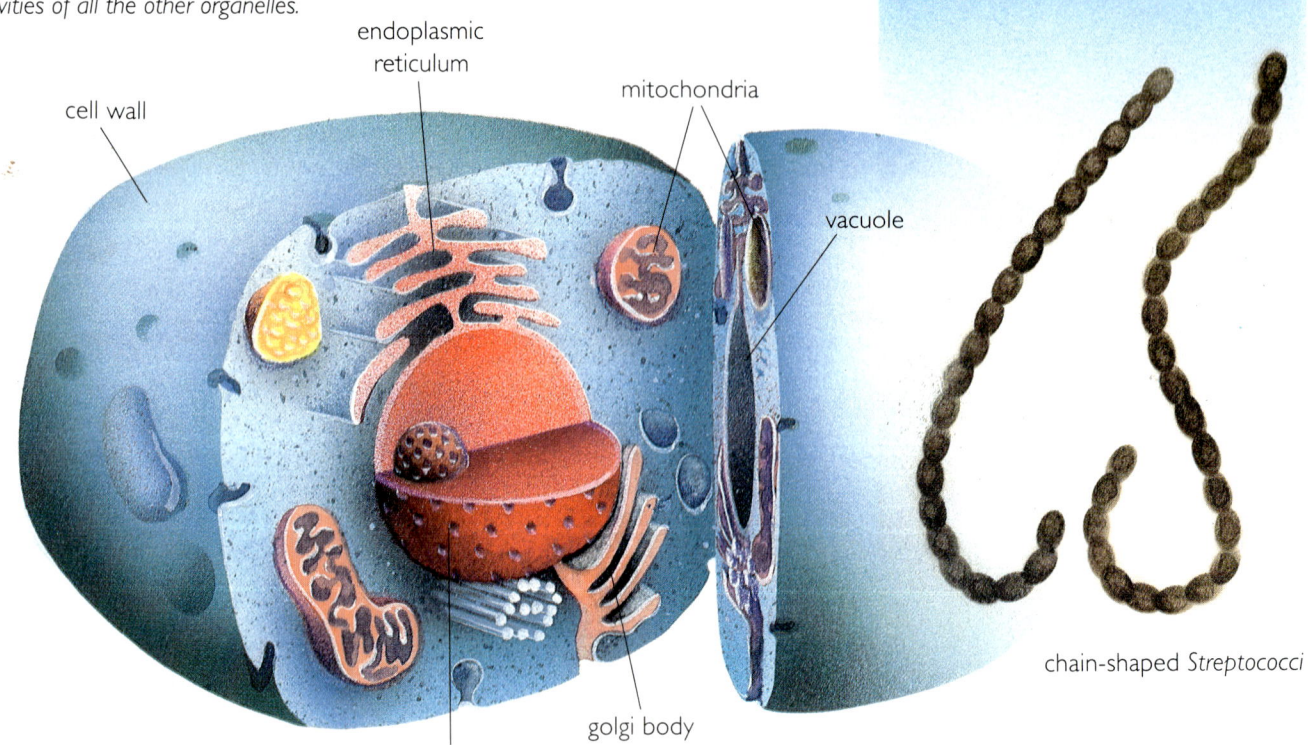

Different kinds of bacteria can be recognized by their shape.

CELLS AND LIFE

Single-celled life

The simplest organisms are those that consist of single cells, and the simplest of these are bacteria. These organisms vary in shape: they may be round, rod-shaped, comma-shaped or twisted into a spiral, and some kinds have their cells arranged in pairs or chains. The nucleus of a bacterium is poorly defined; sometimes there appear to be several nuclei.

Some bacteria cause diseases, such as typhoid fever and cholera. Others are harmless and play a vital role in breaking down dead plant and animal material.

The organisms most closely related to bacteria are the blue-green algae. Their cells have no nuclei at all. The walls contain chemicals like those in the cell walls of bacteria but, like other plants, the cell walls contain cellulose and the cells contain chlorophyll, the green pigment that enables them to carry out photosynthesis.

The class Protozoa contains a variety of single-celled animals.

Single-celled animals are all grouped together in the class Protozoa (first animals). They include the shapeless amoebas, which appear to move by flowing along. Other protozoans have tiny, hair-like cilia, which can be used to row the animal along, or to create water currents in order to gather food. Yet others have long, whip-like flagella to propel them. Radiolarians and foraminiferans have tiny, elaborately constructed shells. Sporozoans (spore-producing protozoans) cause diseases; the parasite that causes malaria is an example.

Actinosphaerium eichorni

Paramecium

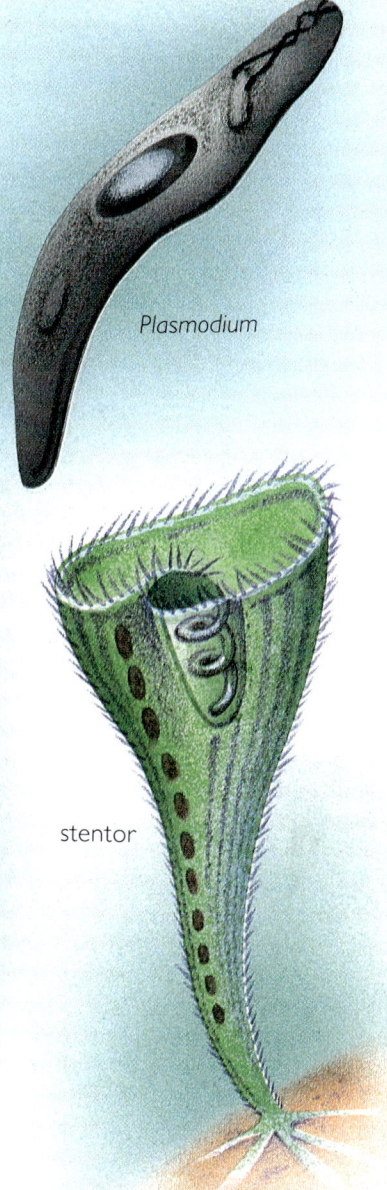

Plasmodium

stentor

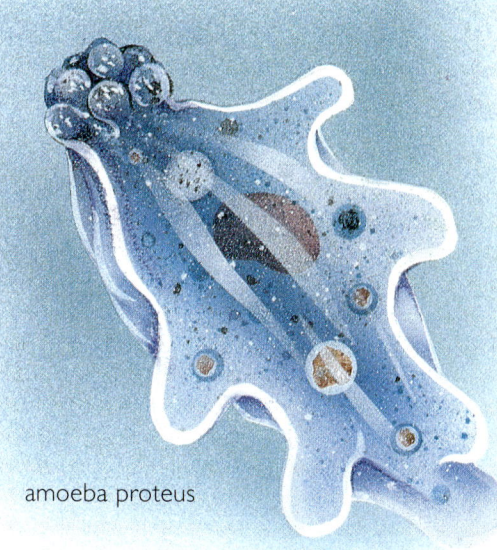

amoeba proteus

FORAMINIFERANOUS MUD

Foraminiferans are single-celled sea animals with shells (often many-chambered) made of calcite (calcium carbonate). Most foraminiferans live on the sea-bed, but some, such as *Globigerina*, float near the surface. *Globigerina* is the most common foraminiferan. Its discarded shells sink to the bottom, where they form a thick mud known as *Globigerina* ooze. About one-third of the ocean floor is covered with this ooze.

Many-Celled Life

> Most living organisms consist of more than one cell. Many have huge numbers of cells, which all work together in a carefully controlled way. But the simplest many-celled organisms contain only a small number of cells that work more or less independently of each other.

Colonies of cells

One of the organisms commonly found in ponds is a single-celled plant known as *Chlamydomonas*, an oval-shaped organism that uses two flagella to propel it through the water. The relatives of *Chlamydomonas* have similar cells, but arranged in small colonies. Within these colonies the cells work together to a limited extent, but they also have a great deal of independence.

Members of this group show a gradual increase in size and complexity. *Pandorina* has 4, 16 or 32 cells arranged in a small round ball and held together by a sticky material called mucilage. *Eudorina* has 16, 32 or 64 cells arranged in a hollow ball. The largest member of this group is *Volvox*, which may have up to 50,000 cells.

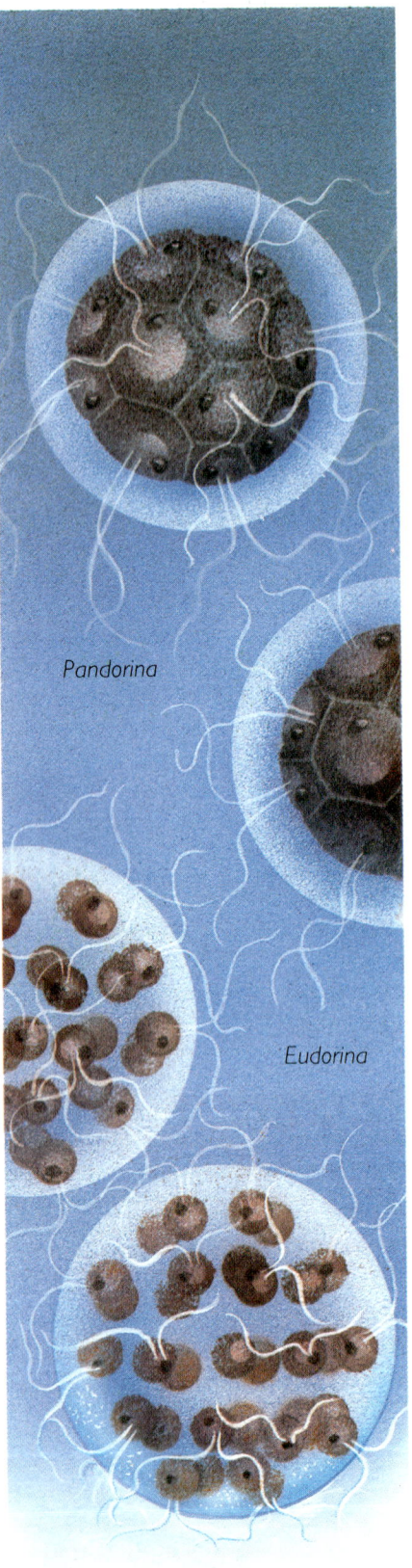

The alga Chlamydomonas *(left) and its relatives show how some early many-celled organisms may have evolved.* Pandorina *and* Eudorina *(above) consist of small balls of* Chlamydomonas*-like cells.* Volvox *colonies (far left) contain thousands of cells.*

MANY-CELLED LIFE 13

Many-celled animals

In other many-celled algae the cells are much more dependent on each other. Such plants have bodies that range from long threads, or filaments, to tubes and sheets of tissue two or more cells thick. Many-celled animals, on the other hand, are more complex and contain more than one type of cell. For example, the tiny, worm-like mesozoans, which form the simplest group, have bodies made up of at least three kinds of cell.

The sponges form the next simplest group of animals. In a sponge the cells still work in a more or less unco-ordinated way, but some cells have specialized tasks.

Collar cells (choanocytes), for example, are equipped with flagella. Groups of collar cells create water currents, which flow through channels in the sponge's body, and capture the food particles in the water. Flat cells called pinacocytes line the channels and form the outer layer of the sponge. Wandering cells called archaeocytes move through the body of the sponge, laying down the material that forms the sponge's skeleton.

Sponges vary a great deal in shape. Some species are formless mats that cling to, or encrust, rocks. Water is drawn in through many tiny pores and passes out through larger, chimney-like openings known as oscula. Some sponges have just one osculum at the end of a tube-like body. Sponges have an internal skeleton of lime and silica.

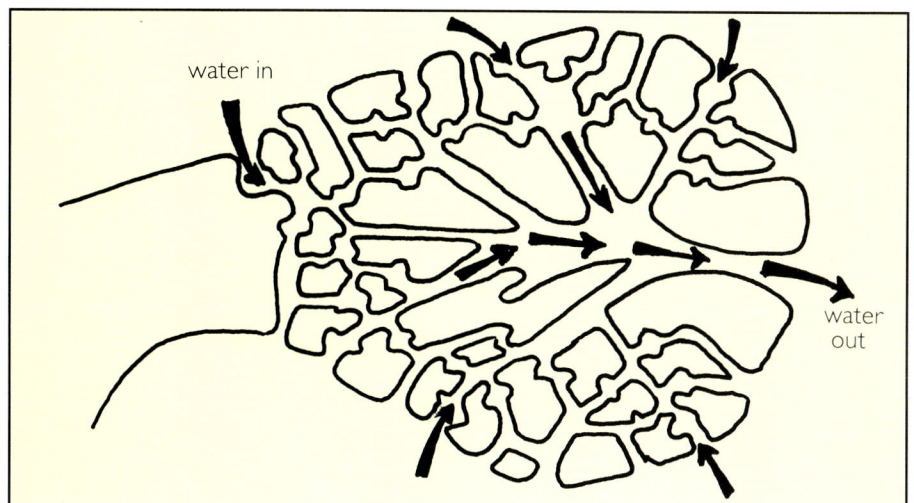

Above: Inside a sponge water currents flow through channels, bringing food and oxygen to the cells. The water is drawn in through a number of incurrent openings, and flows out via a smaller number of excurrent openings.

Although sponges are among the simplest many-celled animals, there is an enormous variety of form and size. Some form thin mats; others look like fingers, branching trees, flasks or goblets.

Fungi

Fungi are an unusual group of organisms. They are often classified as plants, mainly because they are certainly not animals! However, they are not really plants either; their cell walls are not made of cellulose and their cells never contain chlorophyll. Unlike plants, therefore, they cannot manufacture their own food by photosynthesis and must obtain it from other sources. Many are parasites that feed on living organisms. Others break down organic material; they can often be found growing on decaying foods, such as stale bread or rotting fruit.

Some scientists classify fungi in a third, completely separate kingdom, known as the *Protista*. Also included in this group are the bacteria, although there is no obvious relationship between fungi and bacteria. Single-celled organisms are also sometimes included.

Spore producers

The body of a fungus consists of a mass of long threads, or hyphae, that contain many nuclei. The mass of hyphae is known as the mycelium. Fungi reproduce themselves by means of spores, which are produced in a variety of ways. For example, the pin mould, *Mucor*, produces spores in tiny black containers known as sporangia, which form at the tips of long upright hyphae.

Other spore containers are even less easy to see. The mycelium of a rust is located inside the leaves of the plant that the rust has invaded. The rust gets its name from the tiny red spore containers that appear on the surface of the leaves.

Some fungi produce their spores in large, fruiting bodies. Among these are the jelly fungi, cup-fungi and puffballs. The spores of bracket fungi and toadstools are produced on gills, spines or the linings of tiny pores on the undersurface of the fruiting body.

Moulds often form on food left exposed to the air. Pin mould is so called because of the pin-shaped capsules in which the spores are formed.

Below: *Enlarged view of a spore capsule growing on bread.*

FUNGI

Many kinds of fungi produce their spores in large fruiting bodies, such as toadstools, puffballs and jelly fungi.

shaggy ink cap

common puffball

penny bun

jelly fungus

Parasites and partners

A parasitic fungus may cause much damage to its host. As the mycelium spreads through the host, it takes nutrients and damages the host's tissues. Potato blight can destroy a crop of potatoes. Downy mildews attack onions, cabbages and maize (sweetcorn). Powdery mildews attack gooseberry bushes and strawberry plants. Dutch elm disease is caused by a fungus whose spores are carried by a beetle. The honey fungus attacks fruit trees and may eventually kill them.

Some fungi, on the other hand, establish a symbiotic relationship with their hosts, which means they both benefit. Others are useful to us. Yeasts are single-celled fungi used in baking and brewing. Some species of *Penicillium* produce antibiotics; others are used in making blue cheese.

BUGS IN THE BRIE?

Cheese is made by the fermentation of milk by bacteria and fungi. One type of bacterium begins the process by making the milk curdle. Others digest fats or proteins, or make acids. Different types of cheese are made by varying the effects of the various types of bacteria that play a part. Fungi such as *Penicillium camembertii* and *P. roquefortii* are used in the ripening process of Camembert, Roquefort and other cheeses.

References

Algae A group of simple plants containing chlorophyll, which vary in size from microscopic, single-cell organisms to giant seaweeds.

Antibiotic A chemical produced by a fungal mould or other micro-organism that is poisonous to certain bacteria. Antibiotics can therefore cure some diseases caused by bacteria.

Bacteria Microscopic organisms, consisting of single cells or groups of cells. Sometimes grouped with plants, but bacteria lack chlorophyll. Some bacteria are parasites that cause disease. Others are harmless types that feed on decaying material.

Cell All living organisms are made up of one or more cells. Each cell consists basically of a cell wall or membrane that surrounds a jelly-like cytoplasm.

Cell membrane A very thin membrane (about .000001mm thick), composed mainly of fat and some protein, which surrounds a living cell.

Cellulose A chemical substance made up of carbon, hydrogen and oxygen which is the basic material of the cell walls of plants. It is made of long chains of molecules of the sugar glucose, which the plants make by photosynthesis.

Chlorophyll The green pigment in the chloroplasts of plants that enables photosynthesis to take place. It converts the energy in sunlight into chemical energy, which the plants use to build up sugars.

Chloroplasts Tiny green organelles found in some plant cells. Photosynthesis takes place inside chloroplasts, which are mostly located in the layer of cells (known as the palisade layer) that lies just below the upper epidermis, or skin, of each leaf.

Cytoplasm The jelly-like material inside a cell in which all the organelles are suspended.

DNA (Deoxyribonucleic acid) The chemical that is capable of reproducing itself and makes up the hereditary material of every living organism. A molecule of DNA consists of two spiral chains linked by two rows of bases (chemical groups). There are only four types of base, but the order in which the bases are arranged along the chain forms a code that controls the characteristics of the organism. Each characteristic is controlled by a gene, which is simply a long series of bases.

Excretion The removal from the body of unwanted or poisonous waste materials.

Fermentation The process in which certain substances, called carbohydrates, are broken down through the action of proteins called enzymes, produced by living cells. See also **Yeast**.

Gene see **DNA**.

Membrane A thin sheet of tissue, like a skin.

Meteorite A massive lump of stone or metal that reaches the Earth from outer space.

Mitochondrion A cell organelle that is the energy producer, or power plant, of the cell. A mitochondrion uses oxygen and the sugar glucose to produce chemical energy in the form of ATP (adenosine triphosphate), which can be used to power many other cell functions.

Molecule The smallest unit of a chemical substance, consisting of one or more atoms.

Nervous system A system of special nerve cells in an animal by which electrical messages are passed from one part of the body to another.

Nucleus The cell organelle that is the central controller of the cell. It usually contains DNA and sends out messages to other parts of the cell in the form of another nucleic acid known as RNA (Ribonucleic acid).

Organelle One of the tiny structures in a cell that has a specialized function.

Organism An individual living thing – plant or animal.

Parasite An animal or plant that lives wholly or partly at the expense of another, without giving anything in return.

Photosynthesis The process by which a plant makes its own food, by using the energy in sunlight and the green pigment chlorophyll to build up sugars from the simple chemicals carbon dioxide and water.

Protein A complicated chemical made up of carbon, hydrogen, oxygen and, most importantly, nitrogen. A protein is formed by long chains of chemicals known as amino acids, of which there are 21 different kinds. Proteins are needed by all organisms in order to grow.

Radiolarian A single-celled sea animal with a shell made of silica.

Reproduction The process by which new organisms are created.

Respiration The process in which oxygen is used to break down food sugars, releasing energy and carbon dioxide. The energy is in the form of ATP (see also **Mitochondrion**) and can be used to power other processes. Human beings and many other animals respire by breathing.

Senses Name given to the abilities to see, hear, smell, taste and feel.

Vertebrates Animals with backbones, including all mammals, birds, fishes, reptiles.

Yeast A single-celled fungus that, in the absence of air, obtains energy by breaking down sugar into carbon dioxide and alcohol by fermentation. This ability is used in the manufacture of alcoholic drinks. In bread-making, the carbon dioxide produced by yeast in the dough causes the dough to rise (the alcohol evaporates away during baking).

Animals Without Backbones

Animals Without Backbones

Corals and Jellyfish

Corals, jellyfish and sea anemones belong to a many-celled animal group known as the coelenterates, or cnidarians. This name comes from the fact that every member of this group has a single space, or coelenteron, inside its body. An opening, the mouth, leads from the coelenteron to the outside.

Two-layered animals

The body of a coelenterate is made up of two main layers of cells. These are separated by a third layer, usually much thinner than the other two, which consists of a network of nerve cells embedded in a jelly-like material. The coelenteron forms the gut – the region where food is digested (broken down into simple chemicals). In many cases the mouth is surrounded by tentacles used for collecting food. The tentacles are equipped with special stinging cells for capturing small animals.

A typical coelenterate has two main stages in its life-cycle. However, one stage is usually more obvious than the other (in some cases there is only one stage). An adult jellyfish, for example, with its jelly-like bag above a ring of hanging tentacles, is the medusa stage of the animal's life-cycle. The eggs produced by this stage do not develop directly into another medusa. Instead they develop into a tube-shaped polyp, which in turn produces new medusae. At the opposite extreme are the sea anemones. These spend all their lives as polyps; there is no medusa stage. Hydras also lack a medusa stage, although their close relatives, the sea firs, do have one.

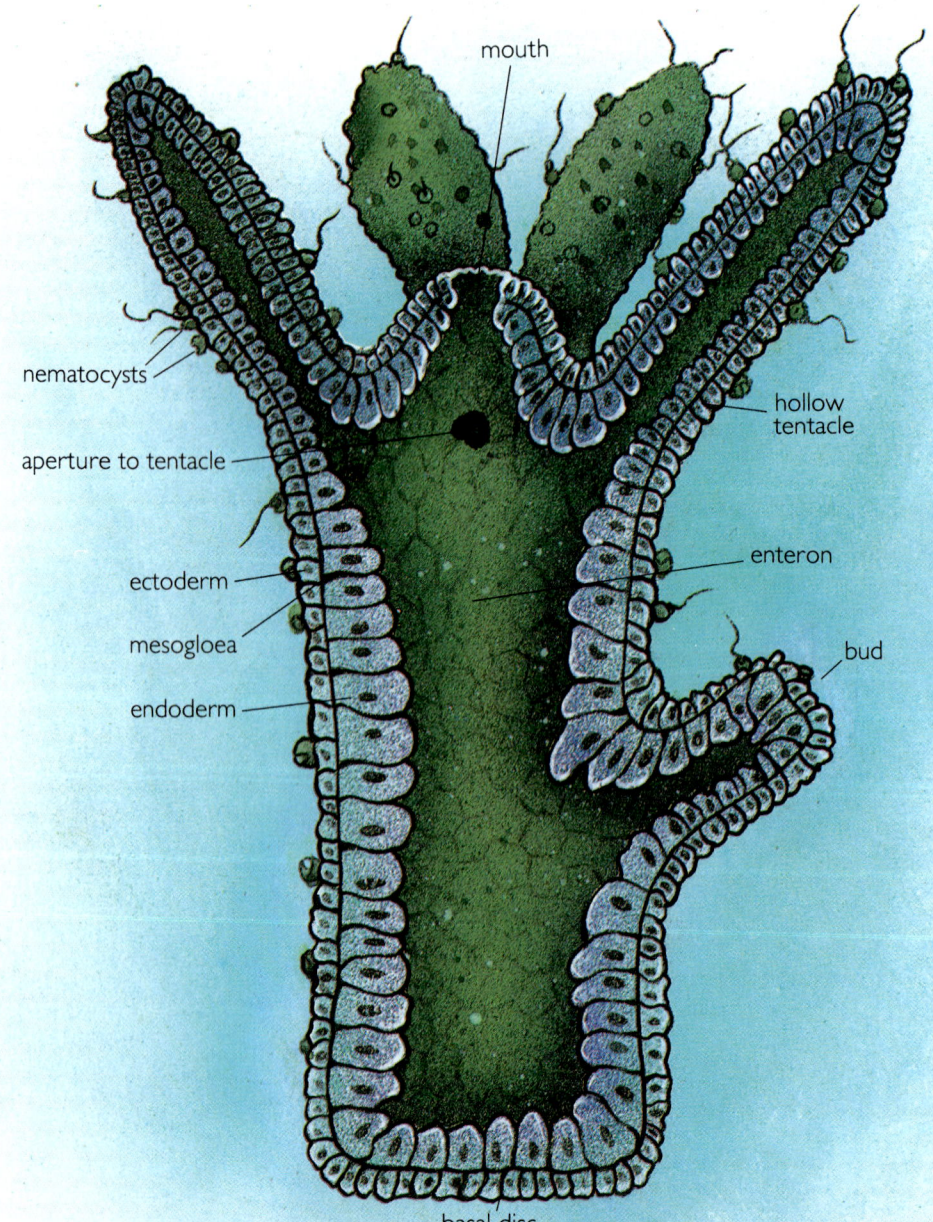

A sea anemone, such as this beadlet, is a single large polyp. There is no medusa stage.

Hydra is a typical example of a polyp-type coelenterate. It can reproduce by budding off daughters from the side of its body.

CORALS AND JELLYFISH

Portuguese man-o'-war

Colonies of polyps

Coelenterates such as sea anemones, hydras and jellyfish are solitary animals. Many others, however, live in colonies. A sea fir consists of a branched colony of many hydra-like polyps. A Portuguese man-o'-war looks like a jellyfish, but is really a colony of polyps suspended under a floating bag of gas.

The largest colonies are formed by the corals. These are coelenterates whose polyps produce a hard, chalk-like skeleton as a support. The corals that can be bought in shops are only the skeletons that remain after the coral animals have died. In a living coral the skeleton is covered by a mass of fleshy polyps, which are often brightly coloured.

The colony begins when a single polyp settles on a rock and produces more polyps by budding. Each new polyp produces a new piece of skeleton and the colony grows rapidly. The polyps remain connected to one another and share the food that is caught by the colony.

jellyfish

A jellyfish is a coelenterate whose adult stage is a medusa. The Portuguese man-o'-war is a colony of polyps, as are the corals that form reefs. The inset drawing shows how individual polyps are interconnected so that they can share food and oxygen.

The Many Kinds of Worm

> The natural world contains many different kinds of worm-like animals, including the familiar earthworm as well as a number of unpleasant parasites.

Flatworms

Among the simplest of these animals are the flatworms which, together with the flukes and tapeworms, form the animal phylum known as the *Platyhelminthes*. Flatworms are free-living, mostly predatory (hunting) animals. Some are found in freshwater streams and ponds; others live in the sea and some land-dwellers can be found in moist, tropical environments. Flatworms are renowned for their ability to regenerate their bodies: a small piece of flatworm may grow into a complete new individual. A number of tropical flatworms are brightly coloured.

Parasitic worms

Flukes and tapeworms are parasites that need two or more hosts to complete their life-cycles. The human parasite bilharzia and the sheep liver fluke, for example, both spend part of their lives in small water snails. The human tapeworm uses the pig as its secondary host. Other tapeworms attack a number of vertebrate primary hosts, ranging from fish to mammals. Roundworms, also known as eelworms or nematode worms, belong to another phylum, the *Aschelminthes*. Some other parasites live on plants or other animals and are the cause of major human diseases, such as river blindness and elephantiasis. They are very common, largely due to the amazing rate at which they breed. A female roundworm of the type that infests human beings can lay 200,000 eggs in a day! Other roundworms are free-living. Many millions live in the soil, and in freshwater and sea muds. They feed on bacteria or on larger prey, such as other nematodes or animals known as rotifers.

Tapeworms and proboscis worms (thorny-headed worms) are parasites that live in the intestines of vertebrate animals, as are some roundworms. A tapeworm produces eggs in every segment. Ripe segments break off and eggs pass out in the animal's dung.

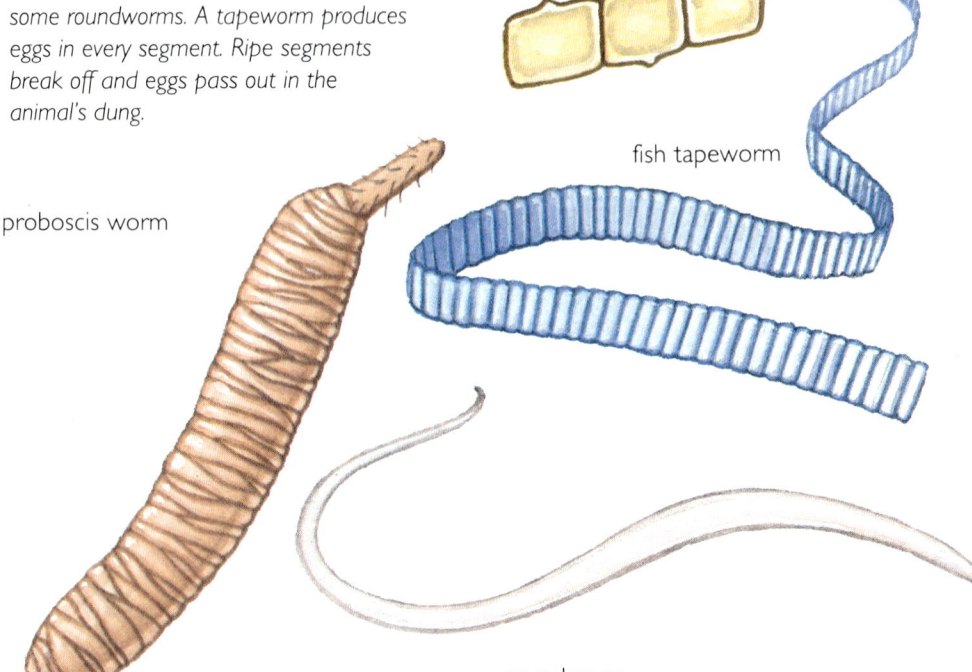

THE MANY KINDS OF WORM

Free-living worms

The most familiar kinds of worm are, of course, earthworms, of which there are over 20 different kinds in Britain alone. They are vitally important to the soil in which they live, as they assist with aeration and drainage and draw down a great deal of organic matter from the surface. There are about 7.5 million earthworms in every hectare of topsoil.

Earthworms belong to yet another phylum, the *Annelida*, which also includes a number of sea worms, such as lugworms, ragworms, bristleworms and fanworms.

The leeches also belong to this phylum. A variety of other worms belong to several smaller phyla. Among these are the horse-shoe worms, thorny-headed worms, ribbon worms, peanut worms, spoon worms, beard worms, acorn worms and arrow worms. Moss animals live in colonies that form tufts or encrust rocks. Lamp shells, or brachiopods, are enclosed in shells and look more like bivalve molluscs than worms.

common earthworm   brandling earthworm

Left: Earthworms tunnel through soil feeding on leaves and other organic material. Below: Lugworms and peanut worms live in sandy burrows. Ragworms and sea mice forage for small animals and carrion.

PARASITES OF SHEEP

The sheep liver fluke is a parasite with a complicated life-cycle, involving two hosts. Eggs are dropped in sheep's dung and in damp conditions they hatch out into larvae, which invade the body of a small water snail. Several stages occur inside the snail's body, and eventually a different kind of larvae are released. These attach themselves to grass and develop a hard coat. If they are then eaten by a sheep, they continue their development into adult flukes in the sheep's liver, causing illness and even death.

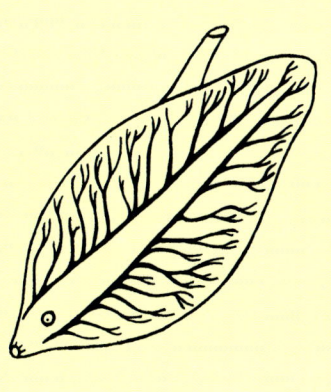

ragworm
lugworm
sea mouse
peanut worm

Animals with Shells

Most of the world's shelled animals belong to the group known as the molluscs (phylum *Mollusca*). For over 500 million years this has been an enormously successful group. Today it contains a greater number and a greater variety of animals than any other group apart from the arthropods.

A typical mollusc has a shell that is produced by a sheet of tissue called the mantle. Attached to the underside of its body is a large muscular foot. At the rear end is a space between the mantle and the body, known as the mantle cavity, which contains a pair of gills, used for extracting oxygen from the water. Just inside the animal's mouth is an organ known as the radula, which is a long toothed membrane used for scraping up food. Among the molluscs there are many variations on this basic plan and the phylum is divided into six classes. The three most important are the gastropods, the bivalves and the cephalopods.

Snails and other gastropods

The gastropods include the snails and slugs, as well as the many sea-dwelling snails with coiled shells, such as topshells, periwinkles and whelks. In these animals the body has been twisted round so that the mantle cavity lies at the front. Other gastropods include freshwater pond snails, cowries, cone-shells, limpets and ormers. Land snails have developed air-breathing lungs instead of gills. Land slugs have lost their shells, as have sea slugs, sea butterflies and sea hares, all molluscs nonetheless.

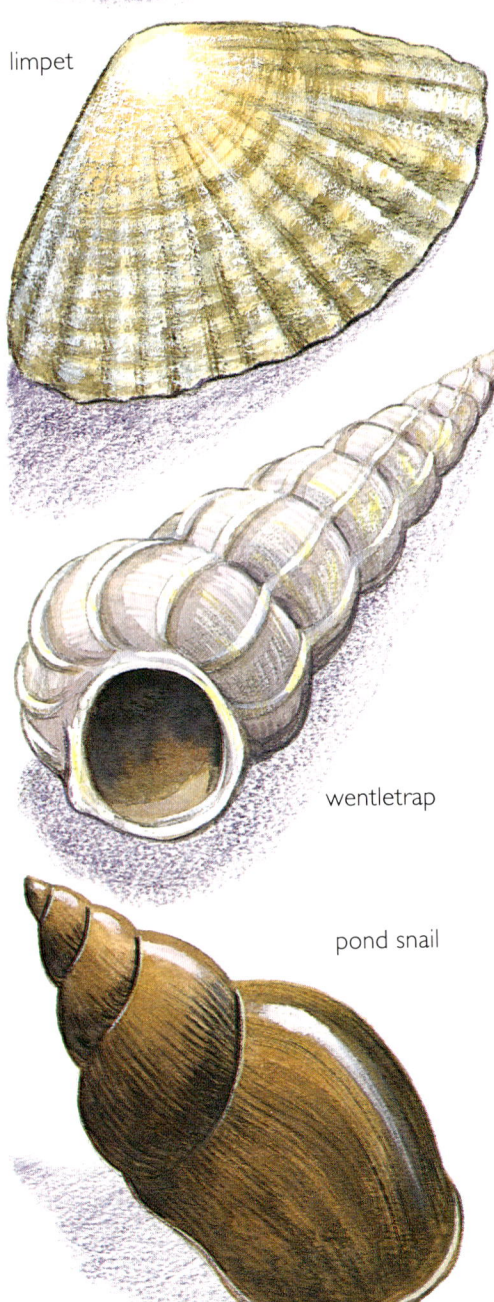

cowrie

limpet

wentletrap

pond snail

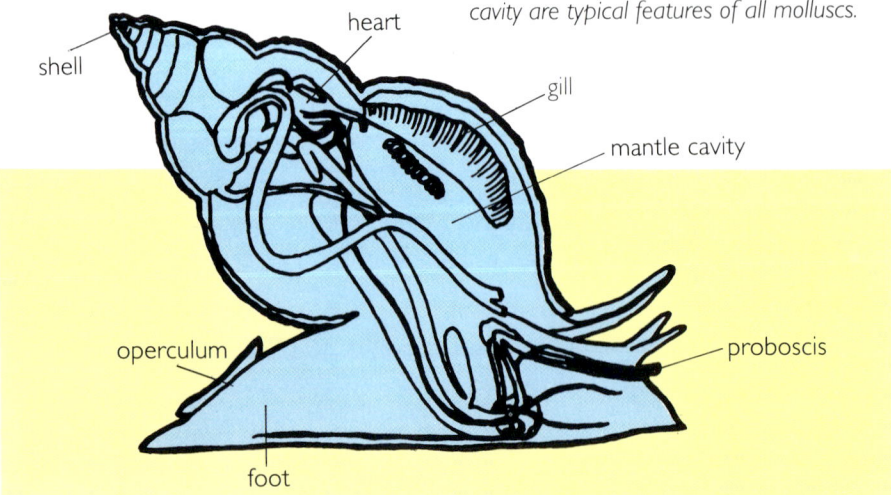

Below: A vertical section through a common whelk. The shell, foot and mantle cavity are typical features of all molluscs.

ANIMALS WITH SHELLS 23

Bivalves and cephalopods

Bivalve molluscs, which have two-part, hinged shells, are equally diverse. Cockles, Venus shells, gapers and razor shells burrow in sand or mud, using a powerful, tongue-like foot. The ship worm tunnels its way through wood (a menace to ships before the days of iron hulls), and the piddock bores through rock. Mussels and oysters live attached to rocks, while scallops swim by a kind of jet propulsion. Bivalves use their gills for filtering food as well as taking in oxygen.

The cephalopods are totally unlike other molluscs. In this group, which includes squids, cuttlefish and octopuses, the foot has been modified into a number of tentacles attached to the head (the name 'cephalopod' means 'head-foot'). These have suckers and are used for catching food. The shells of squids and cuttlefish are inside the animals' bodies, while octopuses have no shells at all. Only the deep-sea nautilus has a visible shell.

Other members of the large and fascinating mollusc group include the primitive *Neopilina*, chitons (coat-of-mail shells) and tusk shells.

Octopus, squid and cuttlefish belong to the group known as cephalopods. Mussels and oysters are bivalves that attach themselves to rock.

Left: *The gastropod group includes cowries and limpets, as well as many kinds of snail.*

Animals with Outer Skeletons

> Soft-bodied animals with thin skins are vulnerable and can survive only in a limited range of environments. Shelled animals have slightly more protection, but the invertebrates with the greatest advantage are those with hard outer skeletons. Such a skeleton provides an animal with a waterproof barrier and helps to prevent its tissues drying out. At the same time it provides a firm anchorage for muscles and thus greatly increases the power of the animal.

Jointed-leg animals

Animals with hard outer skeletons are all grouped together in the phylum *Arthropoda* – a name that means 'jointed leg'. This is the largest group in the animal kingdom. There are well over one million species, most of them insects. Another important, but smaller, group is formed by the arachnids – the spiders and their relatives.

Arthropods are thought to have evolved from annelid worms, and one arthropod, the velvet worm (*Peripatus*), has some of the features of annelids. However, it is possible that the evolution of an outer skeleton occurred more than once and some biologists divide living arthropods into two distinct subphyla, leaving the velvet worm in a separate phylum.

The first subphylum contains the arachnids, together with the sea spiders, which are not true spiders, and the strange king crabs, which are bottom-dwelling sea creatures with a large horseshoe-shaped carapace (shell).

The second subphylum is composed of the insects, the myriapods and the crustaceans. Myriapods include the centipedes and millipedes – long-bodied animals with many legs. Centipedes are fast-moving carnivores (meat-eaters) with flattened bodies and one pair of legs on each segment. A millipede is a plant-eating animal with a more rounded body and two pairs of legs on each segment.

Velvet worms live in dark, damp places in warm parts of the world.

Despite their name, centipedes may have between 30 and 340 legs. Millipedes may have as few as 26 legs and no millipede has more than 400 legs.

ANIMALS WITH OUTER SKELETONS 25

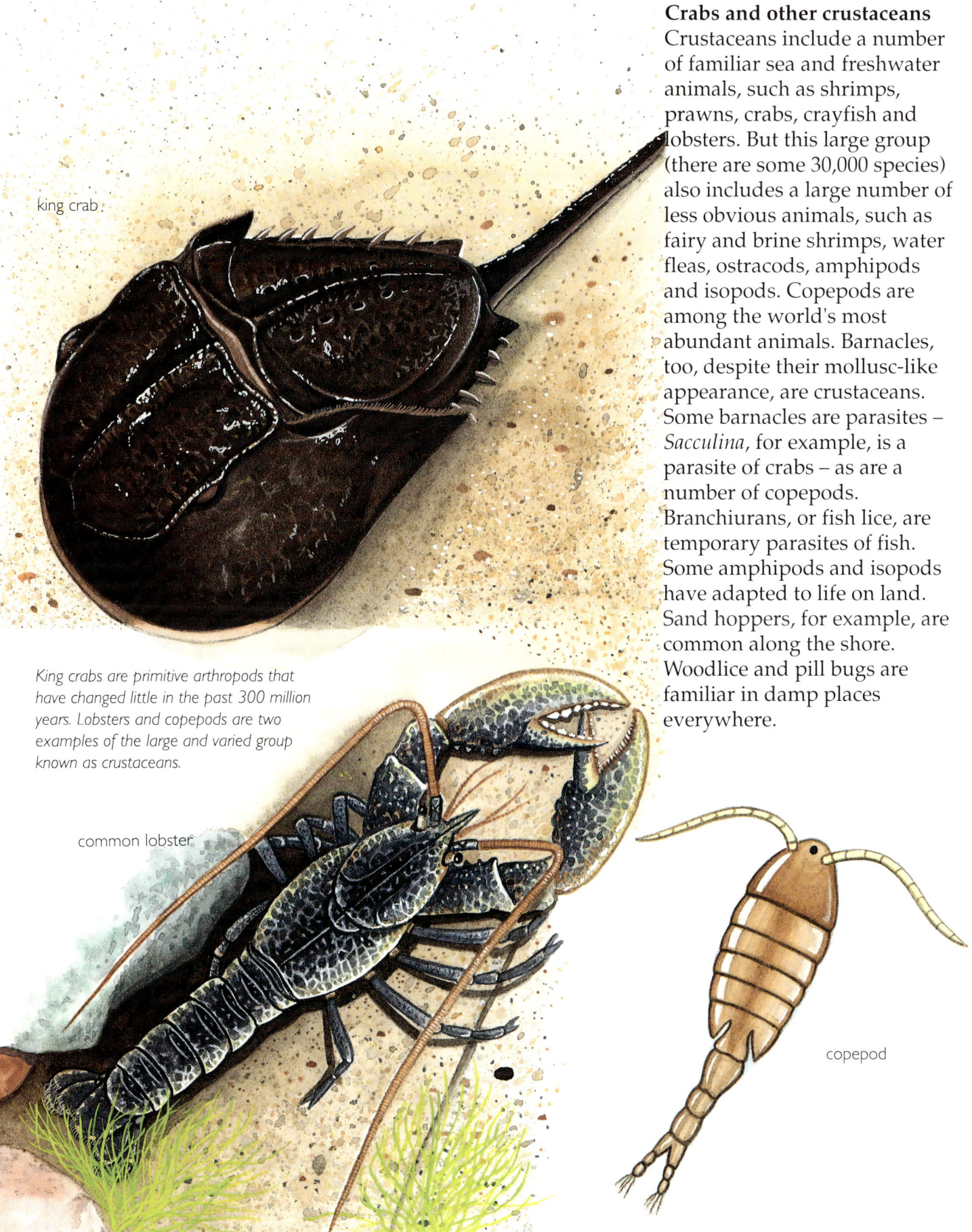

king crab

King crabs are primitive arthropods that have changed little in the past 300 million years. Lobsters and copepods are two examples of the large and varied group known as crustaceans.

common lobster

copepod

Crabs and other crustaceans
Crustaceans include a number of familiar sea and freshwater animals, such as shrimps, prawns, crabs, crayfish and lobsters. But this large group (there are some 30,000 species) also includes a large number of less obvious animals, such as fairy and brine shrimps, water fleas, ostracods, amphipods and isopods. Copepods are among the world's most abundant animals. Barnacles, too, despite their mollusc-like appearance, are crustaceans. Some barnacles are parasites – *Sacculina*, for example, is a parasite of crabs – as are a number of copepods. Branchiurans, or fish lice, are temporary parasites of fish. Some amphipods and isopods have adapted to life on land. Sand hoppers, for example, are common along the shore. Woodlice and pill bugs are familiar in damp places everywhere.

The World of Insects

> Insects are the world's most numerous and most successful animals. There are over a million known species and there may be thousands or even millions more that scientists have yet to discover. Known insects are divided into two main groups – those with wings and those without. Among the more primitive wingless insects are springtails and bristletails, such as silverfish.

Winged insects

Insects with wings are themselves divided into two groups. Members of the group called the *Exopterygota* have young known as nymphs, which look similar to the adults when they emerge from their eggs. In order to grow they undergo a series of moults in which the outer skeleton is sloughed off to reveal a new one underneath.

The new skeleton is soft at first, and the nymph swells up before it hardens. After each moult the nymph becomes more and more like the adult. Insects that have this kind of life history include dragonflies, mayflies, grasshoppers, cockroaches and mantises, termites, earwigs, stick insects, stone flies, lice, thrips and bugs.

Members of the *Endopterygota* have more dramatic life histories. The eggs of these insects hatch out into larvae, which are quite unlike the adults. Typical larvae include grubs and caterpillars. A larva grows by a series of moults, in a similar way to a nymph. However, the outer covering of a larva is soft, which makes growth easier. When the larva reaches full size it undergoes a final moult, but this time the new skin underneath is different. It hardens into a case and the insect becomes a pupa. Inside the case a dramatic metamorphosis (change of form) takes place, and after a few days or weeks an adult insect breaks open the case and emerges into the world. Insects that have this type of life history include butterflies and moths, lacewings, caddisflies, true flies, fleas, beetles, bees, ants and wasps.

The hoverfly has distinctive black and yellow markings which resemble those of a bee or wasp. Despite its appearance, the hoverfly does not sting. Its larvae scavenge amongst decaying organic matter and some eat aphids and other plant pests.

Above: *The dung beetle rolls animal dung into balls which it buries and feeds on. The female lays eggs in dung-balls, which provide food for the larvae.*
Left: *The caterpillar of the large white butterfly feeds on leaves, especially cabbage leaves, where the female has laid her eggs.*

THE WORLD OF INSECTS

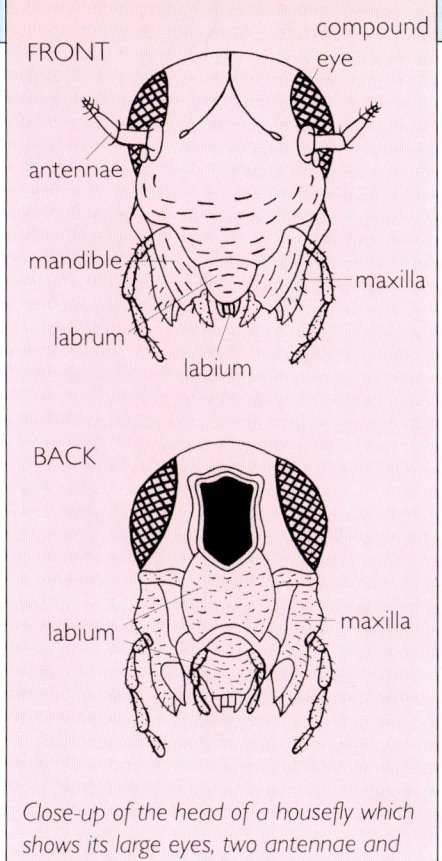

Close-up of the head of a housefly which shows its large eyes, two antennae and mouthparts.

Legs and mouthparts

An insect's body is divided into three parts – head, thorax (chest) and abdomen (stomach). Attached to the outside of an insect's skeleton are a number of appendages. All insects have six legs attached to the thorax. They are generally used for walking, although some insects, such as fleas and grasshoppers, use their large, powerful hindlegs for jumping. Mantises use their fearsome forelegs for catching prey.

Arranged around an insect's mouth are several appendages used for feeding. Insects like the grasshopper or cockroach have mouthparts adapted for biting and chewing. Two powerful mandibles cut off pieces of food and chew it up. A pair of smaller maxillae and a lip-like part called the labium manipulate the food and pass the chewed-up pieces to the mouth. The maxillae and the labium are equipped with sensitive feelers, or palps, and the mouthparts are protected by a large flap called the labrum.

This basic arrangement has been modified in various ways. Some predatory insects, such as the devil's coach horse beetle, have greatly enlarged mandibles for catching prey. In liquid feeders, the mouthparts have been modified to form a long tube, or proboscis. A mosquito uses its proboscis to pierce skin and suck blood, and an aphid sucks the sap of plants. A butterfly has a very long, coiled proboscis that it can extend deep into flowers to find nectar. A fly drinks liquid by means of a sponge-like organ attached to the end of a short proboscis.

Insects feeding. The hawk moth (left) feeds on nectar which it sucks from plants through its long proboscis. The ladybird beetle (bottom left) feeds on aphids while the mantis (right) uses its strong forelegs to catch insects and other small animals which it passes to its mandibles.

ANIMALS WITHOUT BACKBONES

dragonfly

burying beetle in flight

swallowtail butterfly

scarlet tiger moth

common blue butterfly

common field grasshopper

Insect flight

Typically, a flying insect has two pairs of wings, which are simply flat membranes reinforced with a network of veins. An insect virtually rows its way through the air. It flaps its wings in such a way that the air is pushed backwards and downwards, thus creating an equal forward and upward reaction in the insect itself. Not all insects have two pairs of wings. In a beetle, the hind wings have become a pair of hard coverings, or elytra, which conceal and protect the forewings when the insect is at rest. In flies the hindwings have become a pair of balance organs called halteres. These vibrate at high speed during flight and, acting like gyroscopes, enable a fly to change direction very suddenly.

Insects form the largest, most successful group of invertebrates. Their success is due partly to their tough outer skeletons, which allow them to live in dry conditions without losing too much water, but largely to their ability to fly.

THE WORLD OF INSECTS 29

RESPIRATION

Methods of obtaining oxygen vary widely among the invertebrates. Very small animals take in oxygen through their body walls; so do worms. Larger water animals, such as molluscs and large crustaceans, use special structures called gills, and some echinoderms have specially adapted tube feet. On land delicate gills would dry out, so other structures are needed. Land snails have a kind of lung. Some spiders have internal gills known as lung-books, which receive air from the outside via a tiny slit. Other arachnids have long tubes, or tracheae, as do insects.

Social insects

Most insects lead solitary lives, but there are several species whose individuals live together in large colonies. The members of a colony all work together to maintain and defend the colony as a whole. Social insects are found among bees, wasps and ants. All termites also live social lives.

Generally, each community is made up of three or four castes, each of which has a particular job to do. Workers do most of the work, such as building the nest, keeping it clean and feeding the larvae. In some cases a separate soldier caste may defend the colony. Generally, there is a single queen, whose sole task is to lay eggs. Fertile males are produced only when new queens need mates.

A nest of wood ants is a scene of constant activity, with workers involved in cleaning, repair work and transport of food, eggs and larvae.

HOW INSECTS BREATHE

An insect breathes through spiracles – tiny holes in its sides. Each body segment has a pair of spiracles, one on each side. Air passes through the spiracles and into tubes called tracheae. The smallest tubes, known as tracheoles, contain a fluid. Oxygen from the air dissolves in this fluid and passes into the insect's body tissues.

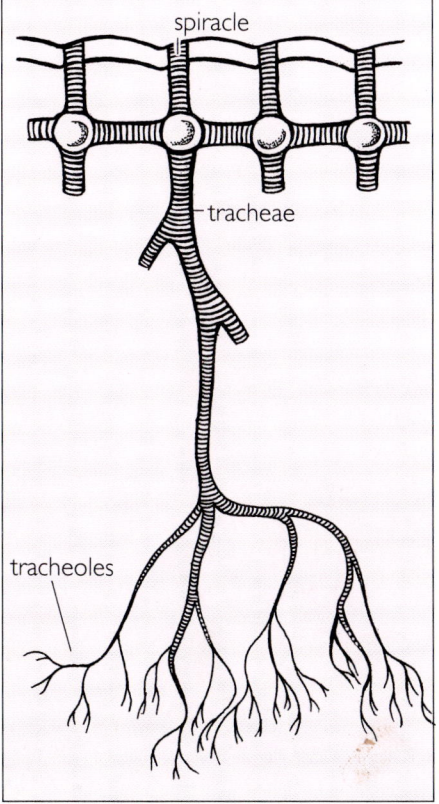

Scorpions and Spiders

> Scorpions and spiders are arachnids. All members of this class have eight legs and their bodies are divided into two distinct parts. Other arachnids include the harvestmen, sun spiders, ticks and mites. There are over 15,000 species of mites. Many of them cause diseases in animals and plants.

A garden spider sits in the middle of its elaborate orb web, waiting for insects to become trapped by the sticky threads.

Poison fangs

Arachnids have less complicated mouthparts than insects and in many cases food is largely digested outside the body. A prey animal is first immobilized, or paralyzed. Then enzymes are pumped into its body. They break down the tissues into a sort of soup, which can then be sucked up.

Spiders have developed this technique to a fine art. A spider immobilizes its prey by first injecting it with some poison through its sharp fangs.

Blood suckers

Ticks and some mites have taken the technique of sucking up liquid food a stage further and have become blood-sucking parasites. A scorpion, however, digests more of its food inside its body. It holds its prey in its huge pincers and chews it up with its fangs. The poison sting carried at the tip of the tail is generally used only to subdue very large prey. Some species use their sting only for defence. They prey at night on spiders and insects.

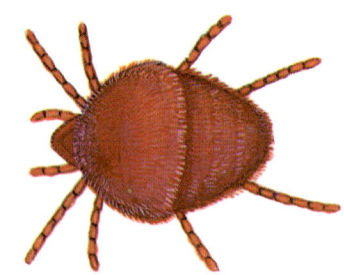

Mites form a very varied group of animals. Among the smallest is a species that lives in the hair follicles of mammals. In contrast the red velvet mite (above) may grow to 10mm long.

Scorpions prey on insects and spiders. Despite its own poison fangs, a spider stands little chance once it has been seized by a scorpion's pincers. If it does offer resistance the powerful sting in the scorpion's tail soon immobilizes it.

SCORPIONS AND SPIDERS

Catching prey

Spiders are well known for producing silk and for the ingenious ways in which they use it. A female wolf spider spins a small web of silk to provide protection for her young after they hatch. Other spiders spin webs as traps for catching prey. A house spider, for example, spins a shapeless web equipped with 'trip wires'. A garden spider creates a beautiful circular web with sticky threads. A trap-door spider lies in wait inside a silk-lined burrow. A bolas spider catches its prey with a sticky blob on the end of a long, thin, silk thread. A water spider spends its time under water in a bubble of air trapped inside a silk 'diving chamber' and darts out to catch any small water animals that pass too close.

Many spiders rely on speed and agility to catch their prey. Wolf spiders and others, such as the large bird-eating tropical spiders, catch prey animals simply by chasing them. A jumping spider stalks its prey and then leaps on it from a distance of about 15mm (about half an inch). Crab spiders, on the other hand, are less energetic. They have camouflage colours and lie unseen in flowers or leaves, waiting for their prey to come to them.

Below: A water spider spends most of its time underwater in a bubble of air. When a potential victim, such as the mayfly larva shown to the left, passes, the spider rushes out to seize it.

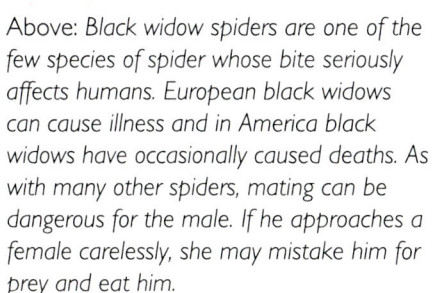

Above: Black widow spiders are one of the few species of spider whose bite seriously affects humans. European black widows can cause illness and in America black widows have occasionally caused deaths. As with many other spiders, mating can be dangerous for the male. If he approaches a female carelessly, she may mistake him for prey and eat him.

Below: A crab spider is so called because it scuttles sideways like a crab. Many crab spiders are brightly coloured and lie in wait for their victims in flowers.

ANIMALS WITHOUT BACKBONES

Spiny-Skinned Animals

> Echinoderms, or spiny-skinned animals, are so called because they have a chalk-like skeleton that forms part of the skin and, in many cases, the skin bears spines. Among the echinoderms are starfish, sea urchins, brittle-stars, sea lilies, feather-stars and sea cucumbers.

Five-sided animals

These animals have bodies constructed on a five-sided plan and lack distinct heads, tails or legs. They have a unique system of tubes filled with fluid, known as the water vascular system. In most echinoderms there are a number of small extensions of this system on the outside of the body, which are known as tube feet. Different echinoderms use them for walking, feeding, feeling, building burrows or taking in oxygen.

The five-sided plan of echinoderms is most obvious in the arms of a starfish. Not all starfish have five arms. Some have ten or any multiple of five up to as many as 50 arms. The arms are flexible – the skeleton consists of many chalky plates and spines embedded in the skin. Underneath the arms are two rows of tube feet, most of which end in suckers and are used for walking and holding prey. A starfish can pull apart the shell of an oyster. The mouth is on the underside of the animal.

comb-star
common starfish
brittle-star
sun-star

SPINY-SKINNED ANIMALS

diadem sea urchin

sea cucumbers

common sea urchin

green sea urchin

Urchins and cucumbers

A sea urchin has a rigid skeleton, known as the test, which is composed of many interlocking plates and bears many long, movable spines. Five double rows of very long tube feet, with suckers, project out through the wall of the test. Sea urchins live on rocks, from which they scrape small animals and plants, using a complicated set of teeth known as an Aristotle's lantern. Sand dollars and heart urchins are close relatives of the sea urchin, but they are sand burrowers.

Brittle-stars resemble starfish, but they have long delicate arms, which they wriggle in order to move about. A sea lily is similar, except that it remains attached to the mud or a rock by means of a stalk and uses its tube feet to help catch particles of food from water currents. Feather-stars are close relatives of sea lilies, but they can move about.

A sea cucumber is very different. With its soft, elongated body, it looks like a large slug – its skeleton is reduced to a few chalky spikes. Around its mouth are a number of branched tube feet, like tentacles, for catching food. Some sea cucumbers can swim, but most use large tube feet to crawl along the bottom.

The echinoderm group contains some 6,000 living species of five-sided, spiny-skinned animals, and a further 13,000 species that exist only as fossils. They include many different kinds of starfish, sea urchins and sand dollars, delicate brittle-stars and basket-stars, sea lilies and sea cucumbers.

SEA URCHINS ON DISPLAY

The dried 'shells' of sea urchins are colourful and attractive objects. They are sometimes sold in seaside souvenir shops. Long, tapering spines are typical of sea urchins. One species, found in the tropical Pacific, may have spines up to 400mm (16in) long. It is known as a hatpin sea urchin.

References

Acorn worm One of about 90 species of worm-like animals found in the sea. One type lives in a burrow in the sand in shallow water. The other type lives in colonies in deep water. Each individual lives in a tube.

Adaptive radiation The evolution of a primitive type of organism into a number of different forms, each adapted to distinct and different ways of life. In the animal kingdom, the best examples of adaptive radiation can be seen among molluscs and mammals.

Aristotle's lantern A complicated structure used by a sea urchin for feeding. It is made up of 40 pieces of skeleton bound together with muscle and other tissue, which supports a ring of five teeth. The muscles move so that the teeth perform a pincer-like action, scraping algae and other organisms from the rock.

Arrow worms A small group of about 75 species of torpedo or arrow-shaped, transparent, worm-like animals that are mostly found floating in the plankton in the sea. They feed on crustaceans and larvae.

Beard worm One of about 160 species of sea-living worm. Beard worms are very long and live in tubes they produce themselves and have a bunch of beard-like tentacles on the head which are probably used in feeding.

Brachiopods Lamp shells – so called because some kinds look like old oil lamps. They are two-shelled animals, attached to rock by a short stalk. They feed by means of a loop-shaped, tentacle-like structure, which creates a current of water and filters out small organisms.

Chelicerae The first pair of appendages of an arachnid. In spiders they are like fangs; in other arachnids, like pincers.

Chitin A type of sugar, containing nitrogen, which has long, fibrous molecules. It is an ingredient of the outer skeleton of insects and other arthropods, and is also found in cell walls of most fungi.

Chitons Coat-of-mail shells, a group of molluscs with a flat body protected by an eight-plated shell, often found on rocky shores.

Enzyme A protein that acts as a biological catalyst; that is, it helps a chemical reaction take place in a living organism without itself being used up in the reaction.

Horseshoe worm One of over 15 species of sea-living worm. A horseshoe worm lives in a tube, partly buried in sand. It collects food by means of a horseshoe arrangement of tentacles.

King crabs A group of arthropods forming the class *Meristomata*. A king crab is protected by a hard, horseshoe-shaped shell, or carapace. The rear end is also well-shielded, by a long spine.

Living fossil A term used to describe an animal or plant that has changed very little over millions of years. Examples include the brachiopod *Lingula*, which has existed for 500 million years, and the molluscs *Neopilina* and *Nautilus*. The coelacanth is another 'living fossil'.

Moss animals A group of animals that form the phylum *Bryozoa*. Moss animals are tiny creatures, no more than 1.5mm long, that form encrusting colonies, like moss. The colonies may be soft or hard to the touch. Each individual, or zooid, lives inside an outer case, or cuticle, made of chitin.

Nautilus A cephalopod mollusc whose body is enclosed in a spiral, chambered shell, like the shells of the ammonites that existed 150 million years ago. The shell acts as a buoyancy device and the animal can be found at 600m (2,000ft) deep in the south-western Pacific.

Neopilina A primitive mollusc. It is the closest living form to the earliest molluscs from which all modern forms evolved.

Organ Any part of the body of an animal which has a special job to do, like the heart, lungs, etc.

Peanut worm One of about 320 species of sea-living worm. Most burrow in sand or gravel, but some can bore into rock or coral.

Pedipalps The second pair of appendages of an arachnid. Their function varies. In scorpions they are sense organs. The pedipalps of male spiders are used for transferring sperm to the female.

Ribbon worm One of about 800 species of long, ribbon-like worms, mainly found in the sea. Most of them are less than 50cm (1.5ft) long, but some can measure up to 30m (90ft).

Rotifers Also known as wheel animalcules, meaning tiny wheel-like animals, they belong to the phylum *Aschelminthes* (the same phylum as the roundworms). Rotifers are tiny, transparent water animals, up to 2mm long. A typical rotifer has a long body that ends in a tail-like foot with two toes. The head bears a crown of cilia which, when they beat, look like a wheel spinning.

Spinneret The organ used by a spider to produce silk. Glands inside a spinneret produce a sticky liquid, which is forced out through a tiny hole and hardens to form a thread.

Thorny-headed worm One of about 750 species of parasitic worms that live in the guts of other animals, anchored by means of a proboscis which is armed with many backward-pointing hooks.

Tusk shells A group of molluscs forming the class *Scaphopoda*. These molluscs have long bodies which are protected by tusk-like shells. They burrow in sand or mud on the sea-bed.

Animals With Backbones

Sea Squirts, Lancelets and Lampreys

Fishes, amphibians, reptiles, birds and mammals are all vertebrate animals. That is, they all have a backbone, or spine, composed of a number of vertebrae. All invertebrate animals lack such a backbone. Originally, vertebrates evolved from invertebrate animals, though no one knows exactly how or when.

Chordate animals
Modern scientists recognize that the vertebrates are quite closely related to the lancelets and the sea squirts. All these groups are therefore included in the phylum *Chordata*. The important feature that all chordate animals have in common is that, at some stage during their lives, they possess a rod-like structure, known as a notochord, along their backs. A lancelet, for example, has a notochord throughout its adult life. A sea squirt, or tunicate, however, only has a notochord when it is a larva, at which stage it resembles the tadpole larva of a frog. All vertebrates also have a notochord at an early stage of their development.

These groups also share some other features of their anatomy. Both sea squirts and lancelets appear to represent stages in the evolution of vertebrates from invertebrates. Many scientists believe that vertebrates evolved from larvae like tadpoles, which failed to develop into adults and became able to breed in their tadpole-like form. But it is also possible that neither of these groups are the direct ancestors of vertebrates. Some scientists think that an extinct group of echinoderms, known as the *homalozoa* or calcichordates, may have been the ancestors of all three chordate groups.

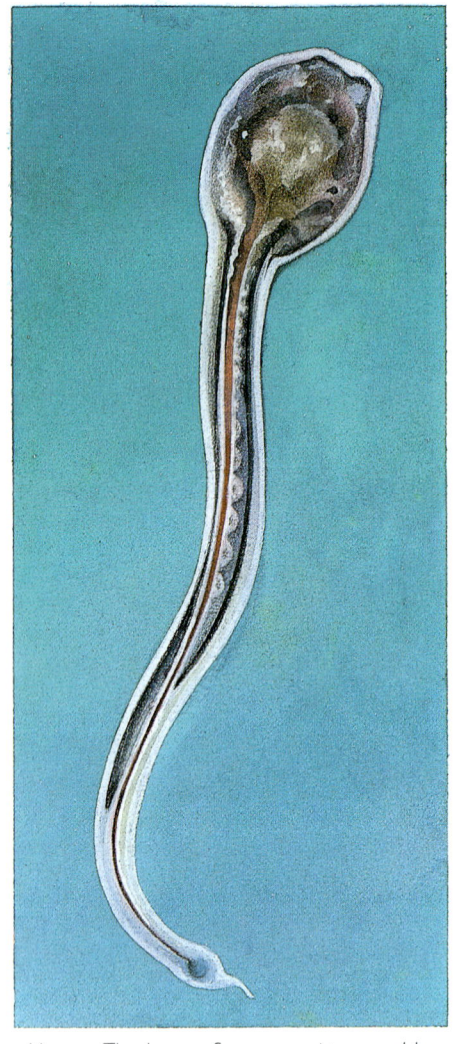

Above: *The larva of a sea squirt resembles a frog tadpole. Unlike the adult sea squirt the larva has a notochord.*

Below: *A lancelet lies with its rear end in gravel or mud. It feeds by filtering particles from the water.*

Sea squirts and lampreys

Whatever the case, adult sea squirts look nothing like vertebrates. They are mostly tube-shaped animals that live singly or in colonies attached to rocks, filtering the water for their food. Lancelets are more fish-like animals that spend most of their time lying tail-downwards in gravel or sand.

The most primitive living animals with true backbones are the jawless fishes – the hagfishes and the lampreys. Hagfishes are eel-like animals that live in the mud. They prey on worms and shrimps, and sometimes emerge from the mud to feed on dead or dying fishes. Lampreys are parasites that attach themselves to other fish with their sucker-like mouths. Inside a lamprey's mouth are several rows of horny, hooked teeth, which the animal uses to rasp away the flesh of its host. Lampreys inflict severe damage, but seldom kill their victims.

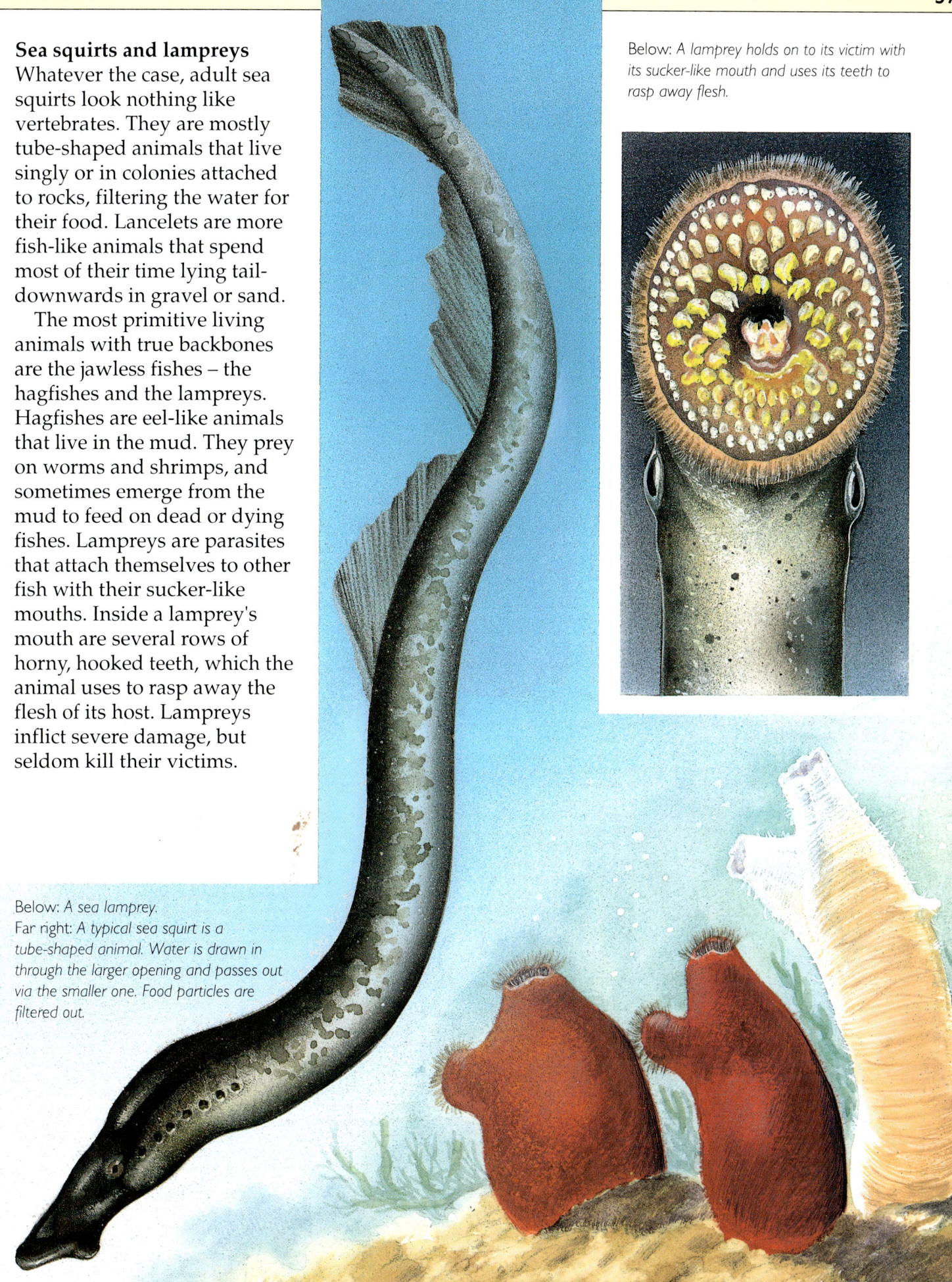

Below: A lamprey holds on to its victim with its sucker-like mouth and uses its teeth to rasp away flesh.

Below: A sea lamprey.
Far right: A typical sea squirt is a tube-shaped animal. Water is drawn in through the larger opening and passes out via the smaller one. Food particles are filtered out.

ANIMALS WITH BACKBONES

Sharks and Rays

Lampreys and hagfishes have no jaws. All the rest of the vertebrates, on the other hand, have movable jaws that form part of an internal skeleton. In most vertebrates this skeleton is made of the hard material we call bone. But the sharks and their relatives have skeletons made of a softer material called cartilage. This is lighter than bone and less strong. But in water, where an animal becomes almost weightless, strength is not very important.

A light skeleton is particularly important to a cartilaginous fish because, unlike a bony fish, it has no organ in its body that enables it to float motionless in the water. In order to stay off the bottom, it has to keep swimming, and its body and fins are shaped like the wings of an aeroplane to provide lift as it moves through the water. Some sharks store large amounts of oil in their livers and this helps to increase their buoyancy.

Predators and plankton feeders

There are three main groups of sharks. The Port Jackson shark is in a group by itself; unlike most sharks it has two kinds of teeth and feeds on crustaceans, molluscs and sea urchins. The true sharks form the largest group. Most are fierce predators and a shark's mouth contains rows of sharp teeth. Some sharks do attack people and even boats, but many stories are exaggerated. True sharks include the man-eater or great white shark, the hammerhead sharks, the sand shark, the mako and the porbeagle.

Not all sharks are predators. The basking shark and the whale shark are huge creatures that feed on plankton and small fish which they catch by straining water through sieve-like organs called gill rakers.

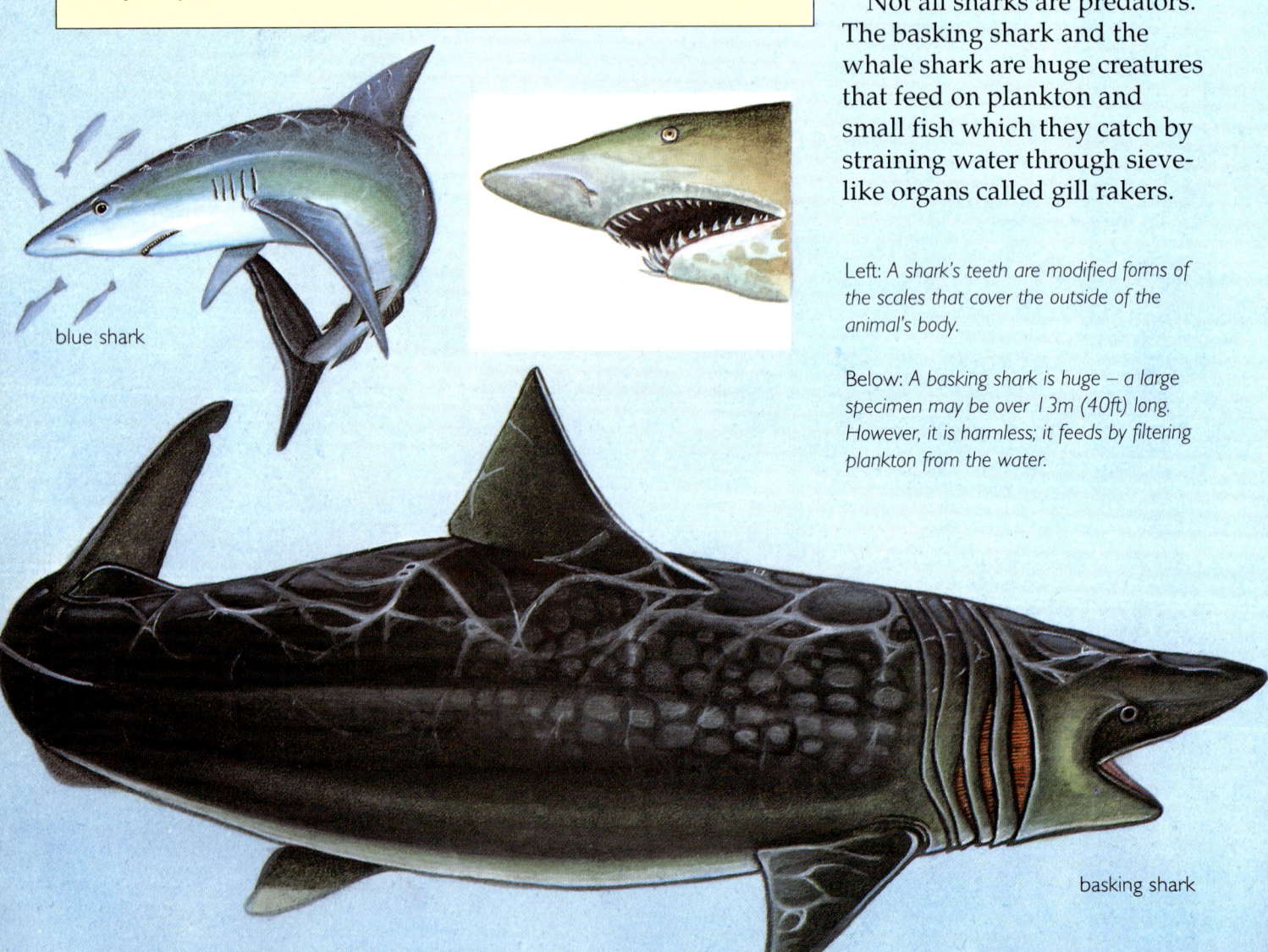

Left: A shark's teeth are modified forms of the scales that cover the outside of the animal's body.

Below: A basking shark is huge – a large specimen may be over 13m (40ft) long. However, it is harmless; it feeds by filtering plankton from the water.

blue shark

basking shark

SHARKS AND RAYS

Dogfish and rays

The last group of sharks are the dogfish sharks. These have shark-like, streamlined bodies, but like skates and rays, they are adapted to living on the bottom. True rays and skates are superbly adapted for bottom-living. Their bodies have become flattened so that, together with the fins, the sides form 'wings'. With these they glide swiftly and gracefully through the water. When they rest on the bottom, camouflage markings often make them impossible to see. And some rays defend themselves; the stingray is armed with a poison spine in its tail, and electric rays can deliver powerful electric shocks. Most rays feed on shrimps and other small crustaceans. Manta rays glide through the upper levels, scooping up plankton through their gaping mouths.

Dogfish sharks and rays mostly live on the bottom, although the huge manta ray is a plankton feeder.

Bony Fishes

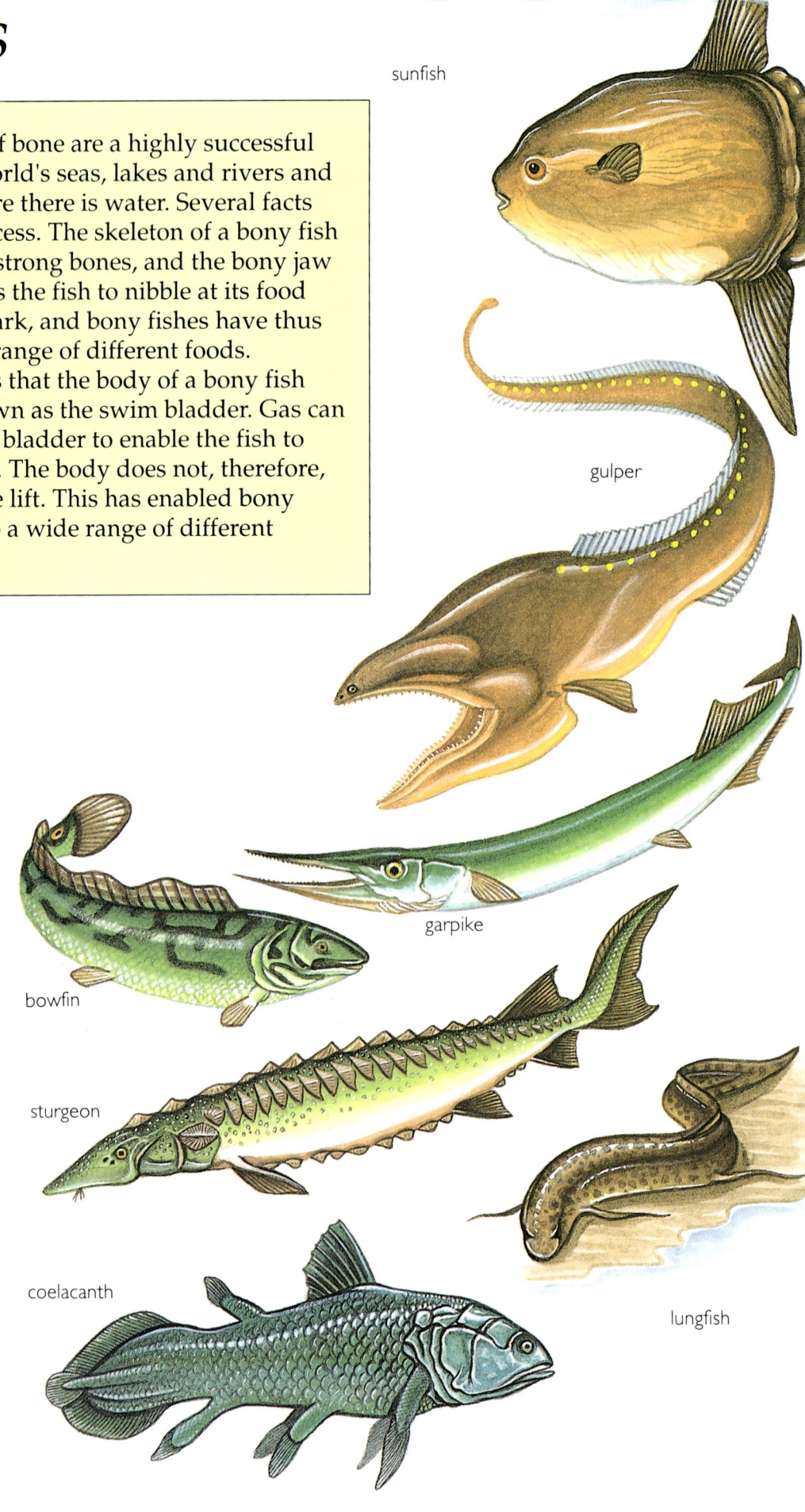

Fishes with skeletons made of bone are a highly successful group. They dominate the world's seas, lakes and rivers and can be found almost anywhere there is water. Several facts have contributed to their success. The skeleton of a bony fish is made up of many tiny but strong bones, and the bony jaw projects forward. This enables the fish to nibble at its food rather than tear at it like a shark, and bony fishes have thus been able to adapt to a wide range of different foods.

Another important factor is that the body of a bony fish contains a gas-filled sac, known as the swim bladder. Gas can be pumped in and out of this bladder to enable the fish to float motionless at any depth. The body does not, therefore, have to be shaped to generate lift. This has enabled bony fishes to adapt their bodies to a wide range of different lifestyles.

Primitive fishes
The most primitive of today's bony fishes include the bichirs, sturgeons, garpikes, bowfins and the two kinds of lobefin that remain. Lungfishes are descended from early fishes that lived in stagnant ponds and developed lungs in order to obtain oxygen. In most later fishes the lung became the swim bladder, but lungfishes kept their lungs and some species can survive out of water in times of drought.

The coelacanth is a lobefin. Before its discovery in 1938 this fish was thought to have died out millions of years ago. It is a puzzle to scientists as it has a notochord instead of a backbone, and its heart and stomach are much simpler than those of other fishes. It appears to have changed very little over millions of years.

BONY FISHES 41

TRAVELS OF THE EEL

Some fish migrate over long distances. The European Atlantic salmon spends most of its life in the ocean, but is born in a river and returns – to the same river – to breed. Eels are born in the Sargasso Sea, in the western Atlantic, and are carried to Europe, as larvae, with the Gulf Stream. They travel up the rivers as small, transparent creatures called elvers, and live in freshwater until they are ready to breed. Then they make the long journey back to the weedy Sargasso Sea. They probably die there, for they are never seen again.

Masters of the sea

Most modern bony fish belong to a group known as the teleosts. These vary in shape and colour according to their way of life. There are, for example, many streamlined predatory fish, built for speed in hunting. Flatfish spend their lives on the bottom, safe from most hunters, while brightly coloured tropical fish swim among coral reefs. Some fish hide themselves in rock crevices; others defend themselves with armour, electric organs, poison spines and warning colours.

Among the strangest fish are those that live in the deepest parts of the oceans, where the water is dark and food is scarce. Such fish often carry their own lights and have huge jaws to make the most of the occasional prey that comes their way.

The success of bony fishes is shown by the enormous variety that exist today. Lungfishes and the coelacanth are relatives of the group of lobefinned fishes that gave rise to the amphibians.

Amphibians

The class of animals we call the amphibians includes frogs, toads, newts, salamanders and caecilians or blindworms. Most of the animals in this group have moist skins and all of them spend at least part of their lives in water. The females produce soft, delicate eggs, which need to be kept damp. They hatch out into larvae, which continue their development in water.

Amphibians live in water or in moist conditions. Most need to lay their eggs in water, although some, such as the midwife toad, look after their eggs in other ways.

Above: A male frog croaks, using his vocal sac, to attract potential mates.

Blindworms

Caecilians are worm-like, sub-tropical animals that spend their lives in burrows in the soil, emerging to seize worms, insects or even small mammals. They have no legs or eyes. A female caecilian lays her eggs in a moist place and looks after them until they hatch.

Newts and salamanders

Newts and salamanders have long bodies with a distinct tail. Four legs stick out from the sides of a salamander's body and it walks with its belly touching the ground. Many salamanders are brightly coloured.

The eggs of newts and salamanders are generally fertilized inside the female's body, with a small packet of sperm dropped by the male during courtship. Some salamanders lay their eggs in moist places, but a female European salamander keeps her eggs inside her body until they hatch. Then she releases the larvae into water. Most newts lay their eggs in water.

fire salamander

crested newt

Alpine newt

AMPHIBIANS

Frogs and toads

Frogs and toads make up the largest group of amphibians. They have short bodies, without tails, and powerful hind legs that are used for jumping or swimming. Frogs are generally slender, agile animals with large eyes. Toads are heavier and clumsier, with warty, sometimes dry, skins. Tree frogs have suckers on their feet to help them climb. Flying frogs use their large webbed feet like parachutes.

Frogs and toads breed in water. A female common frog produces a mass of jelly-like eggs (frogspawn), which are immediately fertilized by the male. Toads generally produce 'ropes' of eggs. The eggs hatch out into tadpoles, which have tails and external gills. As the tadpole develops, the external gills are replaced by internal gills and finally by a lung. Legs develop, the tail is lost and, about three months after hatching, the tadpole becomes a young adult.

Some species take care of their young during part of their development. The male midwife toad carries a string of fertilized eggs wrapped round his legs. When they are ready to hatch, he leaves them in water. A female Surinam toad carries her tadpoles in small pockets on her back while they develop.

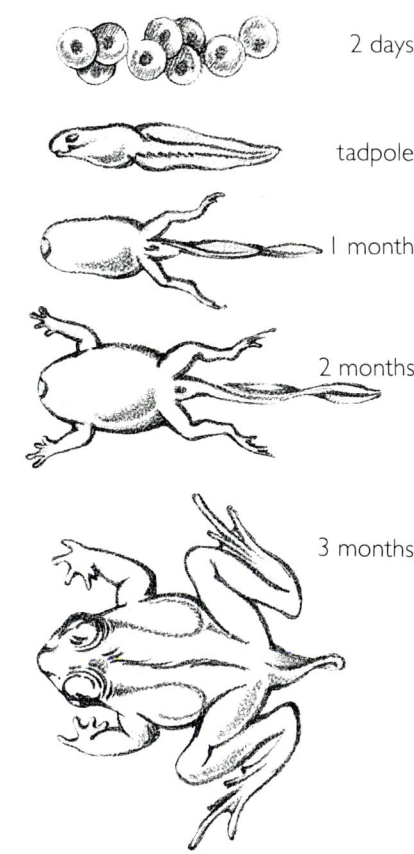

A tadpole goes through a gradual change of form to become an adult.

red-eyed tree frog

midwife toad

HOW A FROG BREATHES

A frog takes oxygen from the air through a lung, which can be closed off from the gullet by means of a muscular slit called the glottis. To take in air, the frog closes its glottis, opens its nostrils and enlarges its mouth cavity. Then it closes its nostrils, opens its glottis and squeezes the air in its mouth into the lung. This has a moist lining in which oxygen can dissolve and pass into fine blood vessels.

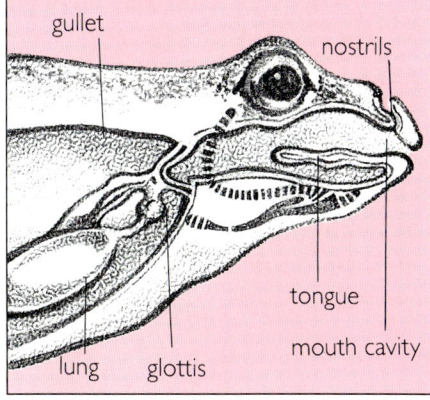

Reptiles

Amphibians, with their soft, moist skins and delicate eggs, can only survive in or near water. They are thus only partly adapted to living on land. Reptiles, on the other hand, are true land-dwellers. They have tough, waterproof skins, usually covered with hard scales, and lay large, shelled eggs that keep moisture in.

There are three main orders of living reptiles: the turtles and tortoises, the crocodiles and alligators, and the snakes and lizards. One of today's reptiles, the tuatara, belongs to a separate order and is the only survivor of a group that was widespread 200 million years ago. All the remaining reptile groups, including the dinosaurs, became extinct long ago.

Above: A crocodile can be distinguished from an alligator by the fact that when its mouth is closed the fourth tooth in its lower jaw remains visible.

Turtles and tortoises are a primitive yet highly specialized group of reptiles.

Turtles and tortoises

Turtles and tortoises protect themselves inside a tough shell. The shell is made up of bony plates covered with a horny material similar to the scales of other reptiles. The bony plates of the top half of the shell, or carapace, are usually fused to the animal's backbone. Most living turtles live in or near water, although they all lay their eggs on land.

Among the largest turtles are those that live in the sea, such as the green turtle and the leatherback turtle. Freshwater turtles are mostly carnivores. Tortoises, on the other hand, are land-dwelling herbivores.

Galapagos giant tortoise

green turtle

diamond back turtle

REPTILES

Crocodiles, snakes and lizards
Crocodiles, alligators, caimans and gavials also spend much of their time in water, which helps to keep them cool. They lie with only their eyes, ears and nostrils above the surface. They feed mostly on fish, but large crocodilians can sometimes catch unwary mammals that come down to the water to drink.

Snakes and lizards form the largest group of reptiles. A lizard, with its four legs held out sideways from its body, is a typical reptile, and there are many different kinds. The common lizard and the green lizard belong to a group known as the lacertids. Other groups include the geckos, skinks, chameleons, iguanas and agamas. Most lizards are carnivores that feed on insects and other small animals.

Snakes probably evolved from a group of lizards that took to burrowing in the ground and lost their legs. Typically, a snake moves by throwing its body into backward-moving waves that push against the ground. All snakes are carnivores, and many kill their prey with fangs that inject poison.

Snakes and lizards are closely related; snakes probably evolved from a group of lizards that burrowed in the ground. Boas and pythons have the tiny remains of hind limbs.

anaconda
green lizard
Turkish gecko
green tree snake

THE PYTHON'S HUG

Pythons, boas and anacondas kill their prey by coiling around it so tightly that it cannot breathe. Like most snakes, they can move their jaws far apart, so that they can swallow an animal bigger than themselves. Some of the largest snakes belong to this group. The anaconda, which lives in tropical America, may reach a length of about 10m (30ft). One species of python (Africa and Asia) is equally large, and can swallow a small antelope.

HOW TO GET AROUND WITHOUT LEGS

A snake moves along the ground in one of four ways. It may throw its body into a series of waves that push against bumps in the ground. On smooth ground, however, a different method is necessary. With its head firmly held on the ground, the snake draws up its body into a number of bends. Then, gripping the ground with its tail, it extends its head and body forward. Some snakes can travel in a straight line by sending waves of muscle movement down the belly while the large belly scales grip the ground. Sand is difficult to grip as it tends to shift. Desert snakes overcome this problem by 'sidewinding' – throwing the body sideways in a series of loops.

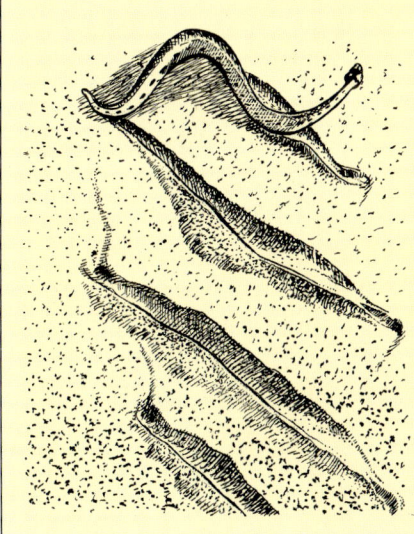

Birds

swift

peregrine

Birds probably evolved from reptiles and, like reptiles, birds lay eggs with hard shells. Reptiles' scales have evolved into feathers and the front legs have become wings.

Birds have one important advantage over reptiles. The body temperature of a reptile varies with the air temperature, and reptiles often have to bask in the sun in order to generate enough body heat. But birds, like mammals, are warm-blooded, which means that they keep their bodies at the same temperature, whatever the temperature of the air. The feathers of birds probably developed originally as a means of keeping precious body heat in. Only later were they used for flying.

Birds of a feather

Modern birds are grouped into 27 different orders. The smallest contains just one species, the ostrich. The largest order, known as the *Passeriformes*, contains over 5,100 species. This includes such birds as sparrows, warblers, starlings, finches, crows, thrushes, swallows, cardinals and many others. Other orders include those of the rheas, penguins, divers, grebes, albatrosses, pelicans, ducks, birds of prey, owls, game birds, waders and gulls, pigeons, parrots, swifts, kingfishers and woodpeckers.

Birds are a very successful group. Apart from bats, they are the only vertebrates that can fly. At the same time they have adapted to a wide range of different land habitats and foods. Their success is due to this combination of mastery of the air and adaptability.

Martial eagle

albatross

BIRDS 47

Above: *Migrating on fine nights and navigating by the stars, birds such as thrushes and finches travel great distances.*

Food, beaks and feet

The ways in which birds have adapted, through evolution, are most obviously seen in their beaks and feet. Meat-eating birds, for example, generally have hooked beaks for tearing at flesh and sharp talons on their feet for catching prey. Birds of prey may feed on anything from insects and small mammals to squirrels and monkeys, according to their size and habitat. Some birds of prey specialize. The secretary bird, for example, preys only on snakes and lizards, and the osprey feeds solely on fish. Also in this group are vultures, which eat carrion. Many vultures have bare necks, which is an advantage to a bird that regularly thrusts its head into the carcasses of dead animals.

Birds that spend much of their time in or on water generally have webbed feet and many of them feed on fish. Penguins, which use their wings to 'fly' underwater, catch fish simply by chasing them. Long, stabbing beaks, like those of a kingfisher, heron or cormorant, are useful for spearing. A puffin can carry up to 30 small fish in its strange beak. A pelican fishes by dipping its huge, scoop-like beak into the water, like a net.

Left: *A bird's wings indicates how it flies. Long narrow wings are used for high speed gliding, while broad wings are needed for soaring high in the air. A peregrine falcon uses its swept-back wings for high speed flight, but a humming-bird can hover.*

Right: *Different kinds of beak are used for obtaining different kinds of food.*

48 ANIMALS WITH BACKBONES

Insects can be found practically everywhere in huge numbers and are therefore the chief food of a wide range of birds. Flycatchers, larks, pipits, thrushes and warblers are among those that forage for insects among the leaves of trees. Tree-creepers use their long beaks to prise insects out of crevices in bark. Woodcocks and hoopoes probe for insects and worms in the soil. A woodpecker drills holes into the bark of a tree and then seeks out insects with its amazingly long, barbed tongue. Other birds, such as swallows, swifts and nightjars, catch insects in the air.

Birds of the world: ostriches (Africa); kookaburra (Australia); pintail duck (Europe, N. America); crossbill (Europe, Asia, N. America).

Wading birds have long legs and widely spaced toes. They use their long beaks to probe for small animals in sand, mud or shallow water.

Some birds have developed ingenious ways of getting at food. A herring gull smashes open mussels by dropping them from a height on to rocks. A Galapagos finch uses a cactus spine as a tool to dig beetle larvae out of dead wood.

A number of birds that feed on insects also eat seeds and fruits. Such birds as tits, starlings, blackbirds, crows and gulls are omnivorous, and the kookaburra of Australia is said to eat anything it can find.

Others specialize in eating plant food. A duck uses its broad, flat bill for cropping grass and water plants. The short, stout beaks of finches are typical of seed-eating birds. Crossbills have very specialized beaks to prise the ripe seeds of conifers out of their cones. Parrots use their slightly hooked beaks and their highly mobile tongues to feed on a variety of tropical fruits and seeds.

BIRDS 49

A male bird of paradise displays to impress a potential mate.

Breeding

Unlike reptiles, birds look after their eggs and young. Breeding often begins with elaborate courtship rituals in which male and female seem to perform to each other. The purpose of this strange-looking behaviour is to confirm that both partners belong to the same species and that they are both ready to mate.

Most birds lay their eggs in nests, which may be simple hollows in the ground or elaborate constructions in trees or bushes. When the young hatch they are cared for by one or both parents. Some chicks can run about and feed themselves within hours or days of hatching. Others are blind and naked and have to remain in the nest for several weeks or even months.

An oystercatcher lays between two and four eggs in a shallow depression scraped in sand or between pebbles.

EXPERT BUILDERS

The weaverbirds are small, mostly seed-eating birds (including the familiar sparrow), some of which build very complicated nests. Using beak and feet, they weave plant fibres into hanging, hollow balls, entered through a tube-like hole. One species builds a very large, thatched nest, which houses dozens or even hundreds of birds.

THE BANDIT CUCKOO

The European cuckoo (and a few other species) lays its eggs in the nests of other, smaller birds. It lays one in each nest, while the owners are away. When the cuckoo chick hatches, although blind and naked, it heaves its foster parents' eggs or chicks (if they have hatched) out of the nest. It then gets the full attention of the parent birds, who continue feeding it until it has grown much larger than they are. They hardly ever recognize that the huge chick is an impostor.

Mammals

Mammals are different from other vertebrates in several ways. Typically they have fur or hair, though some (such as elephants) have very little and whales have none. Nearly all give birth to live young, which feed on their mother's milk. They have a more advanced kind of heart, divided into four chambers, and they are all warm-blooded. This means that they always keep their body at the same temperature, warmer than the temperature outside. Mammals (and birds) can therefore lead a more active life than cold-blooded animals such as reptiles, which can hardly move in very hot or very cold weather.

A cheetah shades her cubs in the heat of the day on an African plain. Like a number of mammals a cheetah loses excess heat by panting instead of sweating.

Saving heat

A warm-blooded animal keeps its body warm by using the heat generated by the chemical processes that go on inside it. However, keeping the body warm uses up a great deal of energy. Saving heat is thus very important.

Most mammals have a covering of fur that provides an effective form of insulation. Very often, there are two layers of fur – a dense layer of fine hairs near the skin that keeps heat in, and a layer of longer, tougher hairs that provides a waterproof outer covering. The hairs are embedded in the skin and can be raised to increase the thickness of the insulation layer.

The insulation provided by hair is often assisted by a layer of fat just under the skin, and in some mammals this is the most important form of insulation. Temperature is regulated by a part of the brain. If the blood gets too hot, blood vessels in the skin expand to allow blood to flow close to the surface, where the air cools it. Many mammals sweat or pant in order to lose heat as moisture evaporates from the skin or tongue. If the blood gets too cold, the blood vessels in the skin shrink, and the body muscles start to shiver in order to generate extra heat.

MAMMALS 51

Parental care

Mammals take greater care of their young than other animals. This means that fewer offspring have to be produced in order to make sure that enough survive. The developing young are raised inside their mother's womb, or uterus. There, in most cases, they receive nourishment from the mother through an organ known as the placenta. The young are born in a well-developed state, and some young mammals can walk within minutes of being born. For some time after birth, all mammal young are fed on milk produced by special glands (mammary glands) in the mother's skin. They are looked after by one or both parents until they are able to fend for themselves.

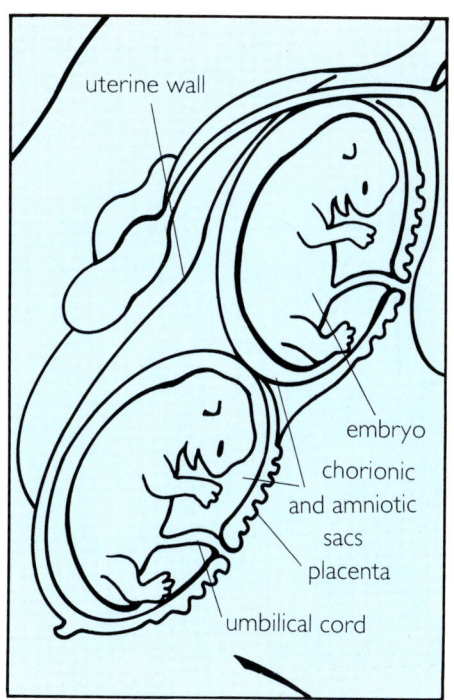

Above: A mammal embryo (in this case a cat) lies protected in membranes inside its mother's womb and receives food and oxygen via the placenta and umbilical cord.

Below: Young mammals instinctively suckle from their mother's teats.

FROM SCALES TO TEETH

The teeth of vertebrates have developed from skin scales. In a shark, for example, there is little difference between the teeth and the scales that cover the animal's body. In other vertebrates the teeth are cemented into the jaws. Teeth are made of a material called dentine and sometimes covered with a harder substance known as enamel. Mammals' teeth have become modified for specialized tasks. In a carnivore, for example, the front teeth, or incisors, are designed for cutting. Behind these are a pair of pointed, canine teeth used for holding and stabbing prey. Towards the back of the mouth are large, carnassial teeth used for slicing flesh. A herbivore, on the other hand, has no canine teeth and the teeth at the back of the mouth have flat crowns for grinding up plant material.

ANIMALS WITH BACKBONES

Monotremes and Marsupials

Mammals evolved from an early group of reptiles over 200 million years ago. Even today, there are a few mammals that still have some reptilian features, one being that they lay eggs.

The platypus (below) feeds on small animals, which it detects using the sensitive skin on its snout. An echidna (right) feeds on termites.

Egg-laying mammals

These primitive mammals are known as the monotremes. There are six species: the duck-billed platypus and five species of echidna, or spiny anteater. The platypus is a water-dwelling animal that is found only in the rivers of western Australia. A female platypus lays her eggs in a chamber at the end of a long, winding burrow dug into the bank of the river. She usually lays two soft-shelled eggs, which she incubates (keeps warm) for seven to ten days. The newly hatched young feed on milk that oozes from slits in their mother's belly and emerge from the burrow after about four months.

The spiny anteaters are all found in Australasia. A spiny anteater looks like a large hedgehog. It uses powerful claws to dig into anthills and termite mounds and picks up the inhabitants with a long, sticky tongue. A female spiny anteater lays a single egg, which she incubates in a shallow pouch on her belly. The young echidna hatches in about ten days. It remains in the pouch, where it is suckled on milk.

MONOTREMES AND MARSUPIALS

Pouched mammals

Marsupials are more advanced mammals. They do not lay eggs but, unlike the placental mammals, their young are born at a very early stage of development. A newly-born marsupial crawls into a pouch on the mother's belly, where it suckles from a teat and continues to develop. Even after it grows too big for the pouch, it continues to receive milk for some time.

Like monotremes, marsupials are mostly found in Australasia, where until recently there were no placental mammals to compete with them. One group of marsupials, opossums, are found in South America and one species, the Virginia opossum, has succeeded in spreading into a large part of North America.

The most familiar Australian marsupials are kangaroos, which are Australia's grazing animals – like deer or antelope in other continents. Another ground-dweller is the bandicoot, which feeds on roots and insects and burrows like a rabbit. Wombats also dig like miniature bulldozers. The numbat feeds on ants, and the marsupial mole is extraordinarily like a placental mole. Tree-dwelling herbivores include such species as the brush-tailed possum and the koala. Among carnivores are the Tasmanian devil (whose diet includes the poisonous black tiger snake), several kinds of marsupial mice and the native cats, which stalk their prey like cats but look more like rodents.

FLYING POSSUMS

There are several species of flying marsupials, the largest being the silky-furred greater gliding possum (or opossum). They have large flaps of loose skin between their front and back legs, which they use like wings to glide from tree to tree, steering with their fluffy tail. Although they don't really fly, they can glide for amazing distances – up to 90m (300ft) – and hardly ever come down to the ground.

The kangaroo is a grazing animal, like deer and antelope in other parts of the world. The Tasmanian devil (right) is a ferocious carnivore.

Hedgehogs, Moles and Vampires

In most parts of the world there are huge numbers of insects. Many animals, such as birds, make use of this practically unlimited source of food. In fact, the earliest mammals were small, insect-eating creatures, and it was from them that all the other groups of mammals evolved.

A hedgehog feeds on insects, slugs and snails and, when possible, young birds, reptiles and amphibians. During the winter it hibernates in a sheltered place.

Insectivores

Modern insectivores are the most primitive group of mammals, after the monotremes and marsupials. The shrews, which form the largest group, are probably most like the early mammals. There are some 300 species of these aggressive, quarrelsome little animals, which spend most of their time among long grass and leaf litter foraging for insects, snails and worms. Being very small, shrews can easily become too cold. To prevent this they have to eat almost all the time: every day a shrew eats an amount of food equal to about three-quarters of the weight of its own body.

Hedgehogs are also members of the order *Insectivora*. These animals are found only in the Old World (Europe, Asia and Africa). A hedgehog feeds on a variety of small animals, and its dense covering of spines makes an effective defence when it rolls up into a ball. Moles, too, are insectivores. A mole spends most of its time underground in a network of tunnels. Its chief food is actually earthworms, but it also eats insect larvae in the soil. A mole has very poor sight, but its senses of smell, hearing and touch are superb.

A mole lives underground using two networks of tunnels. One lies about 10cm below the surface and is temporary. The other is deeper and permanent.

HEDGEHOGS, MOLES AND VAMPIRES

Daubenton's bat

brown bat

short-nosed fruit bat

Serotine bat

vampire bat

Bats

Bats also eat insects, but they are classified in a different mammal order, the *Chiroptera*. They are the only mammals that have truly mastered the art of flying; other so-called 'flying' mammals can only glide. A bat's wing is a flap of skin supported by the front and hind legs, including four long 'fingers' on the front leg. Bats roost upside down to protect their delicate wings and to make take-off easier.

Bats are divided into two main groups. The first, the megachiropterans, are the fruit-eating bats, of which the largest are the flying foxes of southern Asia. The second group, the microchiropterans, are nearly all insect-eaters that catch their prey in mid-air. They find their prey, and avoid obstacles, by producing high-pitched sounds and listening to their echoes, a system of echolocation that works rather like a ship's sonar.

Some microchiropterans have adapted to other forms of food. The fishing bulldog bat of Central America uses echolocation to locate fish underwater. A vampire bat drinks the blood of other vertebrates, such as cattle, dogs, poultry, birds and even humans.

For echolocation, some bats produce sounds via their mouths, but the leaf-nosed bat (above) uses its nostrils. Echolocation is less important in a vampire bat, which locates its victims by scent.

Animals with Backbones

Primates

The primates, the group that includes monkeys, apes and human beings, are thought to have evolved fairly early in the history of the mammals and are thus quite closely related to the insectivores.

bushbaby
colobus monkey
howler monkey
mandrill
ring-tailed lemur

Prosimians and monkeys

The most primitive primates are the prosimians ('before monkeys'). The largest family is that of the lemurs, which are today all confined to the island of Madagascar. Others include the bushbabies of Africa, the lorises of south-east Asia and the tarsiers of the Philippines and Indonesia.

Monkeys are divided into two main groups. Those that inhabit the Old World include baboons, mandrills, patas monkeys, colobus monkeys and guenons of Africa. Langurs and most of the macaques are found in Asia. All Old World monkeys have nostrils that are close together and open to the front.

Monkeys of the New World have broad, flat noses and their nostrils open to the sides. Many of them also have grasping tails that can be used like a fifth hand. New World monkeys include capuchins, howler monkeys, spider monkeys and tamarins.

Tree shrews

Another group of animals, tree shrews, are sometimes classified as primates, because they have a number of primate features. For example, they have good colour vision and depend on sight rather than smell to find food. However, tree shrews, which are squirrel-like animals found in southern Asia, are usually placed in a separate mammal order.

Apes

The most advanced primates are classified in three separate families. The first of these contains the gibbons, which are smaller than the other apes and have particularly long arms. They spend much of their lives in trees, swinging from branch to branch. The second family consists of the three species of great apes – the orang-utan, chimpanzee and gorilla. The orang-utan is a tree-dwelling ape found in Borneo. The gorilla is an African animal that lives in small groups in the rainforest. Chimpanzees are also found in Africa, where they live in large social groups of up to 40 individuals.

The last family contains only one living species, *Homo sapiens*, the modern human being. The enormous success of our species is largely due to our intelligence. We can adapt to a variety of surroundings and often alter them to suit ourselves. At the same time we have developed social behaviour to the point where we share food and divide up the tasks that need to be done.

Primates mostly have flattened faces and their eyes point forwards, giving binocular, or stereoscopic vision. This makes it easier to judge distance. Instead of claws they have flat nails that protect the pads of the fingers and toes.

gibbon

gorilla

orang-utan

chimpanzee

Rodents and Rabbits

Rodents are mostly fairly small animals, but they form the largest of all the mammal orders – there are more than 1,600 species. In contrast, there are only about 60 species of rabbits and hares.

Rodents

The most obvious distinguishing feature of a rodent is its chisel-like front teeth, or incisors. Every rodent has a pair of these in both upper and lower jaws; they are used for gnawing food and other materials. The gnawing action keeps the teeth razor sharp, but at the same time they are constantly being worn down. However, as the teeth also grow continuously from the base, they remain roughly the same length throughout the animal's life.

Most rodents dig underground burrows. Many of them use their front legs to hold food and generally eat sitting on their hind legs. Small rodents often have cheek pouches, which can be used to store food as it is gathered. The food is then taken back to the burrow and eaten at leisure, thus reducing the time the animal needs to spend outside its burrow, where it may be preyed on by other animals. The cheek pouches can also be pushed inwards to close off the mouth when the animal is gnawing at an inedible material such as wood.

Typical rodents include many mice and rats native to the Old World. There are no native mice and rats in America, but there are several American members of the vole family. This is the largest rodent family and includes hamsters, lemmings and gerbils. Squirrels form another large family that includes not only tree squirrels but also a number of ground squirrels, such as the European marmot and the prairie dog of North America. Other rodents include dormice, jerboas, porcupines and the beaver. In South America there are a number of unique types, ranging from the guinea pig to the coypu and the capybara, at one metre (three feet) long the largest of all living rodents.

Left: *A harvest mouse builds a round nest of grass and leaves among the stems of grass or reeds.* Below: *Beavers build a lodge of sticks, grass and mud. The entrance is underwater in a pond, which is created by a dam built by the beavers.*

RODENTS AND RABBITS

CITIES ON THE PRAIRIE

Prairie dogs, which are squirrels, not dogs, live in large underground 'cities', consisting of a mass of burrows with hundreds of entrance holes, sometimes spreading over several kilometres. Unfortunately, the North American prairies have also attracted human farmers, and the prairie dogs have been killed in huge numbers. Not many of their vast colonies are left.

Left: *A prairie dog town consists of a huge network of tunnels and nest chambers. Sentries posted at some of the entrances can give warning of approaching danger.*

Rabbits and hares

Rabbits and hares have long hind legs and long ears. They differ from rodents in having four incisor teeth in the upper jaw. True rabbits make their nests in underground burrows. Hares, on the other hand, do not. Whereas the young of rodents and rabbits are born naked, blind and helpless, the young of a hare are born with open eyes and a covering of fur. To begin with, they are left in a 'form', which is a hollow in the grass. Within a few days they start to nibble grass.

Below: *Hares are generally larger than rabbits. They also have larger ears with black tips. Young hares are born in a 'form' among the grass, while rabbits are born in underground burrows.*

hare

rabbit

Aardvarks and Elephants

There are several mammal orders which have only a few living members. The smallest is that of the *Tubulidentata*, which contains just one species while the order *Dermoptera* contains only two.

Aardvarks and flying lemurs
The aardvark is placed in an order by itself because of its strange and unique teeth. Unlike the teeth of other mammals, they have no covering of enamel and no roots. They do contain many fine tubes – hence the name *Tubulidentata* ('tubular teeth'). Otherwise, the aardvark looks like an anteater. It feeds on termites and its common name, which means 'earth pig' in Afrikaans, is due to its pig-like snout.

The two species of *Dermoptera* are known as colugos or flying lemurs, although they are not related to the lemurs and cannot fly – only glide. The colugos are plant-eating mammals that may share a common ancestor with the bats.

Anteaters, armadillos and sloths
The *Edentata*, or edentates, form a larger order. The name means 'without teeth', but again this is a little misleading as only the anteaters lack teeth completely. The other members of this group, the armadillos and sloths, do have very simple teeth – and some armadillos have up to 100 of them. Anteaters live entirely on ants and termites. Armadillos are omnivorous, feeding on anything from plants and insects to lizards and snakes. Sloths are slow-moving plant-eaters.

The edentates are all found in the Americas, mostly in the south. The anteating animals of the Old World form a separate order, the *Pholidota*. This order contains the pangolins, or scalytails; they have bodies covered in scales, providing protection against attack by ants and soldier termites.

two-toed sloth
giant anteater
aardvark
pangolin

AARDVARKS AND ELEPHANTS

Hyraxes and elephants

The hyraxes (order *Hyracoidea*) are rabbit-sized African animals that at first glance look like guinea pigs. However, unlike rodents, they have blunt hooves instead of claws – a feature that they share with a number of other animals, such as elephants, horses and deer.

Only two species of elephant (order *Proboscidea*) exist today. The largest living land animal is the African elephant, which grows to about 3.5m (11ft) at the shoulder. The smaller Asian elephant rarely exceeds 3m (10ft). An elephant's most remarkable feature is its trunk, which can be used to sniff the air, pick up food and suck up water – either to drink or squirt over the body. An elephant eats grass, leaves, twigs and fruit, consuming up to about 230kg (500lbs) of food every day. It also needs about 180 litres (over 300 pints) of water each day and can dig for water with its tusks.

Hyraxes have a mixture of rodent and hooved mammal characteristics and are said to be the nearest living relatives of the elephants.

rock hyrax

African elephant

Indian elephant

Hooved Mammals

Most of the hooved mammals, or ungulates as they are sometimes called, belong to two orders, the *Perissodactyla* and the *Artiodactyla*. These animals are all plant-eaters, and most are built for fast running. They walk on the tips of their toes, of which there are one, two, three or four on each hoof.

Modern horses are grassland animals that, in the wild, prefer to live in herds. Rhinoceroses and tapirs live more solitary lives, and browse the leaves of many kinds of low-growing plants.

Odd-toed ungulates

The perissodactyls include all the ungulates with an odd number of toes on each foot. Rhinoceroses, for example, have three toes on each foot. Tapirs have three toes on their hind feet but four on the front feet. Horses, the fastest runners in this group, have only a single toe.

Rhinoceroses are the largest living land mammals after elephants. Two species live in Africa and three in Asia. Three of the four species of tapir live in Central and South America, the fourth in Malaysia. Horses all belong to one genus, *Equus*, and the domestic horse is now the most common species. Others include three species of zebra and the wild asses of Asia and Africa.

onager

Malayan tapir

black rhinoceros

HOOVED MAMMALS

Even-toed ungulates
Ungulates with an even number of toes on each foot belong to the artiodactyl order. Most artiodactyls have two-toed, or cloven, hooves. The least agile artiodactyls are the hippopotamuses ('river horses'). Pigs and peccaries form another family. The European wild boar spends its time digging in the ground for roots, bulbs and fungi. Other members of the pig family are the warthog of Africa and the wrinkly-skinned babirusa ('pig-deer') of the island of Celebes (Indonesia).

All the remaining artiodactyls are ruminants. They have four-chambered stomachs, the first of which is called the rumen. These animals 'chew the cud', that is, they bring up lumps of partly digested food from the stomach to the mouth in order to chew it a second time.

Among the ruminants are members of the camel family, which includes the South American llama and its relatives. All the rest belong to the sub-order *Pecora*, whose members have no incisor teeth in the upper jaw. The lower incisors bite against a horny pad. Except for the mouse deer, all pecorans have horns. Giraffes have a pair of bony knobs, deer have horny antlers that are shed once a year, and members of the cattle family have permanent horns with a horny sheath surrounding a core of bone. The cattle family includes sheep, goats and all the antelopes, such as gazelles.

The large artiodactyl group contains a range of very different hooved animals. However, scientists believe that all these animals are descended from a group of animals that existed about 60 million years ago.

Animals with Backbones

Carnivores

Most flesh-eating mammals belong to the order *Carnivora*. Members of this order have teeth and bodies specially designed for catching and eating other animals. However, they do not all rely entirely on meat; for example, bears and raccoons are omnivorous animals that include a large amount of plant material in their diet.

tiger

Like primates, most carnivores have forward-pointing eyes. They can thus judge distance accurately – often very important when catching prey.

ocelot

coyote

hyena

Cats and dogs

The best known carnivores are the cats, all of which have excellent hearing and long-distance vision – necessary for hunting. Big cats can roar, and their eyes have large, round pupils. Small cats cannot roar, but they can purr and breathe at the same time. The pupils of their eyes are usually vertical slits. Big cats include the tiger, which is found in Asia, and the lion, which is largely restricted to Africa. Other big cats include the leopard and the cheetah of Africa and the jaguar of America. Among the small cats are the rare snow leopard of Asia, the European lynx, the serval of Africa and the ocelot of South America. The domestic cat was probably originally bred from the African bush cat.

The dog family includes the wolf and its relatives, such as the domestic dog, the coyote of North America and the jackals of Africa. Also in this family are all the foxes, such as the two red foxes of Europe and North America, the kit fox of the American deserts, the fennec of the Sahara desert, and the Arctic fox.

CARNIVORES

Bears, weasels and seals
Among the bears are some of the largest carnivores; an adult Kodiak bear can weigh more than 500kg (1,100lb). The Kodiak is a race of brown bear, like the fearsome grizzly. Other bears include the American black bear and the polar bear, which lives along the edge of the Arctic pack ice.

The rare and attractive giant panda of central China is probably a bear, though zoologists are not certain. The smaller red panda, on the other hand, is a member of the raccoon family and more closely related to the North American raccoon and the South American coati.

Weasels belong to the mustelid family, along with the stoat, mink, martens, polecats and otters. The largest mustelids are the badgers, skunks and wolverine of northern Canada and Eurasia. Another family, the viverrids, includes such carnivores as civets, genets, suricates and mongooses.

Most carnivores are land animals, but the seals have become adapted to a life spent mostly in water (they return to land to breed). Their bodies are streamlined and their limbs have become flippers. True seals include the common seal, grey seal, leopard seal and the largest of all seals, the elephant seal. Fur seals and sea lions belong to a separate family.

weasel

giant panda

meercats

bear

A weasel eats only small animals, but suricates eat some plant material as well. A bear is even more omnivorous and a giant panda feeds only on bamboo shoots.

Sea Cows, Whales and Dolphins

Some mammals live permanently in water. Most belong to the mammal order *Cetacea*, which includes all the whales and dolphins. Sea cows also live in water, but they are actually more closely related to elephants than to either seals or whales and are therefore placed in a separate order, the *Sirenia*.

Whales are superbly adapted to a life spent in water. Their forelimbs are flippers and the hind limbs form a powerful, horizontal tail or fluke. The nostrils are fused into a single opening on the top of the head. This blow-hole is automatically closed when the whale dives. Instead of fur to keep it warm, a whale has a thick layer of fat, or blubber, under the skin.

Toothed whales

A number of whales are carnivorous animals that catch their prey with their peg-like teeth. Among these are the dolphins, a group that includes porpoises and the killer whale. Dolphins are among the fastest animals in the sea and can reach speeds of over 40kph (25mph).

Larger toothed whales include the beaked whale, the narwhal and the white whale, or beluga. The largest of all is the sperm whale, so called because inside its large, domed forehead is an organ filled with a material known as spermaceti. The purpose of this organ is not known, but it may be concerned with echo-location. Most toothed whales use echolocation to navigate and to find their prey. They produce short bursts of high-pitched sound and listen to the echoes that bounce off other objects in the sea. Ultrasound – sound waves of very high frequency – and audible sounds are also used for communication.

A sea cow is a shy, slow-moving, plant-eating mammal. In contrast a dolphin is a fast-swimming often friendly meat-eater.

blue whale

adult human

sperm whale

humpback whale

orca

minke whale

Most whales are large compared to land mammals, but the blue whale is almost unbelievably huge. This is only possible because the animal's body is supported by the water. If a whale is beached, its weight prevents it from breathing.

Whalebone whales

Whalebone whales are so called because their mouths contain a large number of plates made of a horny material called baleen, or whalebone. The plates are used to filter small crustaceans, particularly krill, from the water.

The largest whalebone whale, the blue whale, may grow up to 33m (108ft) long and weigh over 100 tonnes. Blue whales, which eat about four tonnes of food each day, are the largest animals that have ever lived on Earth. Other whalebone whales include the humpback whale, the right whales (so called because during the 19th century they were considered the 'right whales' to hunt since they were slow swimmers and floated when dead), the minke whale and the sei whale.

Like dolphins, whalebone whales communicate by sound. Some produce very low-pitched sounds that travel hundreds of kilometres underwater. Whalebone whales also migrate with the seasons. Blue whales, for example, move closer to the equator during the summer in order to breed.

FILTER FEEDING

A baleen whale uses its huge whalebone plates to strain from the water small organisms such as the shrimp-like krill. In a shoal of krill the whale opens its mouth and draws in a large quantity of water. The mouth is then closed and the tongue is raised. The water is forced out through the sides of the mouth and the animals become trapped in hair-like growths on the insides of the plates. The whale then swallows the krill.

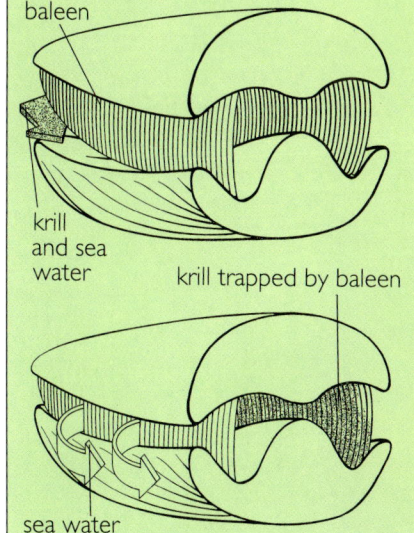

baleen

krill and sea water

krill trapped by baleen

sea water

References

Adaptation A special characteristic developed, or evolved, by an animal (or plant) to help it survive in its particular habitat.

Amphibian Cold-blooded, vertebrate land animal with a moist, often delicate skin that lays soft, vulnerable eggs. Moist or wet conditions are thus essential for breeding and most amphibians breed in water.

Binocular vision Stereoscopic vision. Seeing three-dimensional images. Two forward-pointing eyes, a few centimetres apart, see a scene from slightly different angles and thus two slightly different two-dimensional images are produced in each eye. The nerve signals from the eyes are combined by the brain into one, three-dimensional image.

Bird Warm-blooded, vertebrate animal insulated by an outer layer of feathers. Only the hind legs are used for walking; the front limbs are modified into feathered wings, which in most birds are used for flight. The young are produced in hard-shelled eggs and on hatching are cared for by one or both parents.

Bone The material from which most vertebrate skeletons are made. It consists of fibres (collagen fibres) embedded in a complex chemical compound (bone salt) that consists mainly of calcium and phosphorus (in the form of phosphate). Bone salt makes up 60 per cent of bone and gives it hardness. The collagen gives it strength.

Carapace An external shield of an animal, such as the shell of a tortoise.

Cartilage Tough animal tissue which, in vertebrates, connects and protects the bones. Some animals, such as sharks, have skeletons made of cartilage rather than bone.

Chordate An animal that at some stage during its life has a stiffening rod, or notochord, along its back.

Egg A female sex cell which, after it is fertilized by a male sex cell, develops into an embryo. Part of the fertilized egg becomes a yolk, which feeds the developing embryo until after it hatches. A bird's egg consists mostly of yolk, surrounded by a clear albumen (the 'white') which protects the embryo as it develops on the upper surface of the yolk.

Embryo A young animal in the first stage of its development, such as a bird before it hatches from the egg.

Fish Water-dwelling, cold-blooded vertebrate that swims by means of its tail and fins. The body is covered in scales.

Flying animals Most birds, many insects and all bats can fly, using muscle power to generate lift and stay in the air. All other so-called flying animals can only glide, using their 'wings' like parachutes to slow down their descent towards the ground.

Habitat The type of place or environment in which a particular species lives.

Herbivore An animal that eats only plants, not meat.

Hibernation Sleeping during the winter, so that the animal uses little energy and therefore requires little food. Most reptiles and amphibians, and many mammals, hibernate. They are not really asleep most of the time, and may have periods of activity.

Mammal Warm-blooded, vertebrate land animal insulated by an outer layer of fur and/or a layer of blubber (fat) in the skin. All mammals give birth to active young and suckle their young with milk produced from special skin glands. In a placental mammal the young are nourished in the female's body by an organ known as the placenta.

New World The Americas.

Old World Europe, Asia and Africa.

Oviparous Laying eggs that do not hatch until after they are laid; all birds, for example, are oviparous. Mammals, which give birth to live young, are viviparous. There is also a third category, which includes some reptiles and a few fishes, called ovoviviparous, in which the eggs hatch immediately before the young are born.

Placental mammals Mammals in which the unborn young receive nourishment in the mother's womb through the placenta.

Plankton A large mass of tiny organisms that float or drift in the water, usually near the surface, and provide the main food supply for many fishes, birds and whales. When the organisms are tiny animals, rather than plants, they are called zooplankton.

Reptile Cold-blooded, vertebrate land animal with a tough, leathery or scaly, waterproof skin.

Skeleton A structure or framework that supports the body of an animal. The simplest skeleton is a shell, such as that of a mollusc. Arthropods have an exoskeleton ('outside skeleton') made of chitin. Vertebrates have internal skeletons, or endoskeletons, made of bone or cartilage.

Snake fangs The sharp, hollow teeth of venomous snakes with which they inject poison into their prey. In some snakes the fangs are at the back of the mouth. Such snakes feed on small animals and most are harmless to humans. Snakes with fangs at the front of the mouth, such as cobras and sea snakes, are more dangerous. The long fangs of vipers and rattlesnakes normally lie folded backwards along the jaw but spring upright when the snake opens its mouth to strike.

Spawn Eggs with soft shells that are laid in very large numbers by fish and amphibians.

Vertebrate Animal with a backbone.

The Plant Kingdom

Algae

Plants are organisms that have cells surrounded by more or less rigid walls made of cellulose. They manufacture their own food by the process known as photosynthesis.

We think of plants as having leaves, stems and underground roots, but the simplest plants have no stems or roots. Such plants are all included in the group known as the algae.

All algae require wet or moist conditions in order to survive. Most are therefore found in water, although a few manage to live on land. Algae reproduce very simply. Asexual reproduction is common: pieces of plant body break off and grow, or single cells simply split into two. But most algae also carry out sexual reproduction by producing sex cells. In the most complex algae, plants produce distinct male cells that swim to stationary female cells and fuse with them. The resulting cells grow into new plants.

Green algae

A number of single-celled organisms are classified as algae. Some of them are not necessarily true plants. Others are obviously plants, particularly the green algae (the *Chlorophyta*), such as *Chlamydomonas* and the round-celled *Chlorella* and *Pleurococcus*.

The green algae also include a number of larger plants. Some form threads, or filaments, and are therefore known as filamentous algae. The most common is *Spirogyra*, whose rich green strands can be seen in almost any pond. *Cladophora*, which is found in sea water, has filaments that branch, giving the plant a tree-like appearance. Sea lettuce (*Ulva*) has a flat plant body made up of a two-layered sheet of cells.

Below: *The filamentous alga* Spirogyra *is so named because of the spiral chloroplast in each cell. Its tangled threads form the green scum seen in ponds.*

Above: *The moist green film often found on the bark of trees is formed from millions of cells of the green, single-celled alga* Pleurococcus.

ALGAE

Seaweeds

Among the most familiar algae are the brown and red seaweeds. Brown seaweeds, such as the common bladder-wrack, get their colour from the pigment fucoxanthin, which is another pigment that these plants use to carry out photosynthesis. The kelps, or oarweeds, form underwater 'forests' along rocky shores. The giant kelp has fronds up to 60m (200ft) long. Kelps get their name from the ash they form when burned, which was an important source of certain chemicals in the 19th century. Most brown seaweeds are attached to rocks. However, the Sargasso Sea is named after its floating rafts of *Sargassum* seaweed.

Red seaweeds contain another photosynthetic pigment known as phycoerythrin. This enables them to carry out photosynthesis in places where the light is poor. Red seaweeds are therefore found in shady places and in deep water. Some of them have rather complicated plant bodies.

Marine algae, or seaweeds, are found in the shallow waters around most coastlines. Brown seaweeds are the most common, but there are also red and green species.

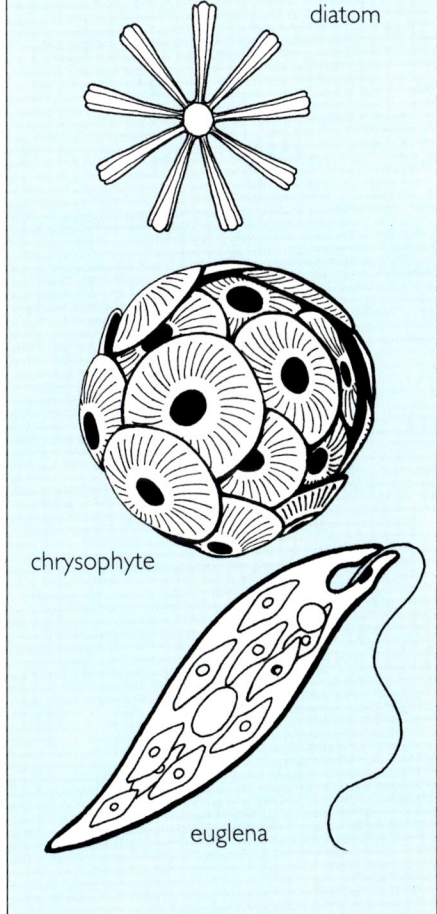

PLANTS OR ANIMALS?

A number of single-celled, plant-like organisms are included in the algae although some of them are not at all like other plants. A diatom, for example, has an outer wall made of silica instead of cellulose. This wall is in two parts that fit together like a box and its lid, and is often sculptured with intricate patterns. Coccolithophores have chalky plates attached to their outer surface. Large numbers of coccolithophores exist in the sea; their chalky plates form thick muds on the ocean floor. A number of single-celled algae are equipped with flagella, which are used for swimming. Among these are the dinoflagellates, which are mostly sea-dwellers, and the euglenoids, which are unusual because they have characteristics of both plants and animals. Like plants, they can make food by photosynthesis, but they do not have cellulose cell walls and can also feed in an animal-like way by taking in food material from outside.

THE PLANT KINGDOM

Mosses and Liverworts

Mosses and their relatives belong to the group known as the *Bryophyta*. The bryophytes are nearly all small, low-growing, land plants. Their plant bodies are fairly simple and they generally prefer moist conditions. Some have distinct leaves and stems, others do not. None of them has true roots. Instead, they attach themselves to rocks, trees or the ground by means of small, root-like threads known as rhizoids.

Leaves and stems

Liverworts are the simplest members of the group. They have delicate plant bodies with no outer covering to prevent them drying out. They are therefore found only in damp, shady places. Thalloid liverworts (without distinct leaves and stems) have flat plant bodies that sprawl along the ground. Leafy liverworts have distinct stems and thin, filmy leaves.

Mosses are much hardier plants. A moss has a thin stem, inside which is a strand of special cells which carries water up the plant. In some mosses the leaves have a thin, waxy covering, or cuticle, which helps to slow down the rate at which water is lost by evaporation.

Mosses are common in damp places, such as woodlands, bogs and tropical rainforests. A few, however, survive in drier conditions – for example, on moorland and dry stone walls. And some live submerged in water, where their fronds may grow to over 1m (3ft) long.

Right: Plagiochila aspleniodes *is a leafy liverwort found in many moist, shady places, particularly in woodlands.*

leafy liverwort

thalloid liverwort

Left: Pellia epiphylla *is a thalloid liverwort that is very common on the shaded banks of streams. In spring this species produces large numbers of tiny black capsules on the ends of stalks. These split open to release spores.*

MOSSES AND LIVERWORTS

Plants with two generations

Bryophytes reproduce themselves by means of spores, and their life-cycles have two distinct generations. The adult plant of a moss or liverwort is known as the gametophyte, because it produces sex cells, or gametes. When the male sex cells are released, they swim through the moisture on the plant's leaves and are attracted by chemicals to the female sex cells.

When a male sex cell fuses with, or fertilizes, a female sex cell, the resulting cell develops into the sporophyte. This consists of a kind of capsule on a stalk and contains spores. When the capsule is ripe, it opens to release the thousands of spores inside. Under the right conditions, each spore is capable of developing into one (in liverworts) or several (in mosses) new gamete-producing plants.

When necessary, mosses and liverworts can also reproduce asexually. Pieces of moss plant that break off may grow into completely new plants. And a number of liverworts produce special cup-shaped structures, known as gemmae, on their leaves. Each gemma may fall off and grow into a new liverwort plant.

Right: Alternation of generations in a moss. The adult plant is the gametophyte generation. The fertilized female cell develops into the spore producing generation, which consists of a capsule on a stalk. The capsule releases the spores and, under the right conditions, each one may grow into a small filamentous plant called a protonema. This develops buds, each of which can grow into a new adult plant.

Some mosses, such as Brachythecium rivulare live in moist places. Others, such as hair mosses, prefer drier places, such as sand dunes and heaths.

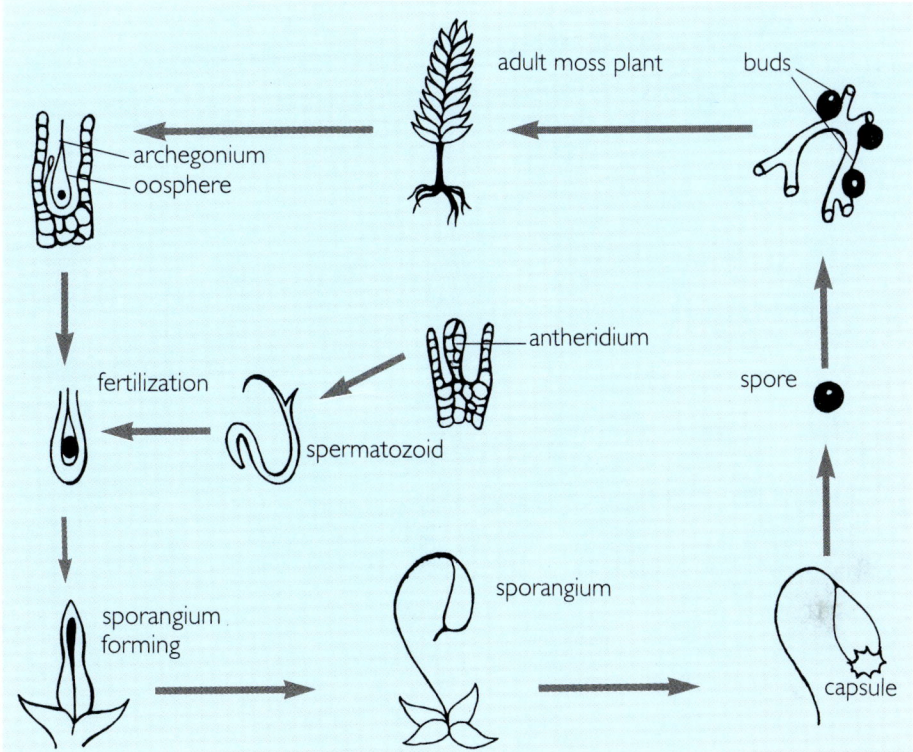

THE PLANT KINGDOM

Ferns

Ferns are larger, more noticeable plants than mosses. Their stems contain several bundles of water-conducting tissue and their leaves have a tough, waterproof covering. Thus, although most ferns prefer to live in damp, shady places, they can tolerate fairly dry conditions. In cool climates ferns may thrive in open, sunny places; bracken is an example.

Epiphytes and tree ferns
Three-quarters of the world's ferns grow in tropical and subtropical forests. In such places very little sunlight reaches the ground. Many ferns solve the problem of too little light by living on the branches of trees. Plants that live like this are known as epiphytes; they are not parasites, as they take nothing at all from the trees. Most ferns are less than 1m (3ft) high, but tropical tree ferns may stand more than 2m (6ft) above the ground. Their 'trunks' consist of the tough bases of leaves that have fallen off, and they are often supported by buttress roots that stick out from the base.

The leaves or fronds of a fern are most often spear-shaped, with a central stalk that holds a number of small leaflets, or pinnae. The pinnae may be lobed or further divided into smaller leaflets known as pinnules.

Ferns with this form of leaf include bracken, the common male fern, the royal fern and the prickly shield fern. The hart's tongue, however, has a strap-like leaf, and the maidenhair fern has delicate wedge-shaped leaves on the tips of long stalks.

A fern has very small roots. The main underground organ is a modified stem, or rhizome. Some ferns have rhizomes that grow horizontally through the ground, putting up new groups of fronds at intervals. They spread rapidly by this method; bracken has become a particular pest in many places.

Above: Bracken is a typical fern, with leaves divided into pinnae and pinnules. It is very common and is rapidly becoming a pest in many areas. Moonwort is found on hillsides and mountain ledges.

Below: Alternation of generations in a fern. The adult plant is the sporophyte. Gametes (sex cells) are produced by the prothallus, which is thus the gametophyte generation.

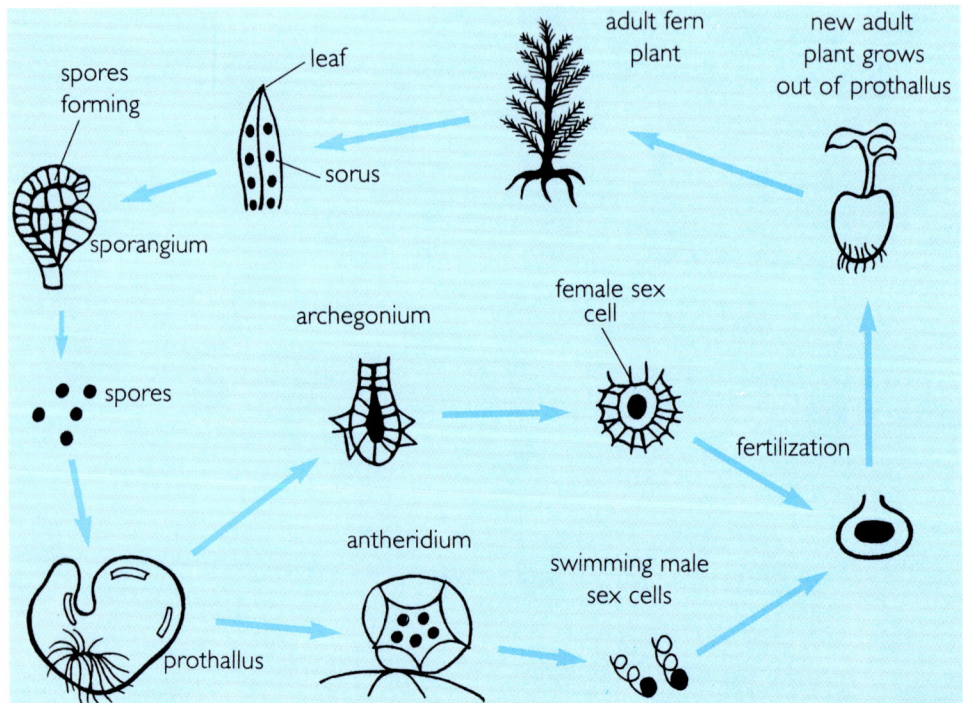

FERNS

tree fern

Above: *Tree ferns grow in tropical and subtropical parts of the world. The 'trunk' of a tree fern consists of the woody leaf bases left behind by previous fronds. New fronds are continually being produced and thus the tree fern grows gradually taller.*

Below: *Hart's tongue fern has tough, strap-shaped leaves. It is very common in Britain and is the only British fern whose leaves are undivided.*

hart's tongue fern

Spores under the leaves

Like a moss, a fern produces spores and its life-cycle involves two generations. But in ferns the spore-producing generation, or sporophyte, is the adult plant. The spores are generally produced on the undersides of the leaves, where the spore-containers lie protected in umbrella-like structures called sori (singular: sorus). When released, the spores are scattered by the wind. If a spore lands on moist ground, it grows into a tiny, heart-shaped structure known as a prothallus. This is the gametophyte generation that produces male and female sex cells. The male sex cells fuse with, or fertilize, the female cells, and each fertilized female cell may develop into a new adult plant.

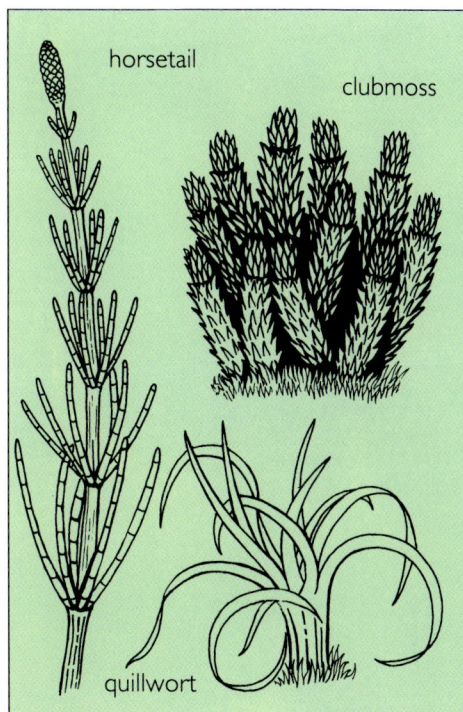

FERN ALLIES

Ferns make up the largest part of the group known as the pteridophytes, which also includes three smaller groups of plants. Clubmosses were once the dominant plants on Earth; around 300 million years ago they formed huge, swampy forests. Today there are only five species left and these are small, moss-like plants.

Closely related to the clubmosses are the quillworts, which were also present 300 million years ago. They have long thin leaves and some modern species live submerged under water.

Horsetails, the last group of pteridophytes, have jointed stems, with rings of small branches at each joint. They look rather like bottle brushes.

THE PLANT KINGDOM

Seeds in Cones

> Two groups of plants reproduce themselves by means of seeds. These are the flowering plants and the gymnosperms. The name gymnosperm means 'naked seed': all the plants in this group produce seeds that are exposed to the air, not protected by a fruit.

Conifers

Most gymnosperms produce their seeds in cones, and most of the cone-bearers belong to the family of trees and shrubs known as the conifers. This group includes the pines, spruces, larches, firs, cedars and cypresses. They generally have leaves shaped like needles, and most are evergreen – leaves are always present. Only the larches and the swamp cypress shed all their leaves at the same time. All the rest shed leaves – and grow new ones – continuously. Each leaf lasts three or four years before it falls.

Conifers can survive in places where other plants find conditions too hard. Their leaves are tough and leathery, which means that, unlike broadleaved trees, they lose very little water and can stand up to cold winds and heavy frosts. Conifers therefore grow in places where water is scarce, such as dry or very cold regions. Most of the world's conifers are found in a broad band that lies just south of the Arctic Circle. Many conifers, especially pines, cedars and the Douglas fir, are important timber trees.

Conifers produce two kinds of cone. Male cones produce pollen grains, which contain male sex cells. Female cones produce female sex cells. In spring, the male cones release their pollen, which is carried by the wind to female cones where fertilization takes place. The fertilized female cells develop into winged seeds that lie exposed to the air on the scales of the cones.

Conifers are easy to distinguish from other trees because of their needle-like leaves and their cones. The female cones are usually larger than the male cones and after pollination may grow larger still.

SEEDS IN CONES

Other gymnosperms

Several other trees and shrubs are included in the gymnosperm group. The maidenhair tree is a 'living fossil' – the only survivor of a group that flourished 130 million years ago. Cycads grow in tropical regions. There are separate male and female trees; the seeds develop in a large cone in the centre of a female tree. Yews have conifer-like leaves, but their seeds are not formed in cones. Each seed develops partly, but not completely, enclosed in a red berry. Other gymnosperms include the switch plants and the *Welwitschia* of the Kalahari desert, which has been described as the world's strangest seed-producing plant. It uses its long trailing leaves to absorb the early morning dew.

The bright red 'berries' of the yew do not quite cover the seeds.

The maidenhair tree has remained unchanged for over 150 million years.

OLDEST AND LARGEST

Among the conifers are the world's oldest and largest living trees. Oldest are the bristlecone pines, which grow on the slopes of the White Mountains in California. The oldest living specimen is thought to be 4,600 years old, and one tree is known to have lived for 4,900 years.

The tallest living trees are the coast redwoods of California. The tip of the tallest known specimen is just over 110m (360ft) from the ground, but its tip is dying and it was probably once taller.

The world's most massive living organism is a specimen of California big tree, or wellingtonia, known as General Sherman. It is over 83m (270ft) high and its base measures over 24m (80ft) in diameter. Scientists have calculated that it weighs about 2,000 tonnes.

THE PLANT KINGDOM

Flowering Plants

Most of the plants we see around us are flowering plants. These are plants that produce seeds completely enclosed in fruits, which are formed in the remains of a flower.

Flowering plants are the world's most successful group of plants. Scientists know of about 380,000 different species of plant, and over 240,000 of them are flowering plants. There are two reasons why they are so numerous. First, their method of reproduction is much more efficient than the methods used by other plants, and this has enabled them to spread very rapidly. Second, flowering plants are very adaptable. They have been able to evolve into forms that are adapted to every type of environment in the world, even to cold, windy mountain tops and hot, dry deserts.

Monocots and dicots

The flowering plants are divided into two main groups, according to the number of seed leaves, or cotyledons, present in their seeds. Monocotyledons have one seed leaf, and fully developed plants generally have long, thin leaves with parallel veins. Dicotyledons have two seed leaves, and the adult plants have broad leaves with a network of veins.

Monocotyledon families include the grasses, irises, orchids, lilies and the palms. Dicotyledons are more numerous. Most are small green plants that grow and die within one or a few years. However, a number have woody stems and some are trees that may live for hundreds of years.

Flowering plants of the monocotyledon group (note their long, thin leaves) which includes grasses, irises, orchids, daffodils, palms and crocuses.

FLOWERING PLANTS

Flowers and pollination

Flowering plants produce their flowers in order to reproduce. A flower may contain male organs (stamens), female organs (carpels) or both. A stamen consists of a stalk, or filament, at the head of which are a group of four small sacs, or anthers. These contain pollen, which in turn contain the male sex cells. The female sex cells are enclosed deep inside the carpels, each of which has a stalk (called the style) which ends in a stigma, the part that receives the pollen. The transfer of pollen from an anther to a stigma is a process known as pollination.

Generally, plants do their best to ensure that pollen is transferred to another flower, or even to another plant (cross-pollination). This helps to produce strong offspring. If it fails, some plants make sure that at least some offspring are produced by transferring pollen to the stigma of the same flower, a process known as self-pollination.

Carnivorous plants

Plants that live on poor soils may have difficulty in obtaining nitrogen, a vital element for all living things. Some plants solve this problem by becoming carnivorous. They get nitrogen by catching small animals.

The best-known carnivorous plant is the Venus flytrap, which catches insects and other small animals in traps formed by pairs of leaves fringed with long spikes. Once trapped, the insect is digested by chemicals produced by the plant. Sundews and butterworts catch insects on sticky leaves. Pitcher plants use fluid-filled pitchers as traps. The bladderwort has underwater bladders and traps its prey by reducing the pressure inside the bladders. When a small animal swims too close, a trapdoor opens and the victim is sucked inside.

A fly has touched one of the fine hairs on the leaf of this Venus flytrap. If it touches another hair, the trap will close.

Flowering plants of the dicotyledon group (note their broad leaves) which includes buttercups, daisies, thistles, ragworts, wild roses and chicory.

THE PLANT KINGDOM

Pollination

Flowering plants go to great lengths to make sure that cross-pollination occurs, and to prevent self-pollination. Some plants use chemicals to prevent pollen grains from developing on the stigmas of the flower in which they are produced. In others the male and female parts ripen at different times. A number of plants produce separate male and female flowers, and some have completely separate male and female plants. In many insect-pollinated flowers the male and female parts are well separated, and in some flowers self-pollination is prevented by an elaborate arrangement of flaps and chambers.

Above: *The spikelets of a grass contain hanging anthers and feathery stigmas.*

Pollen in the wind

Many plants rely on the wind to transfer their pollen. As this is a rather haphazard method, they produce a huge amount of pollen to make sure that at least some of it reaches the stigmas of other flowers. Trees that produce catkins, such as hazel and willow, are typical wind-pollinated plants; the yellow male catkins produce clouds of pollen early in the spring when there are few leaves present to stop the pollen grains reaching the female catkins. All grasses are wind-pollinated; their rather insignificant green flowers have large hanging anthers, which release great amounts of pollen (the cause of hay fever in some people), and large feathery stigmas to catch the pollen of other grass flowers.

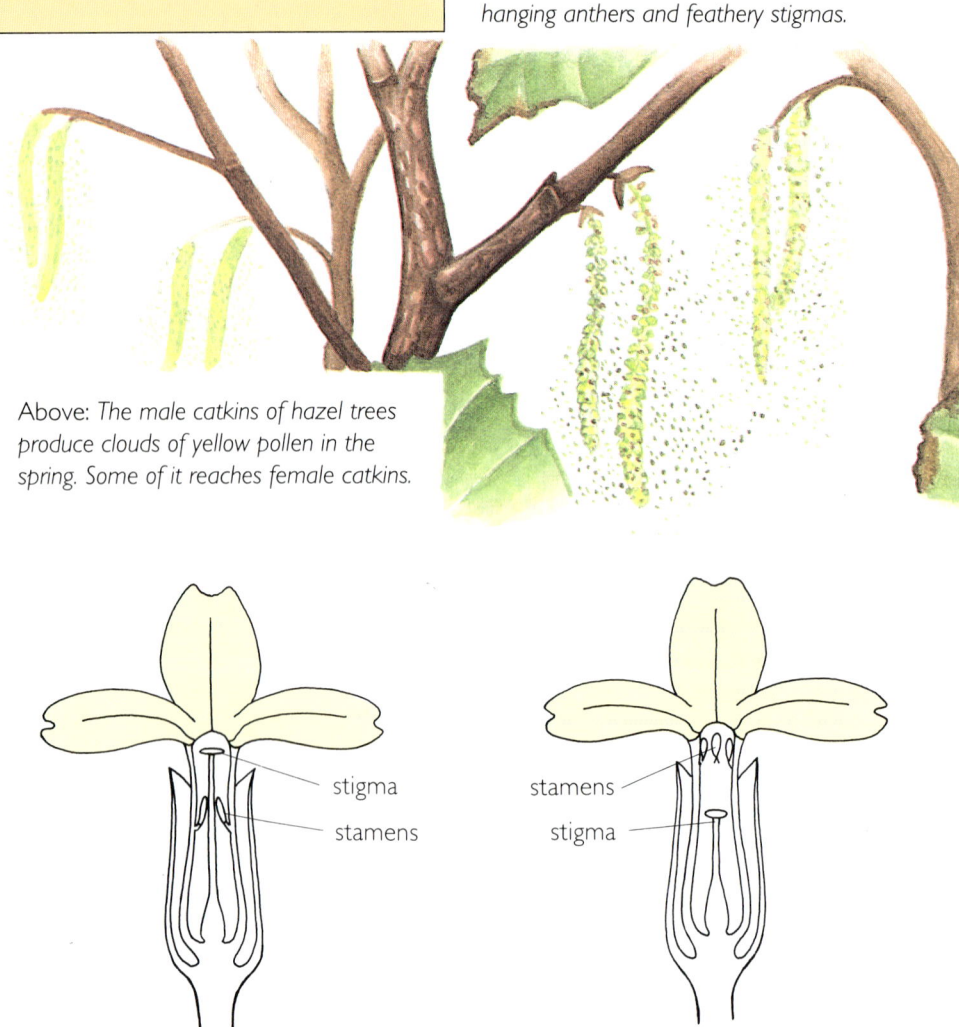

Above: *The male catkins of hazel trees produce clouds of yellow pollen in the spring. Some of it reaches female catkins.*

pin-eyed flower

thrum-eyed flower

In order to ensure cross-pollination the primrose has two kinds of flower. When an insect visits a thrum-eyed flower (right) it picks up pollen on the rear of its body. This can then be brushed on to the stigma of a pin-eyed flower (left).

POLLINATION

Above: *In a foxglove the lower flowers are female, and the upper ones male. It blooms from the bottom upwards ensuring that the female flowers receive pollen from other flowerheads.*

Animal carriers

Most of the world's flowering plants are pollinated by animals, especially insects. Their flowers are generally brightly coloured in order to attract the pollinators. Another frequent attraction is sweet-smelling nectar, which bees make into honey. Many flowers are marked with lines that guide insects towards the nectaries at the bases of the petals. As an insect enters the flower, pollen from a flower it has visited previously may be brushed off on to the stigma. As it leaves, its body is dusted with more pollen from the anthers.

Some flowers attract pollinators with less pleasant smells. Carrion flowers and the vine parasite *Rafflesia* produce smells like rotting meat in order to attract flies or bluebottles. The wild arum, or lords-and-ladies, also does this – then traps the flies overnight in order to make sure that cross-pollination occurs properly.

In tropical and subtropical countries, birds and mammals often act as pollinators. Bird pollinators include hummingbirds, sunbirds, honey-eaters and brush-tongued parrots. Bats pollinate the bell-shaped flowers of the baobab tree in Africa and the Saguaro cactus in America. Rodents pollinate some of the proteas in South Africa. Small marsupials pollinate certain Australian plants.

Left: *Insects are trapped overnight inside the flowerhead of a wild arum plant. After pollinating the female flowers they are showered with pollen from the male flowers. When released, they carry this pollen to other flowers.*

Above: *A sunbird is attracted to a flower by nectar. As it drinks it pollinates the flower, using pollen from a flower visited previously.*

THE PLANT KINGDOM

Fruits and Seeds

After pollination, fertilization takes place. A pollen grain on a stigma produces a long tube that grows down through the style and into one of the ovaries at the base. There a male cell from the pollen grain fuses with a female egg cell and a seed develops.

The fertilized female cell grows into a tiny embryo plant. The embryo is surrounded by a food store and enclosed in a hard case; these three parts form the seed. Around the seed another part of the plant – generally the wall of the ovary – develops into the fruit. The purpose of the fruit is to protect the seed and, later, to aid its removal from the parent plant.

Removing seeds from the parent plant is known as seed dispersal. Ideally, seeds are carried as far away as possible. This helps to increase the numbers of the particular species of plant and to prevent the seedlings having to compete with each other for light and space. Plants have several different methods of seed dispersal.

Explosive pods and wind dispersal

Many plants disperse their own seeds. Some have capsules that split open when ripe. Poppy seeds are shaken out through tiny holes by the wind. Others have pods or similar types of fruits that, as they dry out, suddenly burst open, flinging the seeds through the air for a considerable distance. When pressure builds up inside the fruit of the squirting cucumber, the seeds are fired out in a jet of liquid.

Wind makes an excellent carrier of seeds, and many plants take advantage of it. Orchids produce tiny, very light seeds that are easily carried on air currents. Many plants, such as willowherbs, poplars, thistles and dandelions, have fruits equipped with feathery plumes or parachutes that carry the seeds long distances. Birches, sycamores and ash trees have winged fruits that turn like helicopter blades as the fruits drift slowly downwards. The seeds of the tumbleweeds, which grow in deserts and grassland, are dispersed when large pieces of plant break off and are blown about by the wind.

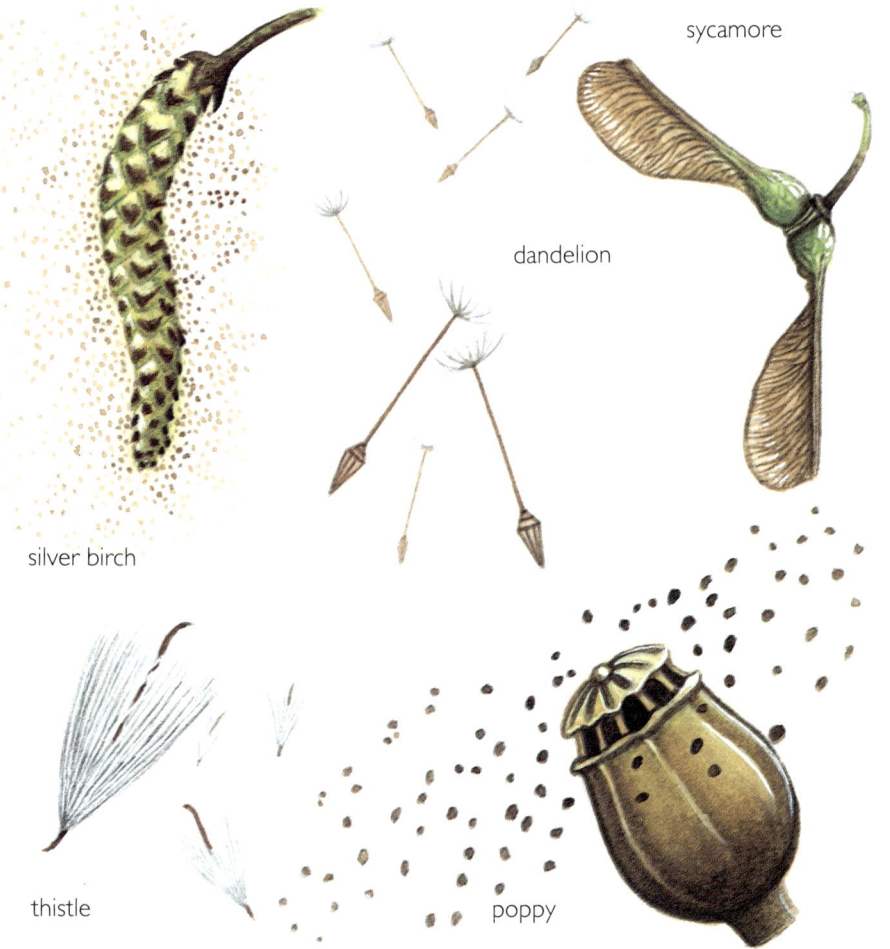

Poppy seeds are shaken out of their capsules. They fall to the ground fairly quickly, but may be carried some distance on a windy day. The small seeds of silver birch have wings to help the wind carry them away, and sycamore seeds have large wings that work like helicopter blades. Dandelion and thistle seeds have plumes that act like parachutes.

Animal dispersal

Animals often unknowingly disperse fruits and seeds. Sweet fleshy fruits are eaten, but the hard seeds inside pass through an animal unharmed and may be dropped a long way from the parent plant.

Sometimes animals such as squirrels take hazelnuts and acorns and store them away. Some stores are forgotten and the seeds inside may grow into new plants.

A number of plants produce fruits that stick or cling to the bodies of animals. Mistletoe fruits stick to the feet of birds. The hooked fruits of burdock and goose grass cling to the fur of mammals. Some tropical fruits have vicious spines or hooks that sink into an animal's flesh.

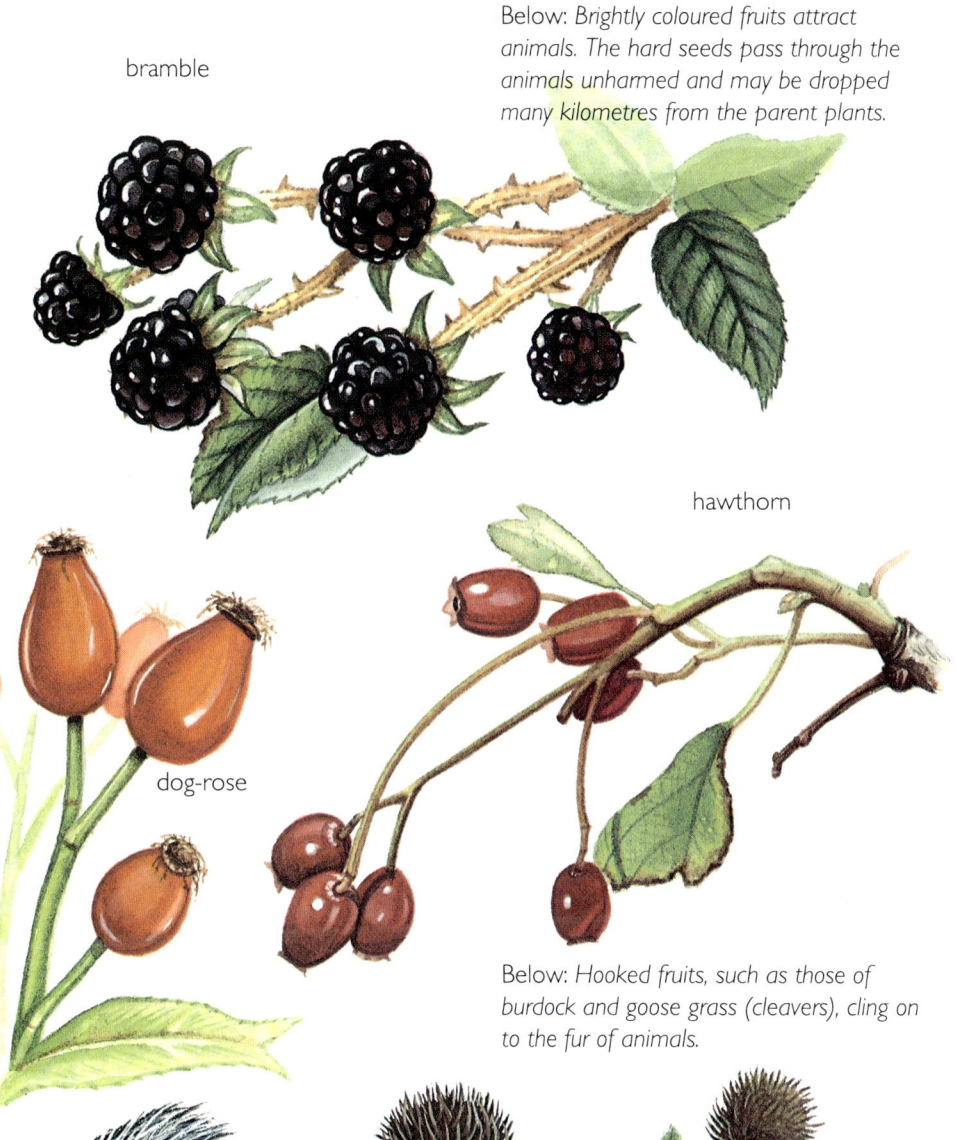

Below: *Brightly coloured fruits attract animals. The hard seeds pass through the animals unharmed and may be dropped many kilometres from the parent plants.*

bramble

hawthorn

dog-rose

Below: *A squirrel may bury several caches of acorns as food stores for the winter. Any acorns that get forgotten may germinate into young oak seedlings.*

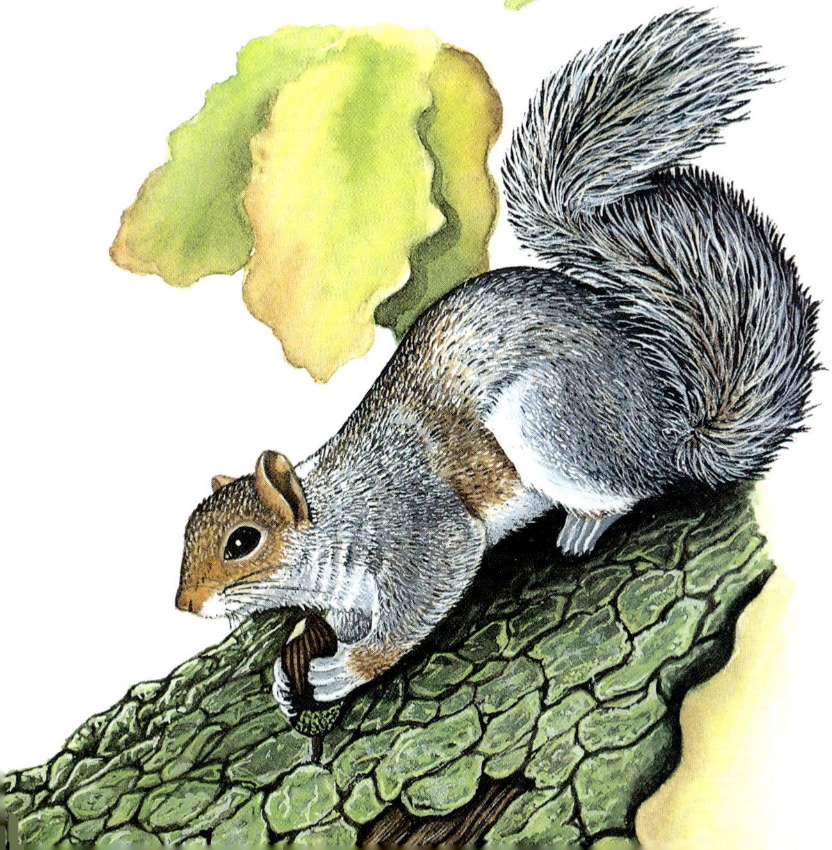

Below: *Hooked fruits, such as those of burdock and goose grass (cleavers), cling on to the fur of animals.*

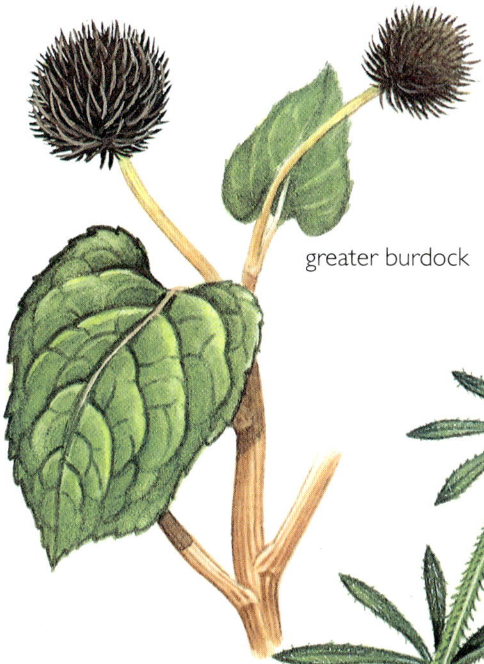

greater burdock

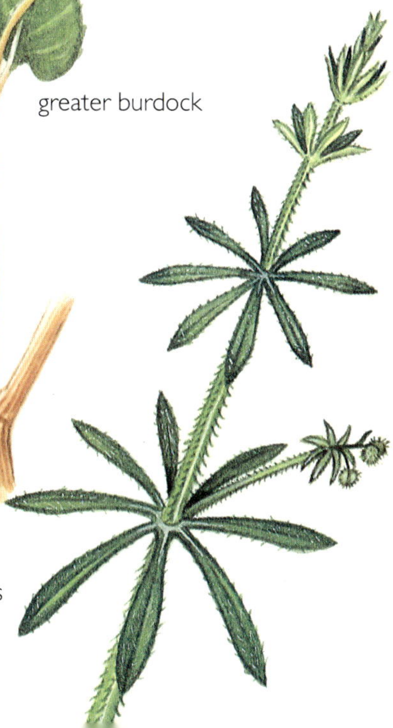

goose grass

References

Angiosperm A flowering, seed-producing plant whose seeds are completely enclosed within fruits.

Annual A flowering plant that grows from a seed, flowers, produces its own seed and dies within a single year.

Anther The head of a stamen, consisting of four sacs containing pollen.

Asexual reproduction Any method of reproduction that does not involve the production of special sex cells.

Biennial A flowering plant that lives for two years. During the first year it grows from seed and develops a food storage organ. This food is used up during the second year, when the plant flowers and produces seed.

Carpel One of the female parts of a flower, consisting of an ovary, style and stigma.

Cotyledon A seed leaf – a leaf-like structure found in all seeds. In some seeds the cotyledons contain the food store and are therefore large and swollen; in others the food store lies outside the cotyledons, which are thin and filmy.

Embryo In plants, a young plant present in a seed. It grows from a fertilized ovum during the development of the seed.

Endosperm *see* **Seed**.

Epiphyte A plant that grows on the branch of a tree in order to get nearer the light. It obtains nutrients from rotting leaves trapped on the branch. Some epiphytes grow aerial roots that take water from moist air.

Evaporation Loss of moisture as vapour.

Fertilization The fusing of two sex cells. In many cases a swimming male cell fuses with a larger, stationary female cell. In a flowering plant, however, a female cell in the ovary is fertilized by a male nucleus from the pollen grain.

Filament A long, narrow structure, such as the plant body of a filamentous alga or the stalk of a stamen.

Flower The reproductive part of a flowering plant. It consists of a ring of petals surrounded by a ring of leaf-like structures, usually green, called the sepals. In the centre of the flower are the sex organs, the stamens and carpels. Some flowers contain only male or female organs. All these parts are attached to the main supporting part of the flower, known as the receptacle.

Fruit The structure that surrounds the seed or seeds of a flowering plant. A fruit may be hard or fleshy, but it is always formed from the ovary wall. Sometimes other structures, such as the petals, sepals or receptacle are involved in fruit formation, but botanists describe such fruits as false fruits.

Gamete A sex cell. In most plants and animals there are obvious male and female cells: small, swimming cells are generally described as male; large, stationary sex cells as female. In some algae, however, all the sex cells are of one kind. Fertilization occurs when two identical swimming cells fuse together.

Gametophyte The stage during the life-cycle of a plant in which gametes are produced.

Gymnosperm A seed-producing plant whose seeds are not enclosed in fruits but exposed, completely or partly, to the air.

Herbaceous plant A green plant with no woody parts.

Nectar A sugary liquid produced in many flowers, usually by the petals, which attracts insects, birds and bats to the flower and encourages pollination as the animal collects nectar from many different plants.

Ovary In plants, the part of a carpel in which the ovum, or egg cell, is located.

Perennial A plant that lives for a number of years, during which time it continues to grow. *See also* **Annual** and **Biennial**.

Pollen The powdery, male sex cells of a flowering plant.

Receptacle *see* **Flower**.

Rhizoids Small, hair-like structures used by plants such as mosses and liverworts to help anchor them to the ground.

Seed A self-contained stage during the life-cycle of some plants. It consists of a hard outer coat, or testa, which surrounds the embryo, together with its cotyledons and food store (known as the endosperm). After it is formed, a seed may need to go through a period of dormancy (sleep) before it will germinate. Then, given water and warmth, it germinates. The food store swells, bursting the seed coat, and the root and shoot develop.

Sexual reproduction Any form of reproduction that involves the fusion of gametes, or sex cells.

Shrub A woody plant whose above-ground parts consist of several branched stems, all of which arise from the base of the plant (the point at which it emerges from the ground).

Spore A self-contained, single- or many-celled stage during the life-cycle of a plant that is capable of developing into a new individual.

Sporophyte The stage during the life-cycle of a plant in which spores are produced.

Stamen One of the male parts of a flower, consisting of a stalk, or filament, and an anther.

Stigma The pollen-receiving surface of a carpel.

Style The stalk that emerges from the top of an ovary and bears the stigma at its tip.

Thalloid Having a thallus, a simple plant body not divided into root, stem and leaves.

Tree A plant with a single woody stem emerging from the ground.

Prehistoric Life

Prehistoric Life

Fossils

Scientists believe that life on Earth began some 3,500 million years ago, and that since then living organisms have slowly evolved into their present forms. At various times in Earth's history animals and plants have appeared and disappeared. The evidence that such animals existed comes from the study of fossils.

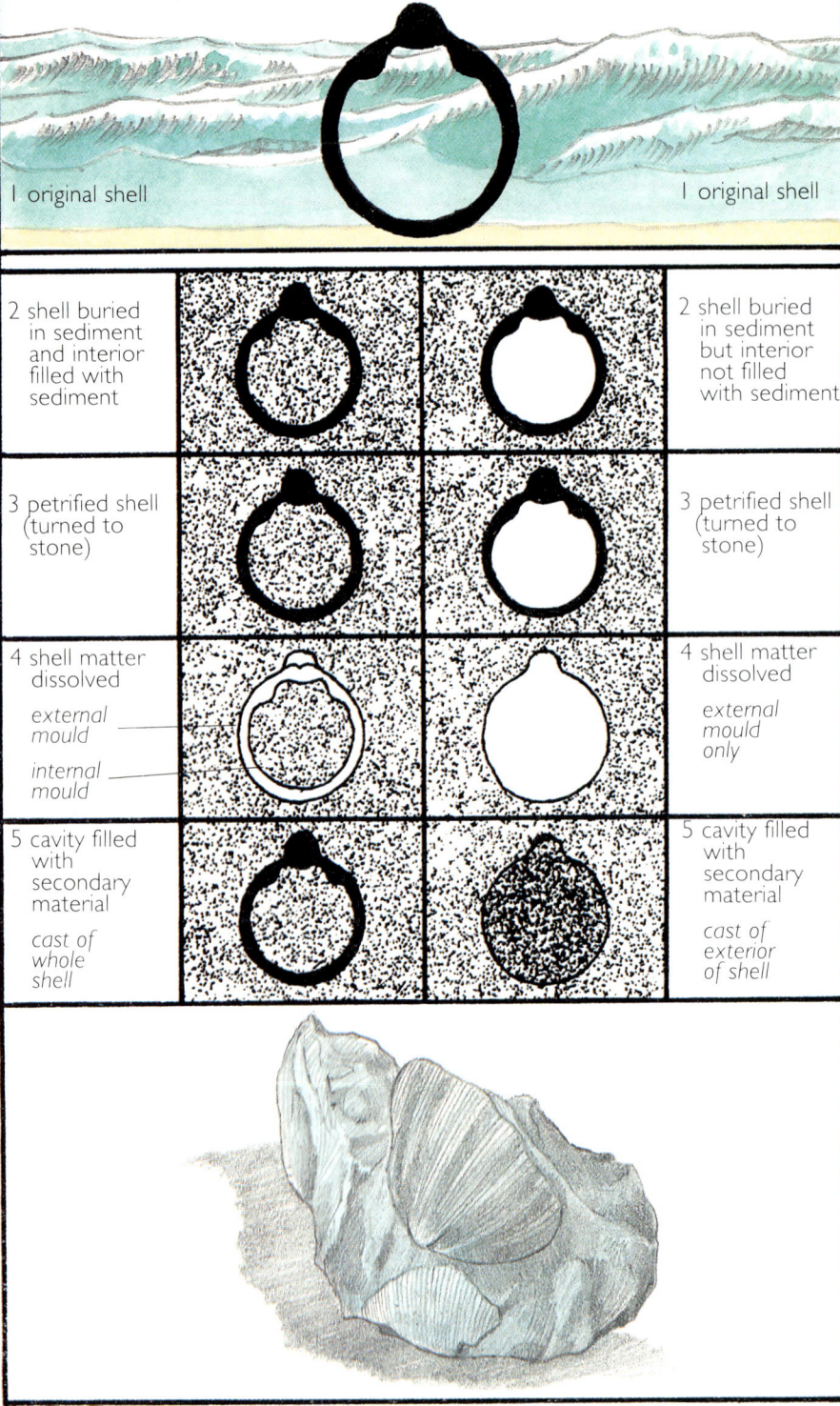

What are fossils?

Fossils are the remains or traces of organisms that were once alive. Most fossils occur in sedimentary rocks – rocks formed from hardened sediments such as mud, sand or deposits of lime. Most of these sediments were formed originally as material settled on the bottom of seas or lakes. Later, when they were buried by further sediments, they were turned into rock. A few deposits, such as coal and desert sandstones, were formed on land.

The process of fossilization begins when an animal or plant dies and becomes buried in a sediment. Very special conditions are necessary for fossilization to occur, and the remains of most animals and plants are lost for ever. But occasionally the bodies of the animals and plants are preserved in a sediment long enough for a fossil to form. It is usually only hard parts, such as bones, shells and teeth, that become fossilized, as soft parts decay too quickly.

Fossils form in a variety of ways. In some cases the pores (tiny holes) that exist in the hard parts of animals may be filled with mineral from the sediment. The hard part thus becomes more stone-like in

The diagrams show two ways in which a shell can become a fossil. In each case the shell must first be buried in sediment (2) and then become petrified (turned to stone) (3). This happens when minerals from the water in the sand slowly replace the original material of the shell. If the shell is then dissolved, moulds and casts can be formed (4 and 5).

appearance. Most commonly, shell, bone and wood becomes petrified (turned to stone). This happens as the original material is slowly replaced, atom by atom, until none of the original material remains. Alternatively the animal part may be dissolved away, leaving a cavity, or mould, in the hardened rock. This may then be filled with another mineral, producing a cast of the original part.

Very occasionally an impression of the soft parts of an animal such as a jellyfish may be preserved in rock, and the remains of animal burrows and trails are known as trace fossils. Some animals and plants are preserved as thin films of carbon in the rock.

More recent animals are sometimes preserved in other ways. Mammoths and woolly rhinoceroses have been found deep-frozen in the Arctic, in ground that has never thawed since the Ice Age, 40,000 years ago. Other mammals have been preserved in the remains of tar pits that existed 15,000 years ago.

Some fossils can be used to help date rocks. From studying rocks whose age *is* known, geologists can tell that certain creatures existed for a fairly short period of time. The presence of those fossils in other rocks therefore indicates the age of the rocks. Such fossils are known as index fossils. Among them are ammonites, brachiopods, belemnites and graptolites, and especially certain microfossils, such as foraminiferans.

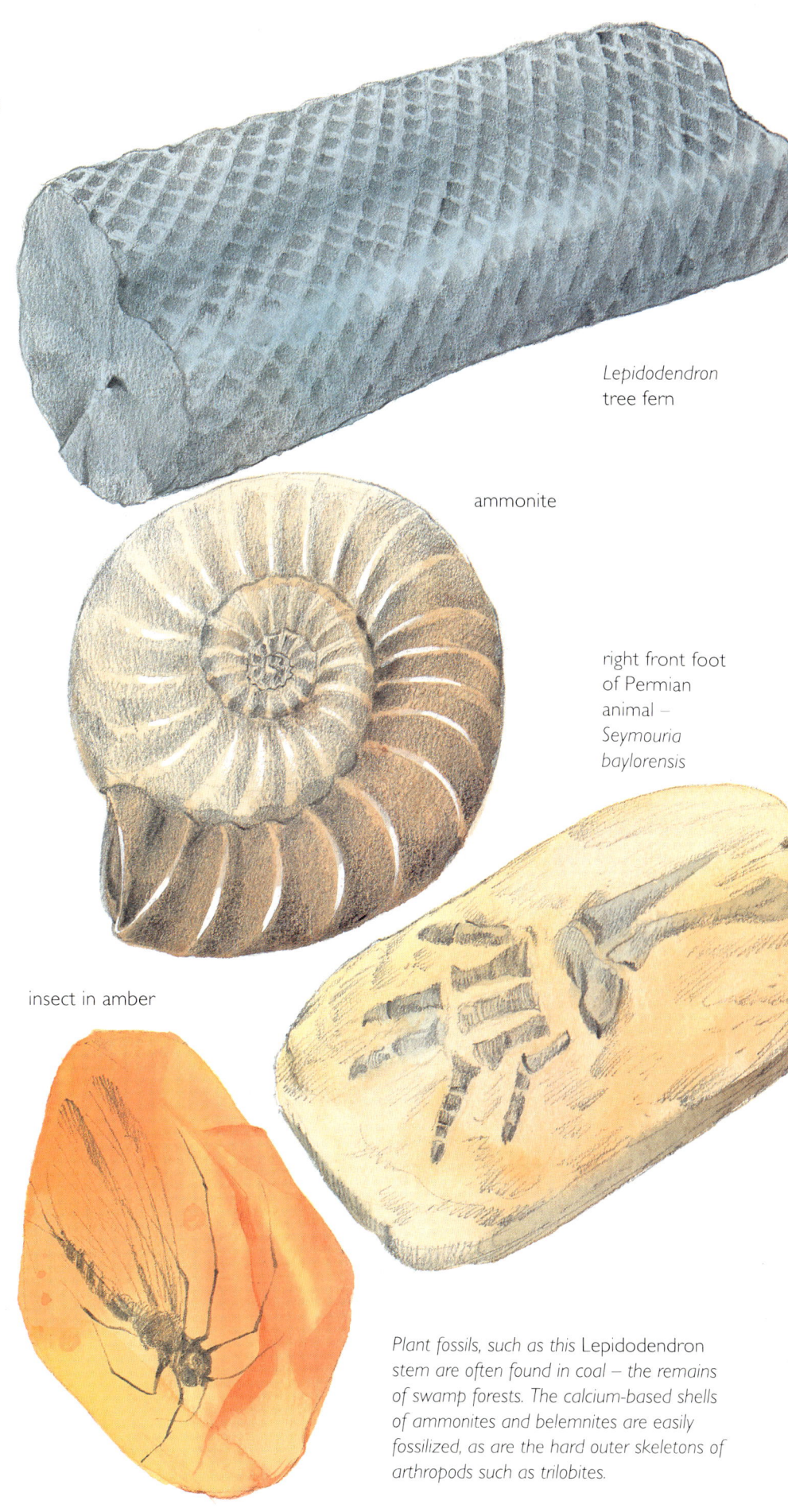

Lepidodendron tree fern

ammonite

right front foot of Permian animal – *Seymouria baylorensis*

insect in amber

Plant fossils, such as this Lepidodendron stem are often found in coal – the remains of swamp forests. The calcium-based shells of ammonites and belemnites are easily fossilized, as are the hard outer skeletons of arthropods such as trilobites.

Prehistoric Life

Evolution

The animals and plants that exist in the world today are thought to have evolved gradually from other organisms that existed in the past. This is known as the theory of evolution. Most people believe this theory to be correct.

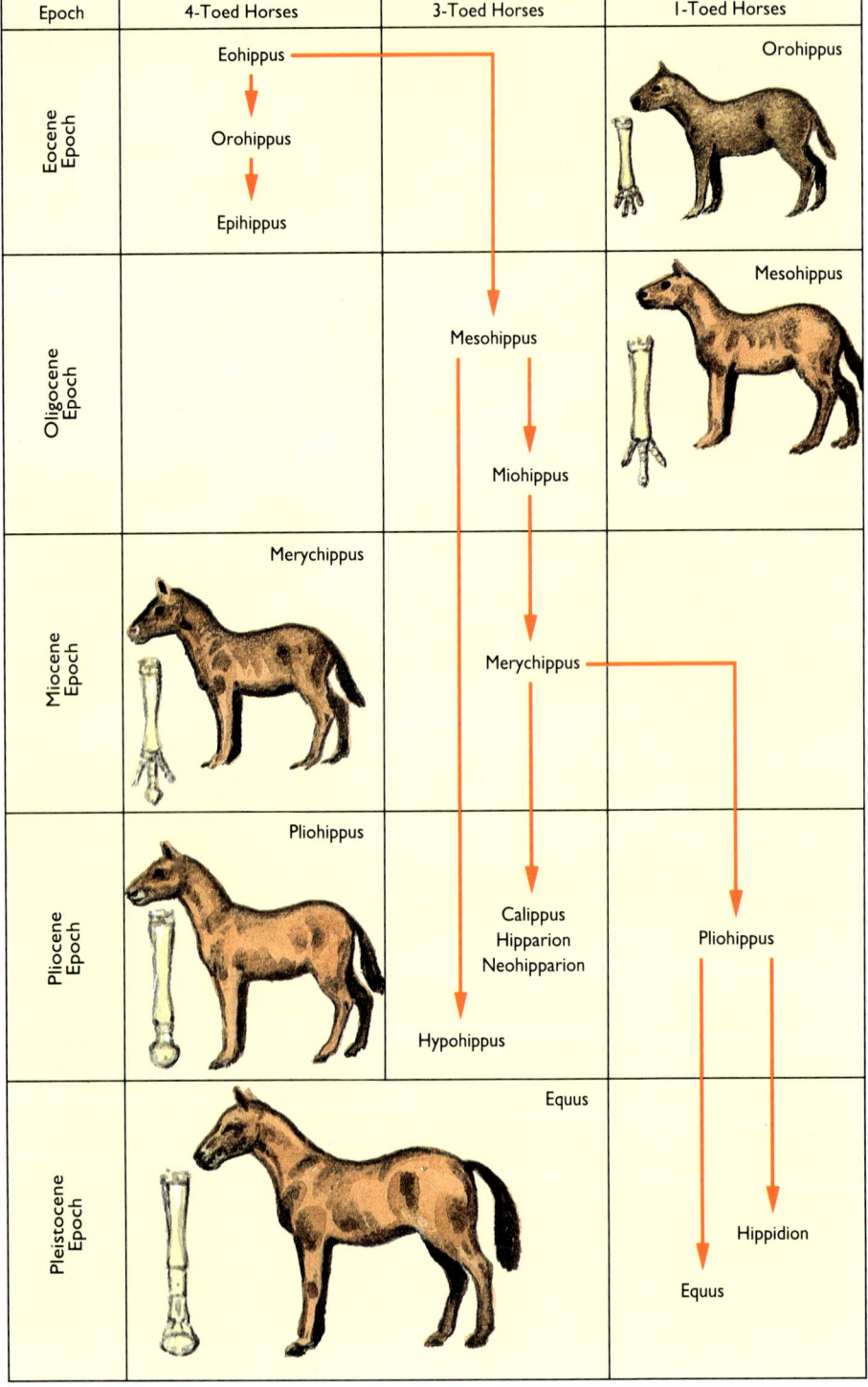

Natural selection
The process by which evolution takes place is known as natural selection. Organisms vary slightly from one generation to the next, and in some cases characteristics may change dramatically. In the natural world, organisms with characteristics most suited to their environment tend to survive, while those with the least useful characteristics die out. In this way nature selects the most suitable organisms.

Environments also change and, when this happens, only those with characteristics suited to the new environment survive. The remainder become extinct. During the history of life on Earth there have been a number of major environmental changes that have caused mass extinctions among the animals and plants that existed at the time.

Evidence for evolution
Not everyone believes the theory of evolution, but there is a good deal of evidence to support it. Much evidence comes from the study of fossils; for example, the fact

The modern horse evolved from an animal known as Eohippus, *or* Hyracotherium, *a small, dog-like, woodland animal with four toes on each foot that existed at the start of the Eocene epoch. Among the descendants of* Eohippus *were the three-toed horses of the Oligocene and Miocene epochs.* Mesohippus *and* Miohippus *were both woodland horses, but* Merychippus *lived on the plains, grazing grass. It walked on a large central toe and could run quite swiftly. Most of the descendants of* Merychippus *were three-toed, but* Pliohippus *had one toe. This was the ancestor of the modern horse,* Equus.

that *Archaeopteryx*, the first known bird, had features like those of reptiles suggests that the birds evolved from the reptiles. Other fossils show the gradual evolution of certain kinds of animal; for example, it is possible to trace the evolution of the horse.

Other evidence comes from the study of living animals. Similarities in the bodies of different animals indicate that they may have had a common ancestor. The various kinds of legs, flippers and wings found among vertebrates, for example, are all based on the same structure – a five-fingered limb. Other similarities can be seen by studying the embryos (very young stages) of animals. Finally, the study of animals and plants in places separated by natural barriers, such as the oceans, has also shown how natural selection can produce several different species from a single ancestor.

The theory of evolution is constantly being modified. According to one recent idea, evolution does not take place gradually and smoothly, but in a series of stages, in between which little or nothing happens. But whatever mechanism has been at work, there is little doubt that the organisms we know today have evolved over millions of years. By studying fossils and other evidence, scientists have worked out a 'family tree' of the animal kingdom. We also have some idea of how the world's main plant groups have evolved.

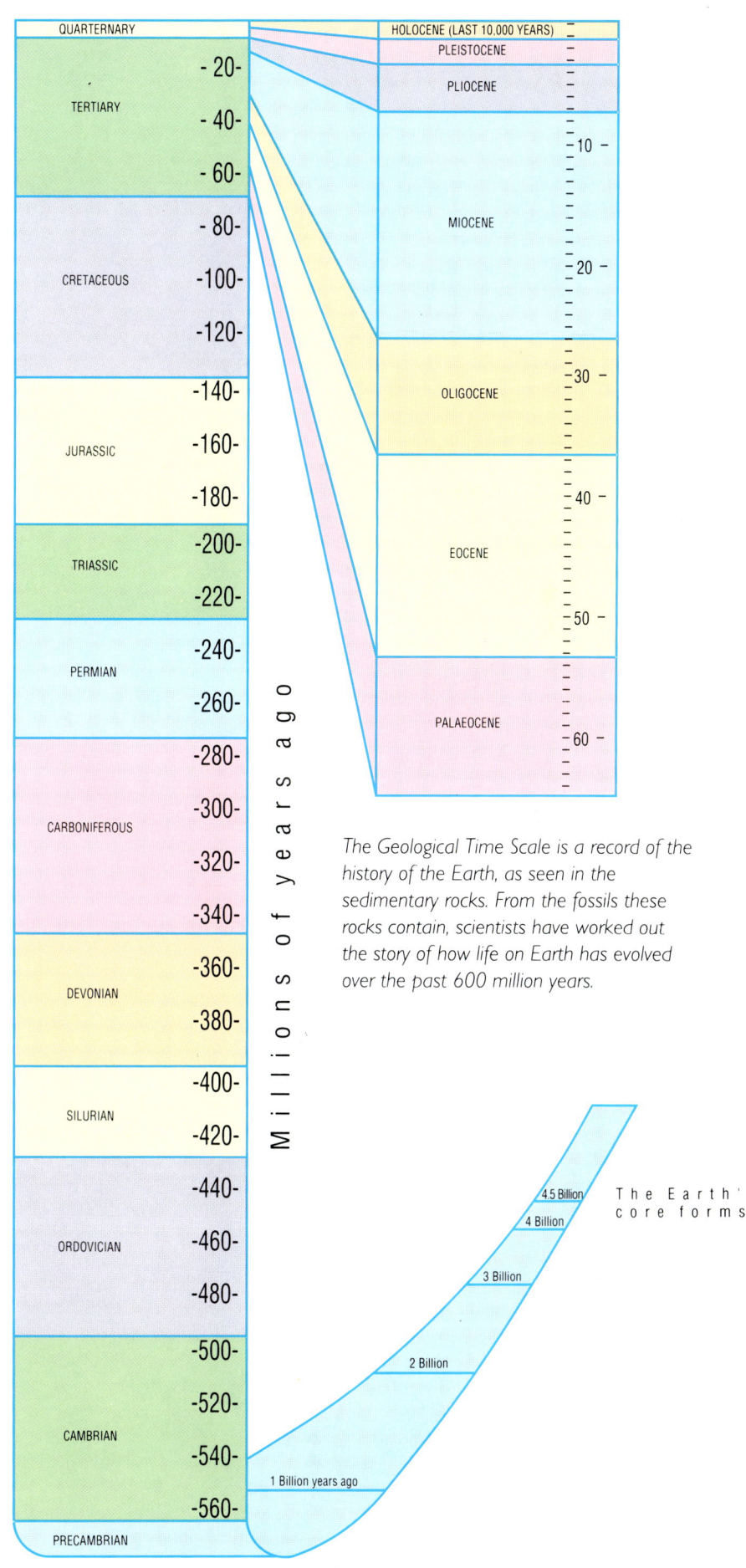

The Geological Time Scale is a record of the history of the Earth, as seen in the sedimentary rocks. From the fossils these rocks contain, scientists have worked out the story of how life on Earth has evolved over the past 600 million years.

The Earth's core forms

Ancient Life

The fossil record begins in rocks formed some 3,500 million years ago. However, because the earliest forms of life had no hard parts, very few fossils are found in such rocks. Only very occasionally, and under very special conditions, were fossils formed.

About 600 million years ago, the first shelled animals appeared, and rocks dating from this time onwards are rich in fossils. Geologists therefore originally made this time the starting point of the Geological Time Scale. This time scale contains three eras, which are divided into periods. The first era is known as the Palaeozoic, or 'ancient life', era. It is divided into six periods, beginning with the Cambrian period. Rocks over 600 million years old are known as Pre-Cambrian rocks.

Invertebrates and fishes

During the Cambrian period, living organisms flourished in the shallow seas that existed then. Most of the main groups of invertebrates appeared, and a group of arthropods known as the trilobites were particularly common. Sea invertebrates continued to spread during the Ordovician period, which began 510 million years ago.

The first vertebrate animals – jawless fishes – also appeared during this period. They had heavy, armoured coverings, which were necessary to protect them from the giant sea scorpions, some of which grew to 2m (6ft) long. The first jawed fishes appeared during the Silurian period, which began 440 million years ago.

During the first three periods of the Palaeozoic era, life in the seas gradually became more complex. Invertebrates of many kinds abounded and by the end of the Ordovician period there were jawless fishes.

ANCIENT LIFE   91

The Devonian period, which began 410 million years ago, is sometimes known as the age of fishes. Cartilaginous and bony fishes spread rapidly. At the same time the first amphibians evolved from a group of lobe-finned fishes and moved on to the land.

The first known land plants appeared in the Silurian period. Land animals – insects and amphibians – then appeared during the Devonian and Carboniferous periods. By the end of the Permian period the land was becoming hot and dry.

Coal forests and reptiles
Plants meanwhile had also been making progress. and by the end of the Devonian period, 355 million years ago, there were a number of land plants. The Carboniferous period that followed is so named because of the vast deposits of coal (composed largely of carbon) that formed from the remains of the swamp forests that existed then. In these swamps the amphibians spread and gave rise to the first reptiles. Insects also appeared and increased, taking advantage of the plant food that was so widely available.

The Permian period, which lasted from 290 to 250 million years ago, was warmer and drier. Many plants, such as the giant clubmosses and horsetails, became extinct, while conifers increased. The reptiles, too, increased, but in the seas many animals became extinct, including many fishes and all the trilobites.

SILURIAN   DEVONIAN   PERMIAN

The Age of Reptiles

The Mesozoic, or 'middle life', era was truly the age of reptiles. During the whole of this era, which lasted for 185 million years, reptiles dominated the land, sea and air.

Other groups of animals were present. For example, the first mammals, little shrew-like creatures, appeared early in the Mesozoic era. They evolved from mammal-like reptiles, which had flourished during the Permian period. Birds, too, first evolved during the Mesozoic era. But, like the mammals, they remained a small, insignificant group. The reptiles dominated the world.

Rise of the reptiles

The Mesozoic era is divided into three periods. The Triassic period lasted from 250 to 205 million years ago, and saw the rise of most of the major reptile groups. A number of reptiles returned to the sea: turtles, mesosaurs, ichthyosaurs, nothosaurs and placodonts fed on fish, crustaceans and molluscs. Ammonites, a group of cephalopod molluscs, flourished throughout the Mesozoic era. Their shells left many fossils.

On land were lizard-like reptiles known as thecodonts, and by the end of the period this group had given rise to the 'ruling reptiles', or archosaurs. Among these were the dinosaurs ('terrible lizards'), pterosaurs ('flying lizards') and the crocodiles. True lizards also appeared during this period.

Ruling reptiles

For about 130 million years the archosaurs truly ruled the world. During the Jurassic period, which lasted from 205 to 135 million years ago, there were plant-eating dinosaurs, such as *Stegosaurus* and the sauropod *Brachiosaurus*, and meat-eating carnosaurs, such as *Allosaurus* and *Megalosaurus*. During the Cretaceous period, which lasted until 65 million years ago, some of the best-known dinosaurs appeared. Among these were the sauropod *Brontosaurus* and the carnosaur *Tyrannosaurus rex*. Other Cretaceous dinosaurs included the armoured, duck-billed, bone-headed and horned dinosaurs.

Diplodocus was a Triassic sauropod, *Stegosaurus* lived in the Jurassic period and *Styracosaurus* was a horned dinosaur that lived in the late Cretaceous period.

THE AGE OF REPTILES 93

The sea during these two periods was dominated by the fish-like ichthyosaurs and the plesiosaurs. In the air, there were pterosaurs, such as *Rhamphorhynchus* and *Pteranodon*. The first known bird, *Archaeopteryx*, is known from fossils found in Jurassic rocks, and by the end of the Cretaceous period there were several kinds of bird.

The rule of the dinosaurs came to an end 65 million years ago. At the same time flying reptiles, most sea reptiles and a number of other groups, such as the ammonites, also disappeared. We do not yet understand why this happened, but the most likely explanation is a major change in the world's climate.

WARM-BLOODED DINOSAURS

Although today's crocodiles are, like all reptiles, cold-blooded animals, there is reason to believe that dinosaurs may have been warm-blooded, which means that, like mammals, they may have been able to keep their body temperature constant and higher than the temperature of the surrounding air. However, it is unlikely that they did this in the same way as mammals. And, in fact, the greatest problem for the really large dinosaurs would have been getting rid of heat rather than keeping it in.

Coelophysis

Deinonychus

Allosaurus was a late Jurassic carnosaur. It preyed on smaller dinosaurs, such as the ornithopod Dryosaurus. Pteranodon was a late Cretaceous pterodactyl.

Pteranodon

Allosaurus

Dryosaurus

Prehistoric Life

The Age of Mammals

When the dinosaurs disappeared, the mammals took advantage of the living space that became available, and they began to spread and evolve rapidly. Within 20 million years there were 27 different orders of placental mammals, of which 18 still exist today.

New Life

The last era, the Cenozoic, or 'new life' era, is divided into two periods, the Tertiary and Quaternary, which are themselves divided into epochs. The Tertiary period opened with the Palaeocene epoch which lasted just 11 million years. Among the mammals that appeared then were such animals as tillodonts, amblypods, notoungulates and condylarths. These were all herbivorous animals that evolved to take advantage of the flowering plants, which were also spreading rapidly at that time. The herbivores were preyed upon by creodonts, which included animals that looked like modern cats, wolves and bears. Primates also evolved during the Palaeocene epoch.

The Eocene epoch that followed lasted until 36 million years ago. By the middle of the epoch all the remaining mammal orders had appeared, including whales, rodents and the ancestors of today's elephants. Hooved mammals also appeared and became the most widespread land animals during the remainder of the Tertiary period. During the Oligocene epoch (36–23 million years ago) there were horses and a variety of rhinoceroses, including the mighty *Indricotherium*, which stood 5.5m (18ft) high at the shoulder and was the largest land mammal that has ever lived.

Indricotherium

Moeritherium

Andrewsarchus

Andrewsarchus *was a condylarth that lived in Mongolia during the late Eocene epoch.* Moeritherium *was an early type of elephant, and* Indricotherium *was a huge type of rhinoceros.*

THE AGE OF MAMMALS

During the Miocene epoch (23–5 million years ago) the world's temperate regions began to cool down, and this resulted in the spread of grasslands. Herds of grazing animals, such as entelodonts, giraffes, camels and the ancestors of today's antelope and cattle, appeared. Apes evolved at this time and so did the early ancestors of human beings. During the Pliocene epoch (5–1.6 million years ago), the last epoch of the Tertiary period, the climate continued to cool. Cattle and antelope spread across the world, but many other kinds of mammal began to die out.

The Quaternary period is divided into just two epochs. At the start of the Pleistocene epoch the climate became much colder in the north and the Arctic ice cap spread southwards. Some of the Pleistocene animals migrated south, others evolved and adapted to the new conditions. Pleistocene mammals that evolved in cold regions included woolly rhinoceroses, mammoths, cave bears, reindeer and polar bears. New kinds of plants adapted to cold also appeared.

Meanwhile human ancestors had been evolving. Pleistocene types included Neanderthal Man and *Homo erectus* ('upright man'). By the beginning of the Holocene, or recent epoch, the modern species, *Homo sapiens*, had appeared.

Mammoths evolved in the Pliocene epoch and continued into the Pleistocene, when some species became adapted for life in tundra conditions. Mammoths were probably hunted to extinction about 12,000 years ago.

References

Amblypods A group of large, hippo-like and rhino-like mammals that appeared during the Palaeocene epoch, but died out by the end of the Eocene.

Ammonites A group of cephalopod molluscs with coiled shells. True ammonites existed during the Mesozoic era and ranged in size from less than 10mm (0.5in) to over 1m (3ft) across.

Archosaurs The name given to the ruling reptiles, including all the groups descended from the thecodonts – the dinosaurs, the pterosaurs and the crocodiles. (Birds are also probably descended from thecodont ancestors.)

Belemnites Squid-like animals that existed from the Carboniferous period to the end of the Mesozoic era. They had large internal shells, of which the pointed end, or guard, is often found as a fossil.

Carnosaurs One of two groups of flesh-eating dinosaurs. Carnosaurs were all large animals, whereas the other group, the coelurosaurs, were much smaller and faster.

Cladistics A system of classification in which animals are grouped together according to how recently they appear to have evolved from a common ancestor.

Coal The remains of the plants that lived in ancient swamp forests.

Condylarths A group of herbivorous mammals that existed from the Palaeocene to the Miocene epochs and gave rise to all the later hooved mammals.

Creodonts A group of Palaeocene carnivores that in many ways resembled modern carnivores. However, they began to die out during the Oligocene epoch, when the true carnivores appeared, and they became extinct during the Miocene epoch.

Darwin, Charles (1809–82) British scientist who put forward the theory of evolution by natural selection in his book *The Origin of Species*, published in 1859.

Geological Time Scale The time scale of Earth's history based on the order in which fossil-bearing rocks were formed. In recent years, methods of dating rocks have made it possible to add dates to this time scale, extending it back to the time the Earth was formed, 4,600 million years ago.

Geology The study of the Earth, its rocks, structure and history.

Graptolites Small colonial animals that existed during the early part of the Palaeozoic era. Their colonies had distinctive skeletons that were preserved in rocks as fossils.

Homo erectus 'Upright man', the species of human that evolved from early ape-like men and eventually gave rise to modern humankind, *Homo sapiens* ('thinking man').

Ichthyosaurs A group of fish-like reptiles that existed during the Mesozoic era.

Index fossil A fossil that, because it is known to exist only in rocks of a certain period, can be used to date rocks of unknown age.

Limestone A sedimentary rock consisting mainly of the chemical calcium carbonate. Some limestones are produced when chemicals in seawater become solid and sink to the bottom. Others are formed from the skeletons of once-living organisms, such as corals, gastropods and echinoderms. Chalk, the purest form of limestone, is formed from the skeletons of coccoliths – microscopic, single-celled algae – together with the remains of small animals, such as foraminiferans.

Mammal-like reptiles A group of mostly Permian reptiles that had several characteristics normally found in mammals. The last members of the group died out in the early Triassic period, but by then they had given rise to the true mammals.

Mesosaurs A group of Permian sea reptiles with crocodile-like heads, long necks, lizard-like bodies and long tails.

Neanderthal Man An early form of *Homo sapiens* who lived in Europe between about 100,000 and 35,000 years ago. They were not the direct ancestors of modern humans and they may have died out as a result of competition with them.

Palaeontology The study of fossils.

Petrification 'Turning to stone', the process of fossilization, in which the remains of a living organism are very gradually converted into rock by being replaced with minerals. If the process takes place very slowly, the detail of the original organism may be faithfully preserved. Shells and tree trunks have been preserved in this way.

Plesiosaurs A group of Mesozoic sea reptiles. There were two types. Long-necked plesiosaurs had small heads and caught fish. Short-necked plesiosaurs had large heads and fed mainly on squid.

Sandstone A rock consisting of grains of sand that have been pressed and cemented together.

Sauropods A group of very large, herbivorous dinosaurs with long necks and small heads.

Sediment A material deposited at the bottom of a river, lake or sea. Sedimentary rocks are formed from hardened sediments.

Tar pit A pool of sticky tar, formed when crude oil seeps out of the ground.

Thecodonts The group of reptiles that gave rise to the dinosaurs, the crocodiles and probably the birds.

Tillodonts A group of Palaeocene mammals that resembled large rodents.

Trilobites A group of arthropods that existed from the Cambrian to the Permian periods. Most were between 20–100mm (0.75–4in) long. Their hard outer skeletons were often preserved as fossils.

Survival

Food and Energy

Every animal and plant needs food in order to survive. Food provides the chemicals needed to build up new body material. It also provides chemicals that contain the energy needed to power the processes that take place in body cells.

Above: *The green colour of plants dominates the countryside.*

Energy from sunlight

Animals and plants do not create energy; they obtain it from their surroundings. Nearly all the energy in the world comes, in the first place, from the Sun, in the form of heat and light. Heat from the Sun creates an environment warm enough for plants and animals to live in. However, it is the Sun's light that provides the energy used for body processes.

Only green plants can make direct use of light energy. They are therefore the world's food producers, without which life on Earth could not exist. Plants create food materials in a process known as photosynthesis, a term that comes from Greek words and means 'putting together with light'. Plants contain the green pigment known as chlorophyll, which captures light energy and converts it into chemical energy. This is then used to power a series of chemical reactions in which carbon dioxide and water combine together to form food sugars and oxygen. The carbon dioxide is taken from the air, and the oxygen that is produced is released back into the air.

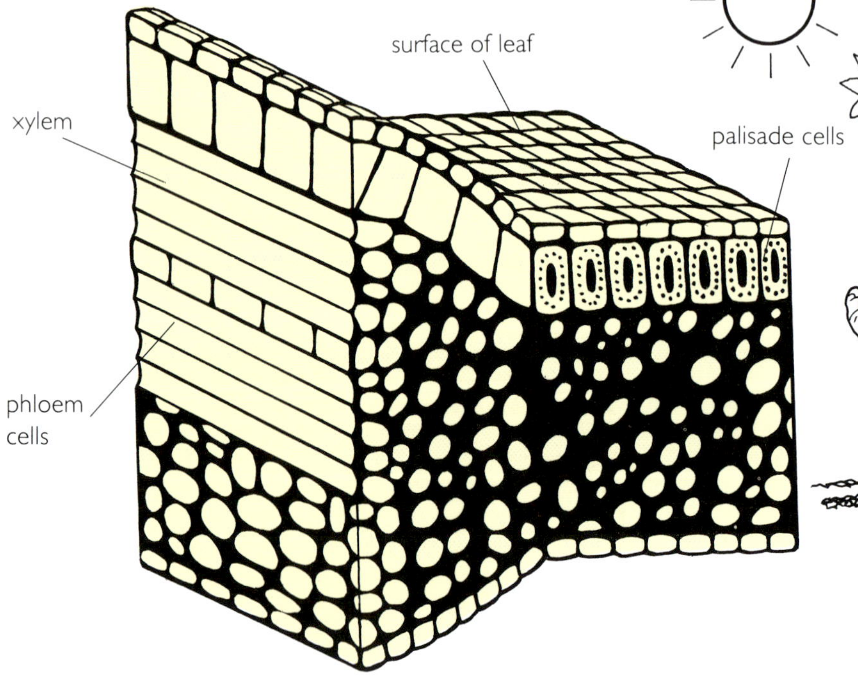

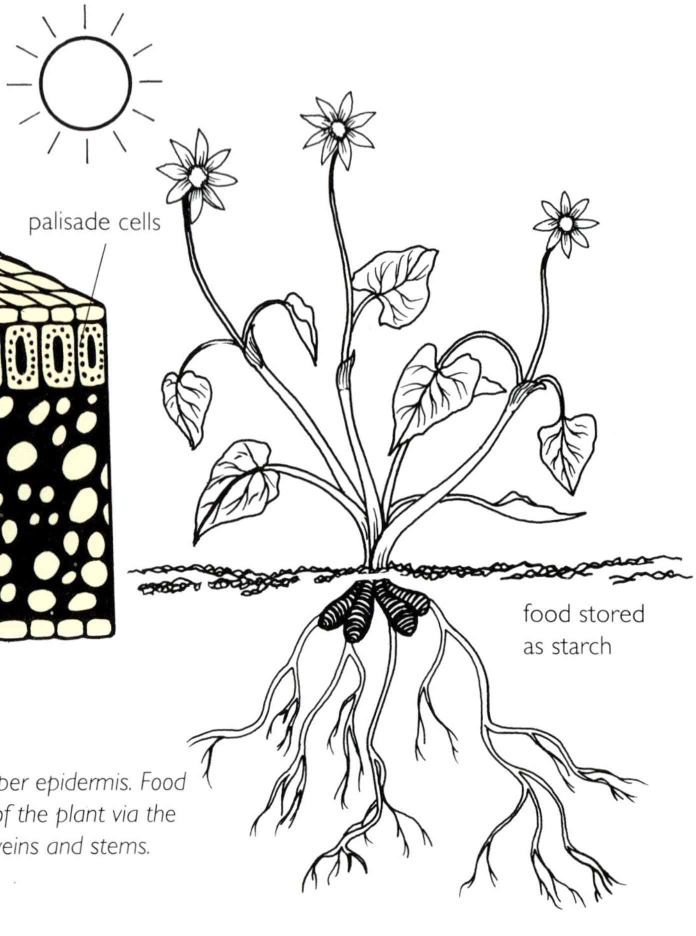

Photosynthesis takes place in cell organelles called chloroplasts, most of which are found in leaves in a layer of cells called palisade cells just beneath the upper epidermis. Food is carried to other parts of the plant via the phloem cells of the leaf veins and stems.

FOOD AND ENERGY

The cycle of life

All other organisms make use of the energy stored by plants. Animals are the consumers of the natural world. Many, such as caterpillars, rabbits or deer, eat plant material and use the chemicals to build up their own bodies. Others eat the plant-eaters and other animals, while some feed on animal remains. Many plant-eating insects, for example, are preyed upon by different, carnivorous insects, which may themselves become the food of insect-eating birds. Because animals generally prefer certain foods, the relationships between living things can be shown in the form of a food chain, or web.

Finally, there are nature's decomposers – the last link in the chain. These are mostly bacteria and fungi, which break down waste material and the remains of dead plants and animals. In doing so they release carbon dioxide into the air and minerals into the soil, recreating the raw materials that can be used by plants, the original food producers.

Right: *Many animals take advantage of the food materials created by plants. Here a dormouse benefits from the energy stored as sugar in a blackberry.*

Below: *All plants and animals form part of a food web, in which animals that eat plant materials are eaten by other animals, who may in their turn be eaten by others.*

SURVIVAL

Feeding and digestion
Most animals specialize in eating certain kinds of food, and it is usually possible to see what kind of food an animal prefers by looking at the structure of its body, particularly the mouth and its surrounding parts. Inside an animal's body, food is broken down into simple chemicals in the process known as digestion. The breakdown process is aided by special chemicals known as enzymes, produced by the body.

Plant material is less easy to digest than animal material, as very few animals can produce the enzyme necessary to break down cellulose. Many plant-eaters therefore have special methods of dealing with their food. Inside the gut of a plant-eating mammal are special bacteria that help break down cellulose. The gut of a termite contains protozoans that help the animal digest wood. The caterpillars of butterflies and moths have enzymes that can penetrate cell walls in order to digest the contents. In grasshoppers and cockroaches, part of the gut is specially designed for grinding up coarse food into a pulp.

Above: *Lions are carnivores that often hunt in groups, or prides. Each pride needs a large territory in which to hunt, as it takes a large number of prey animals to keep each lion adequately fed.*

Below: *The pike is the pond-life equivalent of the lion. It is a voracious predator, feeding on most other kinds of fish (including young pike), as well as frogs, water birds and water rats when possible.*

FOOD AND ENERGY

Animal populations
The number of a particular kind of animal in any one area depends on how much food is available. When food is scarce, the population falls, but when food is plentiful, the population rises. Sometimes, when food supplies are particularly good, a species may be so successful that its numbers become too great for the food supply to support. A huge population explosion of this kind may be followed by a mass movement away from the usual feeding area, as the animals search for food. Many starve to death and the population eventually returns to normal. Lemmings, small rodents found in cold northern areas, have such population explosions every three or four years. At the same time the number of predators, such as Arctic foxes and snowy owls, also increases, as their food becomes more plentiful.

The population of a species also depends to a large extent upon its position in the local food chain. Animals convert very little of the food they eat into body materials. Most of it is converted into energy that is used for movement and other body processes and is eventually lost as heat. Thus an animal needs to eat many times its own weight in food in order to survive. This means that the total weight of the animals at the top of a food chain is much less than the total weight of the animals farther down the chain. There are therefore fewer animals at the top of the food chain than at the bottom. For example, on the plains of East Africa, many tonnes of grass supports a relatively smaller weight of grazing animals. But the number (or total weight) of grazing animals is much greater than the number of the carnivorous mammals that prey on them.

This food pyramid illustrates that a large number of plants and plant-eating animals are needed to support just one sparrow hawk. Leaves are eaten by caterpillars and other insects; small birds eat the caterpillars; the sparrow hawk eats the small birds.

Survival

Movement and Senses

The ability to move from one place to another is one of the things that generally distinguishes an animal from a plant. Most animals move in order to obtain food. At the same time movement is often useful for escaping from predators and avoiding being eaten.

False feet and cilia

Very simple animals move about by various means. An amoeba flows along by putting out pseudopodia ('false feet') in the direction it wants to travel. Another single-celled protozoan called *Paramecium* is covered with tiny hairs, known as cilia. These beat to and fro, rowing the animal through the water. Other single-celled organisms propel themselves through the water with one or two long whip-like structures called flagella.

Some ciliate protozoans use their cilia in a different way. The animals remain fixed to a rock or other object and the beating cilia draw a current of water towards them. Food particles in the water are then filtered out. Filter feeding, using cilia to create food-bearing water currents, is often found in many-celled animals as well. Sponges, tube-dwelling sea worms, most bivalve molluscs, sea lilies, sea squirts and lancelets all feed in this way.

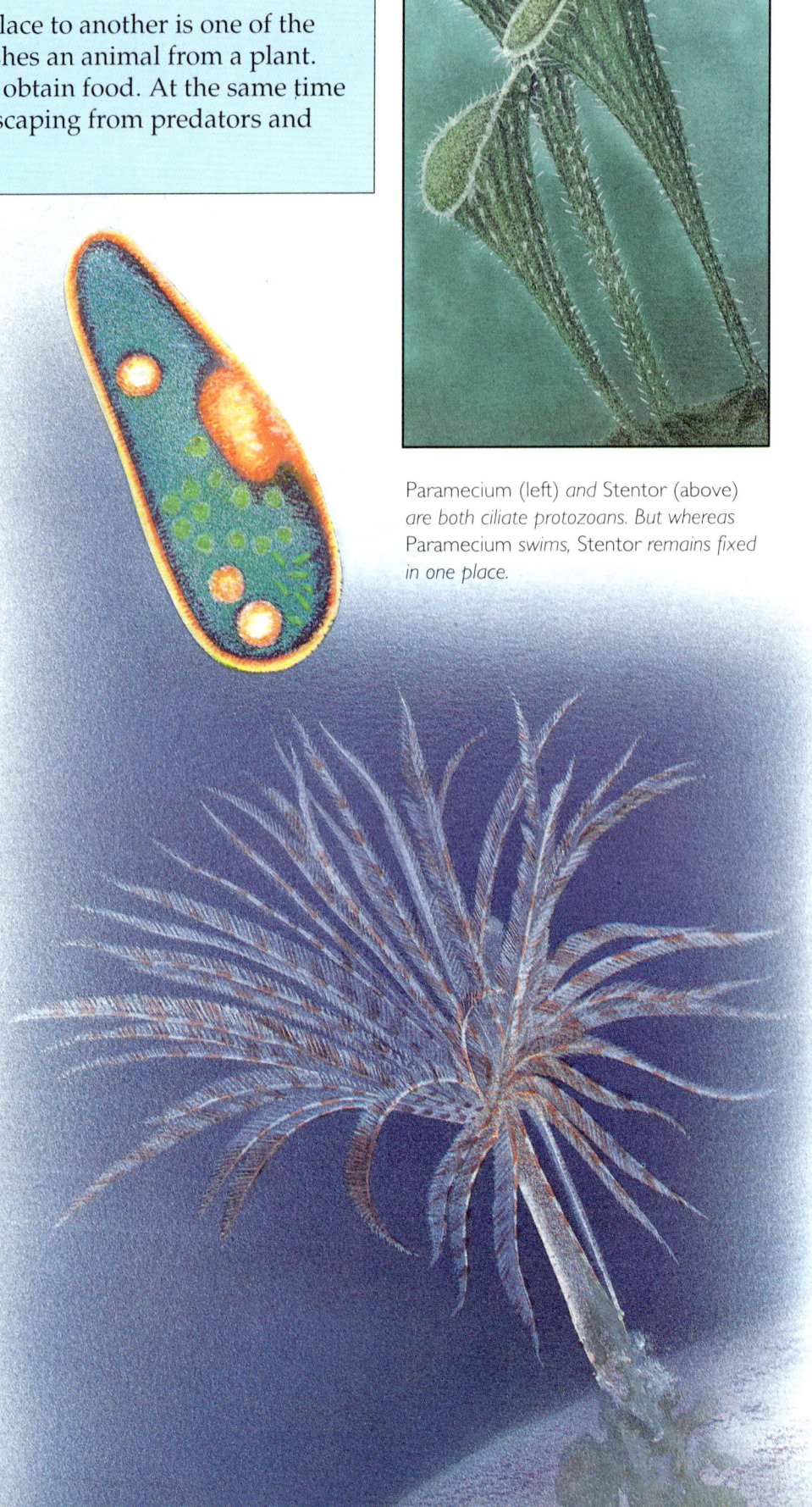

Paramecium (left) *and* Stentor (above) *are both ciliate protozoans. But whereas* Paramecium *swims,* Stentor *remains fixed in one place.*

Right: *A fan worm lives inside a tube. Its delicate arms are equipped with cilia, which beat and draw food-bearing water currents towards the animal.*

MOVEMENT AND SENSES 103

Waves of movement
Other animals have more familiar methods of movement, such as swimming, walking, running or flying. Many animals simply crawl but, whatever the method, animals' bodies are usually well adapted to their method of movement.

In many cases waves appear to travel along the bodies of moving animals. The cilia of *Paramecium*, for example, lie in diagonal rows, and each row beats just after the one in front. A wave of movement therefore appears to travel from the front to the back of the animal.

An earthworm tunnels through the ground by alternately shortening and lengthening the segments of its body. Each segment is equipped with tiny bristles. When a segment shortens it becomes thicker, and the bristles grip the surrounding soil. The worm moves by first shortening the segments at the front of its body. These segments then start to expand, one by one, and at the same time segments farther back shorten. A wave of contraction thus passes down the animal, while the segments in front of the wave lengthen and move forward. Several waves may be passing along the worm's body at the same time.

Wave-like movements are used by many other animals. The typical movement of a snake, for example, is to throw its whole body into a series of waves. An eel swims in the same way. A mollusc crawls by passing waves of muscle contraction along the base of its large foot.

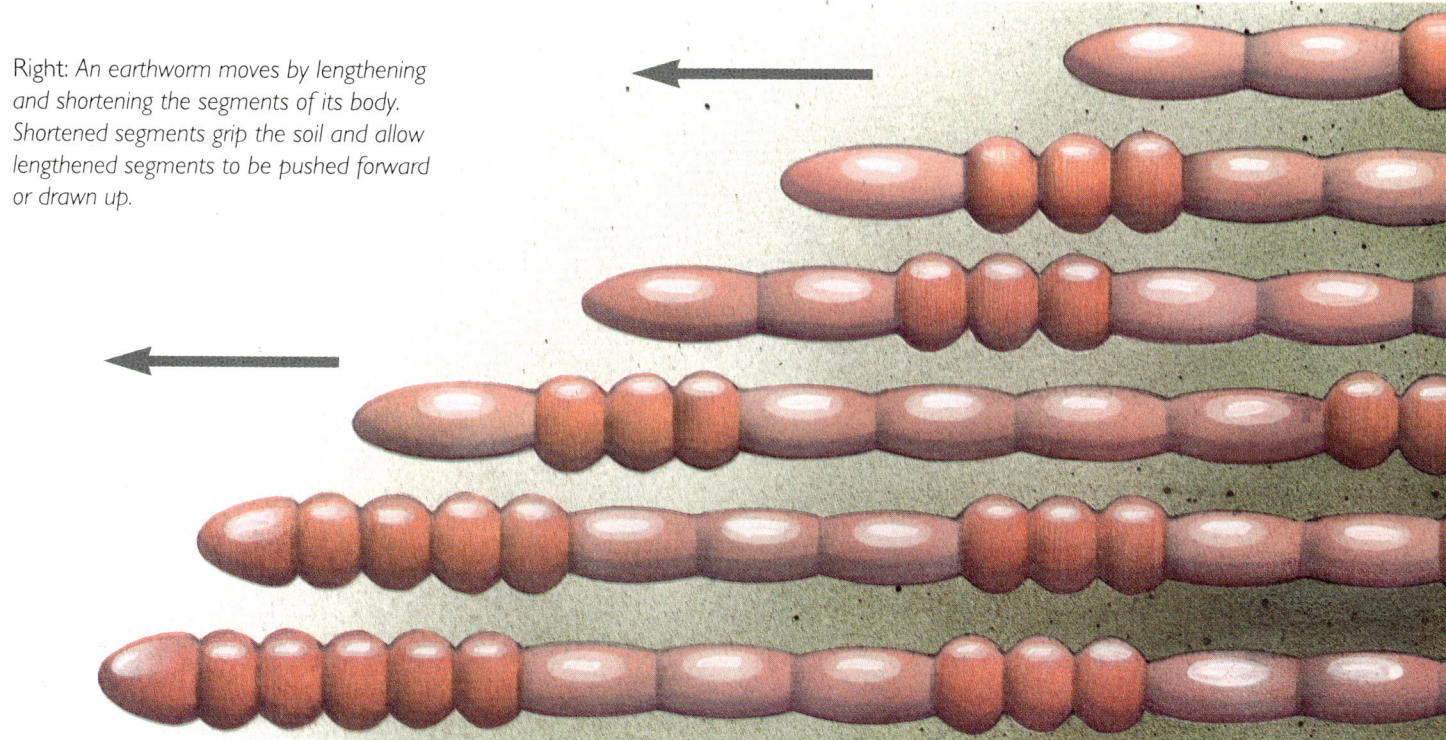

Right: *An earthworm moves by lengthening and shortening the segments of its body. Shortened segments grip the soil and allow lengthened segments to be pushed forward or drawn up.*

Below: *An eel swims by throwing its body into a series of waves. It uses the same method to move across land between streams.*

Above: *Wing shape indicates how a bird flies. Thin, swept-back wings are needed for fast flight. Broad wings produce more lift.*

Flying

Flight is achieved by generating a forward force, known as thrust, and an upward force, known as lift. In an aeroplane, thrust is produced by propellers or jets driven by its engines. Lift is generated by a specially shaped wing. The pressure of the air passing under the wing is higher than the pressure of the air passing over it, and the wing is therefore pushed upwards.

Insects have very light bodies and most have little difficulty in getting off the ground. A bird's wing beats downwards and forwards. The inner part of each wing generates most of the lift in the same way as an aeroplane's wing. Most of the thrust is generated by the outer parts of the wings.

The shape of birds' wings varies according to the type of flying they do. Albatrosses have long, pointed wings that enable them to glide easily over the oceans. A buzzard soars high in the air with its large, broad wings. Swifts and swallows have swept-back wings for high-speed flying. Birds that live in woods, such as sparrowhawks or pheasants, have short, broad wings and long tails for taking off rapidly and manoeuvring among the branches.

Flying uses up a lot of energy, but birds have several special features that make it easier. Their skulls are small and light, without teeth. Their bones are also light, because they are hollow (they are strengthened with cross-struts). The flight muscles are very large. Birds also have special air sacs that drive a continuous stream of air through the lungs. This ensures that there is plenty of oxygen available to break down food sugars and provide the energy needed for flight.

MOVEMENT AND SENSES

swift

mallard

Swimming

Animals that live in water propel themselves along by exerting some sort of force against the water. A fish, for example, pushes against the water with its tail fin, which it moves rapidly from side to side. In some fishes extra force is supplied by waves passing along the body. (The other fins are used for steering and braking.) Whales and dolphins move forward by beating their tails, or flukes, up and down. Swimming animals have many different 'styles'. A water beetle, for example, rows itself along with its large hind legs.

A sea butterfly (a type of gastropod mollusc) swims with its two large, membrane-like wings. Turtles 'fly' under water in the same way as birds do in the air, using their flippers like wings. Penguins use their wings for swimming in the same way. A squid swims by passing waves down a fin on each side, but it also has a method of jet propulsion. It produces a jet of water by contracting a cavity in its body in order to move backwards rapidly. A scallop swims in a similar way by forcing jets of water out between its valves.

Below: *Water provides more support than air and swimming is therefore easier than walking or flying.*

bass

fiddler ray

great diving beetle

scallop

Legs for walking

Arthropods and most vertebrates get about on legs. Animals that use this form of movement have two main concerns – speed and stability. Arthropods solve the problem of stability by ensuring that they always have enough legs on the ground. Insects have six walking legs, but they always keep at least three touching the ground.

Most amphibians and reptiles have legs that stick out sideways from the body and turn down at the knee. This provides great stability, but holding the body off the ground requires a great deal of effort. These animals therefore tend to walk with their bellies trailing along the ground.

Mammals and birds, on the other hand, have legs that extend straight downwards from the body. This makes them less stable, but enables them to run more quickly. For stability they depend on careful co-ordination, using the senses and the brain to keep their balance.

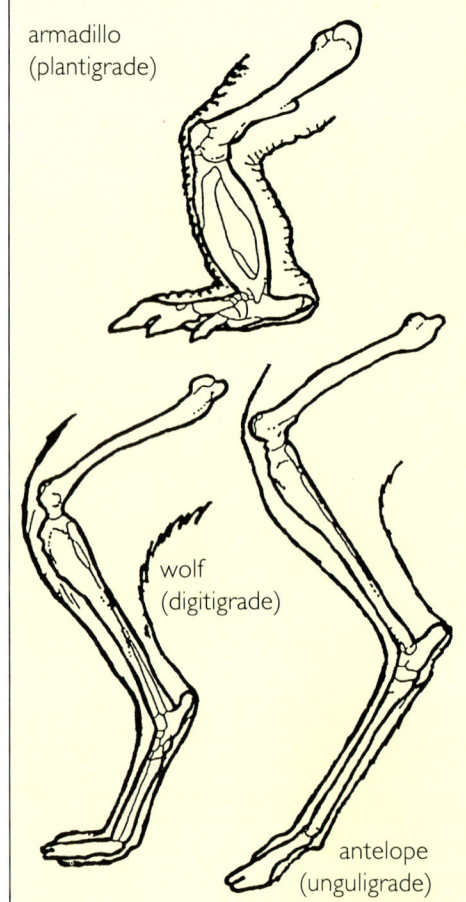

FAST, FASTER, FASTEST

The way in which mammals walk and run is related to the speeds they can achieve. Basically, the speed depends on the length of the animal's stride, which in turn depends to a large extent on the length of the leg.

Animals in which the whole foot touches the ground have relatively short legs and therefore a fairly slow top speed. This is known as the plantigrade posture and examples of animals that adopt it include rodents, edentates and primates.

Carnivores have what is called a digitigrade posture; only their toes, or digits, touch the ground. The heel is raised to add extra length to the lower part of the leg.

The fastest animals are the hooved mammals, which have an unguligrade posture. In this, only the tips of the toes (that is, the toenails, or hooves) touch the ground. The rest of the foot forms over a third of the total length of the leg, which enables the animal to run at high speed over considerable distances.

The rear walking legs of a grasshopper are modified for jumping and it can make prodigious leaps.

A lizard, such as this land iguana, rests on its belly. Holding the body clear of the ground all the time would take a lot of effort and thus would be very wasteful of energy.

MOVEMENT AND SENSES

Using senses

Senses are also important in helping an animal to find food and to avoid attackers. Small animals generally detect their food by sensing the presence of chemicals. In more advanced animals this is developed into the senses we know as smell and taste.

The sense of touch is also important. Many single-celled animals use this sense, as do all the more advanced animals.

A number of small animals also have simple organs for detecting the presence and direction of light. In more advanced animals this is developed into the sense of vision, in which pictures of the surroundings are registered by the eyes. Advanced animals usually also have a sense of hearing for detecting sound.

All five senses are well developed in vertebrates, and some animals have extra senses. All fishes, for example, have a sense system in the lateral line, which runs along their sides. This picks up vibrations in the water and enables them to detect the movements of other creatures.

Some animals probably have extra senses of this sort which we do not yet understand. For example, sharks seem to have special organs to help them detect possible sources of food.

A bat uses its sensitive ears to detect sounds (produced by the bat itself) reflected from objects and flying insects. A male emperor moth, using its feathery antennae, can detect the scent of a female several kilometres away. The feathers on the face of an owl are arranged so that the slightest sounds are directed into the ears.

Attack and Defence

Predatory animals have evolved many ingenious methods of catching and killing their prey. Prey animals often have equally ingenious ways of avoiding being eaten.

Catching prey

Many animals rely simply on speed and agility to catch their prey. Some creep up on their victims stealthily; others lie in wait. A crocodile, for example, lies motionless, waiting for an unsuspecting fish or other animal to come within reach of its jaws. A trapdoor spider rushes from its underground burrow in order to seize passing prey. A chameleon catches unwary insects by means of a long, sticky tongue – nearly as long as the whole of the rest of its body – which it can flick out of its mouth and back again faster than the human eye can see. A spitting spider aims two streams of sticky material at its prey while moving its head rapidly from side to side, so that the unfortunate victim is pinned down by two zig-zag threads.

Many spiders go a step further and set traps for their victims. Insects that blunder into a spider's web are usually doomed. A few kinds of spider hold their webs between the tips of their legs and cast them like nets over their victims.

Above: A trapdoor spider constructs a silk-lined pit and seals it with a silken lid camouflaged with small stones and other debris. When a prey insect comes near, the spider rushes out to seize it.

A chameleon's sticky tongue is used to catch prey using a catapult mechanism to shoot it out. The tongue may be 14cm (5in) long, but it can be extended in just one-sixteenth of a second and withdrawn again in just a quarter of a second.

ATTACK AND DEFENCE 109

Above: *The peacock butterfly is well camouflaged when it hibernates among dead leaves.*

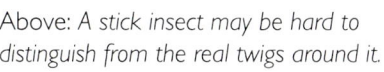

Above: *A stick insect may be hard to distinguish from the real twigs around it.*

Camouflage

Animals that stalk or lie in wait for their victims often make themselves almost invisible by means of camouflage, colours and shapes that break up the body's outline. A lion, for example, is hard to see in the sandy-coloured vegetation of the African savannah. A tiger's stripes help it blend with the vegetation in an Asian jungle. A brightly coloured crab spider can lie in wait for its insect victims in similarly bright flowers. Other predators that use camouflage include mantises and several kinds of snake.

Camouflage also works well for prey animals that wish to avoid being seen by predators. Many moths and butterflies have wing patterns that enable them to remain unseen against such backgrounds as the bark of a tree or fallen leaves. Other insects are masters of disguise and may look exactly like leaves, twigs or pieces of straw, complete with the blemishes that are usually found on real plant material.

In the sea, fishes take on a wide range of camouflage colours and disguises. Many fish have dark backs that make them hard to see from above, while their silvery sides and light-coloured bellies make them less obvious from below. Many flatfish that rest on the bottom have markings that look like the pebbles or sand on which they lie. Anglerfish and stonefish can only be distinguished from rocks when they move. The body of a sargassum fish has many branches, which break up the outline of its body and make the fish difficult to see among the seaweed in which it lives.

Above: *A leafy seadragon is more like a fragment of seaweed than a fish. It lives in warm waters, especially near Australia, and is well camouflaged among fronds of seaweed.*

110 SURVIVAL

Poisons

Once a predator has caught or trapped its victim, it must subdue it. In many cases this can be achieved simply by superior strength, combined with an effective weapon such as teeth or claws. However, many predators catch prey that is the same size – or even larger – than themselves. Such animals generally have other ways of subduing prey.

A few fish stun or kill their prey using electric organs. The most powerful of these is the electric eel of South America, which can produce a 550-volt shock. However, the most commonly used method of killing prey is by injecting poison. Spiders, scorpions and many snakes do this. Cone shells harpoon fish with poison-carrying teeth mounted on movable stalks. Squids and octopuses paralyse their prey by injecting venom through parrot-like beaks. Jellyfish and sea anemones catch prey with their stinging tentacles.

Most of the animals that kill their prey with poison also use it to defend themselves against attackers. Others use poisons only for defence. Examples are the stingray, which carries a poison spine on its tail, and the marine toad, which has two poison glands on its head.

The electrical discharge produced by an electric eel is effective for both attack and defence, as are the bite of a cobra and the sting of a wasp. Burnet moths and arrow-poison frogs, however, use their poisons just for defence. Their bright colours warn potential predators, as do the wasp's yellow and black markings.

ATTACK AND DEFENCE 111

Warnings and bluffs

Animals that are poisonous or unpleasant to taste often advertise the fact with bright warning colours, so that predators will avoid them. Once a bird has tasted a cinnabar moth or a monarch butterfly, it will not attempt to eat another one. Other animals with warning colours include arrow-poison frogs, coral snakes, wasps and bees. Sometimes different species adopt the same colours. The black and yellow colours of wasps are also worn by other poisonous animals, such as the caterpillars of cinnabar moths. Predators soon learn to avoid all animals with such colours.

Some animals cheat. Even though they are not poisonous themselves, they adopt the colours of animals that are. For example, hoverflies have black and yellow markings and are therefore avoided by birds.

Other animals try to bluff their way out of trouble. Several kinds of moth and butterfly have spots like large eyes on their wings. If these are suddenly exposed, a predator may be startled into thinking that it is facing a much larger animal. By the time the predator realizes its mistake, the insect has escaped.

The markings on the wings of a hairstreak butterfly and the eye spots of an eyed hawkmoth are designed to confuse predators. The eye spots of some frogs are thought to perform the same function. A non-poisonous false coral snake protects itself by resembling a true coral snake, which is poisonous. Although it is harmless, the tiger beetle has black and yellow markings, a code that is widely used in the natural world to indicate danger.

Partnerships

Many animals and plants help to ensure their survival by forming a partnership with another animal or plant. A partnership may benefit both partners or just one. In some cases one partner actually lives at the expense of the other.

Hitch-hikers and cleaners
The simplest form of partnership is one in which one animal simply uses another as a means of transport, like a hitch-hiker. A number of arthropods, such as mites, attach themselves to birds or insects, without harming or benefiting their hosts in any way. Other hitch-hikers are more useful. Sea anemones and bryozoans, for example, often travel about on shells occupied by hermit crabs. They get a good supply of food and provide the crab with extra protection. In Africa, oxpecker birds ride about on the backs of herbivorous mammals, such as zebra and antelope. They benefit their hosts considerably by removing ticks and other skin parasites, which they eat.

In the sea, cleaner fish perform the same service for large fish. Client fish queue up to have parasites and other unwanted material removed from their skins and even from inside their mouths and gills.

Other animals share their homes. The innkeeper worm shares its burrow with two kinds of crab, a goby fish, another kind of worm and a small bivalve mollusc! The innkeeper worm generates a current of water that provides all the occupants of the burrow with food and oxygen. Whether or not the worm benefits is not certain.

Above: A sea anemone rides on the shell of a hermit crab, placed there by the crab itself.

Oxpeckers are small birds that feed on the parasites that live on the skins of antelopes, such as the eland.

PARTNERSHIPS 113

Plants and animals

A partnership in which both partners benefit more or less equally is known as a symbiotic relationship. Such partnerships are common between plants and animals. For example, many flowering plants rely on animals to pollinate their flowers, and in some cases plants rely on just one or two species to do the work. A yucca flower, for example, can only be pollinated by a certain kind of moth. The moth, too, relies on the yucca plant for its survival, as its larvae feed on part of the fruit.

Another example of an animal forming a close relationship with a plant is the symbiotic arrangement between certain African ants and the kinds of acacia plant known as whistling thorns. The ants live in homes provided by the thorn bush – large, hollow bulbs that form at the bases of some of the plant's spines. The plant also provides them with food, in the form of nectar and little sausage-shaped food bodies that it produces at the tips of leaflets. In return, the ants defend the plant against caterpillars and other plant-eating animals.

Above: *The yucca and the yucca moth are totally dependent on each other. Neither can survive without the other.*

Right: *The swollen bulbs on the branches of a whistling thorn provide homes for ants, which defend the bush against all kinds of plant-eating animals.*

14 Survival

Plants and fungi

Some of the closest symbiotic relationships are formed between plants and fungi. A lichen, for example, may look like a single plant, but it is actually a combination of a fungus and a single-celled alga. The fungus benefits from the ability of the alga to make food by photosynthesis. The alga is kept moist and gets protection from bright sunlight.

In other cases, the mycelium (mass of threads) of a fungus becomes closely attached to the roots of a flowering plant. A number of toadstool-producing fungi form associations with particular kinds of tree, such as a pine, spruce, larch or birch. The fungus receives food from the tree and in return helps the tree take up water and minerals from the soil.

The birch bracket fungus is a parasite that can also live on dead organic matter. It is always found on dead or dying birch trees. Lichens are tough pioneers that can survive where other plants cannot. The yellow, crusty lichen (Xanthoria aureola) and the grey-green, leafy lichen (Parmelia saxatilis) are common on walls and stones.

birch bracket fungus

leafy lichen

crusty lichen

Parasites

In many cases a symbiotic relationship is only a short step away from a parasitic one. In this type of relationship, one partner, the parasite, receives all the benefit and gives nothing in return to its host. Many parasites harm their hosts, which may even die. Some parasites attach themselves to the outside of their hosts, some live inside a body cavity and some invade the host's own cells. The simplest parasites are the viruses and bacteria. They invade the bodies of animals and plants, causing a wide variety of diseases. Many fungi are also disease-causing parasites.

Several kinds of flowering plant have also taken up a parasitic way of life. Common mistletoe, for example, is found growing on trees such as apple, hawthorn and willow. It is only partly a parasite because, although it takes water from its host, it provides itself with food in the normal way by photosynthesis. Other plants are complete parasites. Examples include the dodders, broomrapes and toothworts, all of which have small leaves that contain no chlorophyll.

Above: *Mistletoe grows on the branches of trees. It buries outgrowths into the wood of its host, but takes only water. Its sticky seeds are carried on the feet of birds.*

Among the animals, the only truly parasitic vertebrates are the lampreys. Some birds, such as the cuckoo, are described as brood parasites because they lay their eggs in the nests of other birds and then rely on the host birds to raise their offspring for them. Most animal parasites are small invertebrates; there are parasitic protozoans, coelenterates, flatworms, annelid worms, roundworms, molluscs, crustaceans, arachnids and insects. Some kinds of wasp are parasites only during part of their lives. They lay their eggs near the eggs of insects or spiders and, when the larvae hatch out, the parasite larvae feed on the bodies of the host larvae, which eventually die.

broomrape

A female cuckoo lays a single egg in the nest of a host species, such as a reed warbler. After the cuckoo chick hatches, the host parents feed it, instinctively believing that it is their own offspring.

Migration

In extreme conditions, such as freezing cold and drought, food is often scarce. Some animals put up with such conditions, but others avoid them by migrating to places where food is more plentiful. Many animals move from an area in which they normally breed to an area that is used just for feeding.

Some animals migrate over enormous distances. This habit may have developed over many millions of years. Originally, there was perhaps only a short distance between their breeding and feeding areas. But movements in the Earth's crust caused them, very slowly, to drift apart. The animals, however, continued to make the journeys they had always made, even though they became a little longer each year.

Migration on land

The best-known migratory animals are birds. In autumn many northern insect-eating birds fly south from their summer breeding areas to warmer places where insects are more plentiful during the winter. Some butterflies make similar journeys. In North America, monarch butterflies migrate south in huge numbers in the autumn, to spend the winter in Florida or southern California. They move north again in the spring.

Other seasonal migrations that occur on land include the movements of herds of plant-eating mammals around the African savannah. As food and water become scarce in one area, the animals move on to where the seasonal rains have refilled the waterholes and caused the grass to grow again.

Above: *In the autumn, golden plovers in Iceland and Scandinavia migrate south to join the resident populations in Britain and other parts of Europe.*

Above: *In North America colonies of monarch butterflies migrate south in autumn, returning again in the spring.*

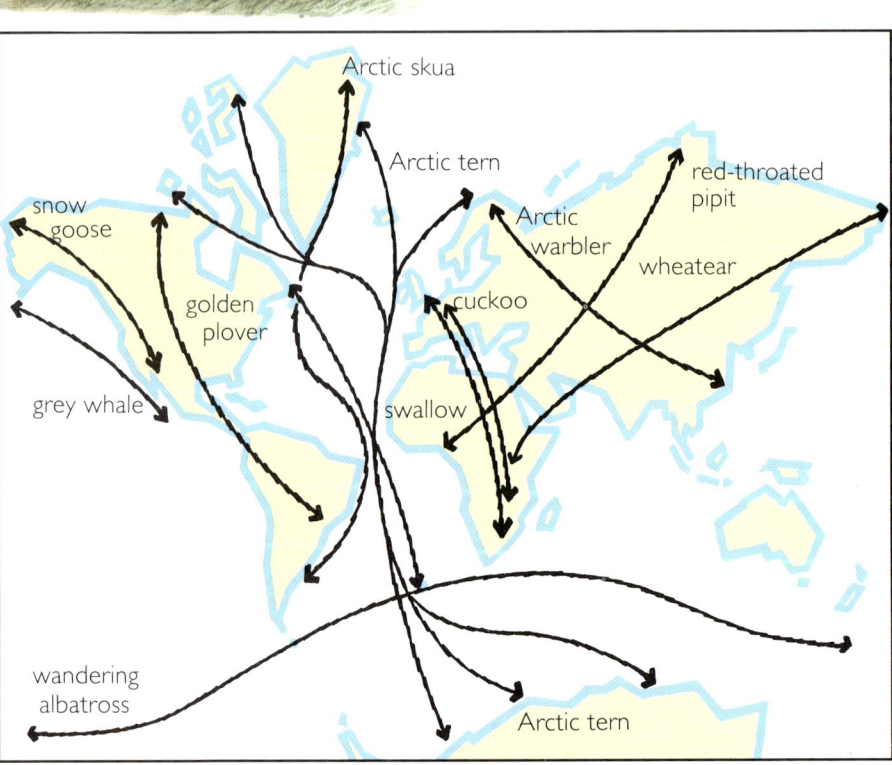

MIGRATION 117

FINDING THE WAY

Animals find their way from one place to another in several ways. Visual clues may tell an animal where it is, and a sense of smell is often useful. A salmon finds its way from the sea to the river in which it was hatched by smelling the water that comes from the river.

Over long distances many animals probably navigate by the Sun and stars – migrating birds certainly do. Pigeons are known to have tiny magnetic particles in their heads. They may use these to orientate themselves using the Earth's magnetism. Other organisms that can detect magnetism include certain bacteria, honey bees, dolphins and sharks. Humans may also have a magnetic sense.

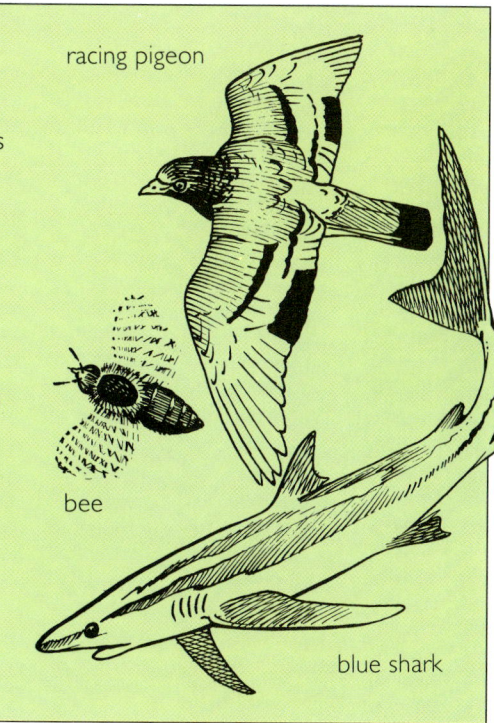

Migration at sea

In the sea, shoals of fish and other sea animals migrate around the oceans. This is not a seasonal migration; the fish are merely following the huge masses of tiny animals and plants known as plankton, which drift around the ocean with the currents. The fish in turn are followed by squid, dolphins and sea birds, such as petrels and albatrosses.

Sea animals that do make seasonal migrations include many of the huge baleen whales, which move to warmer waters near the equator in the autumn. The longest migration is made by a sea bird, the Arctic tern, which breeds in the Arctic during the northern summer and then flies south to the Antarctic, in order to avoid the northern winter.

Some sea animals feed in deep water but move to shallow water in order to breed. Sea turtles lay their eggs on land, and females return to the same breeding beaches year after year. Some fishes spend part of their lives in the sea and part in freshwater. Salmon, for example, migrate from the sea to the rivers in which they originally hatched, in order to breed themselves. Eels breed in the Sargasso Sea, having migrated from freshwater streams in North America and Europe.

Left: Determined to reach the head of the streams in which they themselves were hatched, salmon hurl themselves up waterfalls, trying again and again until they succeed.

References

Bacteria A group of single and many-celled organisms that are neither plants nor animals and whose genetic material is not contained inside nuclei. Some bacteria cause disease. Others break down dead organic matter and are essential to the living world.

Balance In an animal, the ability to remain upright when its centre of gravity is above its centre of mass, which gives it a tendency to fall over. The balance organs of a vertebrate are canals filled with fluid that form part of the inner ear. Most other animals have simple organs for detecting their position relative to the downward pull of gravity.

Bipedal Walking on two legs, like humans and many dinosaurs.

Camouflage Colouring or pattern that makes an animal difficult to see against a background.

Cilium (plural: cilia) A microscopic, hair-like structure embedded in the wall of a cell. The internal arrangement of its fibres enables it to beat to and fro.

Commensalism A type of association between different kinds of animal in which one or more of the partners obtains some benefit from the relationship, but all the individuals remain capable of living independently.

Energy The capacity to perform some sort of work, such as moving something or carrying out a chemical reaction. In the process, one form of energy is generally converted into another. All the energy used by living things comes from the Sun. The Sun's heat maintains the planet's surface and atmosphere at a reasonable temperature, and the Sun's light is converted by plants into chemical energy. This chemical energy is transferred to animals, which use it to power their body processes. Ultimately, all this energy is converted into heat.

Enzyme A biological catalyst. A substance that speeds up or assists a chemical reaction without itself being used up.

Flagellum A long whip-like structure embedded in the wall of a cell. It has the same internal structure as a cilium, but is much longer. The beating of a flagellum produces a lashing movement along its length.

Food chain A chain of organisms along which energy is transferred, usually as a result of one organism eating the one below it in the chain. Green plants are usually at the foot of the food chain. They are eaten by plant-eaters which in turn are eaten by meat-eaters.

Food pyramid A diagram which shows how many prey organisms are required to provide enough food for consumer organisms higher in a food chain. A large number of organisms at the bottom of the pyramid are needed to sustain a much smaller number of predators at the top of the pyramid.

Food web Several interlinked food chains. A food web shows in diagram form all the predator–prey relationships that exist in a particular type of living area.

Haustorium An outgrowth produced by a parasitic plant in order to extract food and water from the tissues of the host plant.

Hearing An animal sense in which the vibrations caused by sound waves produce a response in specialized sense cells. Hearing organs are found in some arthropods, but the sense of hearing is best developed in land vertebrates.

Migration The movement, temporary or permanent, of an animal from one area to another in order to find food or to breed. Migration is best known amongst birds and some species of fish.

Mimicry The adoption by an animal of a particular form or colouring that makes it look like another species, or part of another species. A non-poisonous animal may mimic a poisonous one. Two or more poisonous species may adopt the same colouration (Mullerian mimicry). Other animals mimic leaves, twigs, etc.

Mycorrhiza A very close symbiosis between a fungus and a flowering plant or conifer. In some cases the mycelium (mass of threads) of the fungus surrounds the roots of the plant. In other cases the threads actually penetrate the roots.

Parasite An organism that lives wholly or partly at the expense of another, without giving anything back in return.

Parasitoid An insect whose larva feeds on the body of another young animal, such as another insect larva, spider, or crustacean.

Photosynthesis A process in green plants in which the energy in sunlight is used to build up sugars from water and carbon dioxide.

Poison A chemical that destroys or prevents the functioning of one or more kinds of cell in a living organism.

Quadrupedal Walking on four legs.

Symbiosis A close association between two or more living organisms, in which both or all the partners equally benefit.

Touch A sense in which cells respond to pressure from an outside object. The response is transmitted through the organism which may take avoiding or defensive action as a result.

Vision An animal sense in which cells respond to light. In many cases such cells form part of an eye, which creates an image that can be registered by the animal's nervous system, or brain.

Warning colouration Colouring, usually bright, that warns predators that the animal is bad to eat.

Ecology and the Environment

ECOLOGY AND THE ENVIRONMENT

Biomes and Ecosystems

Animals and plants do not live alone. They live in communities, in which every individual plant and animal affects all the others, and is affected by them. Each species benefits from the presence of others, and in many cases the presence of one species may be essential for the survival of others. The continued existence of such species is therefore necessary to keep the community going and maintain what is called the balance of nature.

The surroundings in which an animal or plant lives is known as its environment. In many ways the environment is created by the community of plants and animals that share it.

Biomes of the world

The world's major communities are known as biomes, and different biomes are identified by the plant life they contain. In turn, this plant life is to a large extent decided by the climate – temperature, rainfall, etc.– of the region. For example, in temperate regions of the world, where the temperatures and rainfall are moderate, the dominant plants are deciduous trees; hence the biome is known as deciduous forest. In colder regions, such as the area just below the Arctic circle, the dominant plants are coniferous trees, and the biome is known as coniferous forest. Farther north still comes a region known as tundra, in which only plants that can tolerate extreme cold can grow. Mountain regions often have similar plants, but the kinds of plants and animals found on mountains also depend on their geographical location.

In warmer, drier regions, nearer the Equator, trees give way to temperate grassland and tropical grasslands. The hottest, driest regions are deserts, in which only a few specially adapted plants and animals survive. In very warm places where the rainfall is high, the rich jungle of plants that grow there is known as tropical rainforest.

Ecosystems and habitats

Within a biome there are millions of smaller communities. These are known as ecosystems, and each one is a completely self-contained community of animals and plants together with the immediate environment. Ecosystems vary greatly in size. A single ecosystem can be as large as a forest or as small as a pond or even a single tree.

Within an ecosystem animals and plants have their preferred living areas, or habitats. In woodland, for example, the many different habitats include such places as the tree canopy, leaf litter, rotting branches, clearings and small pools of water. Every animal and plant is adapted to survive in a particular habitat and is thus adapted to its environment.

The North American prairies are temperate grasslands where huge herds of bison used to roam.

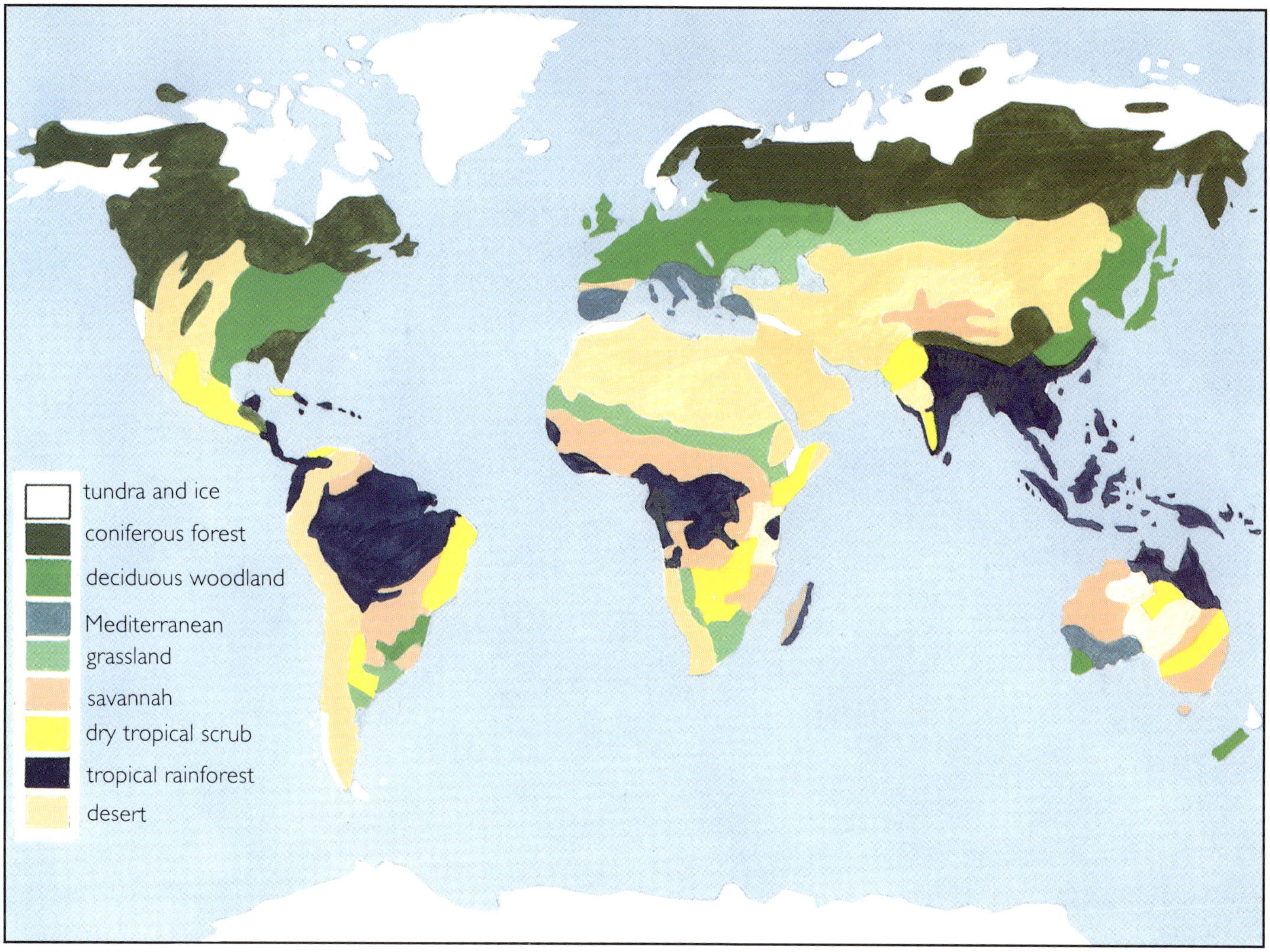

BIOMES AND ECOSYSTEMS 121

- tundra and ice
- coniferous forest
- deciduous woodland
- Mediterranean
- grassland
- savannah
- dry tropical scrub
- tropical rainforest
- desert

Above: *Biomes of the world.*
Below: *The Amazon rainforest is probably the world's richest biome. Thousands of different plants support several million different kinds of animal.*

macaw · spider monkey · tree porcupine · toucan · humming-bird · morpho butterfly · window-pane butterfly · jaguar · coral snake

ECOLOGY AND THE ENVIRONMENT

Geographical Distribution

As well as being restricted to particular biomes, animals and plants are generally found only in certain parts of the world. For example, giraffes and hippopotamuses live only in Africa, while anteaters and most armadillos are restricted to South America. The skunk is found in North America but not in Europe; hedgehogs in Europe and Asia but not in North America.

A number of animals now exist only in the Ethiopian region – Africa south of the Sahara desert. Some used to be more widespread. For example, 100,000 years ago hippopotamuses roamed where London now stands.

Zoogeographical regions

The reason for these differences can be understood by studying the geography of the world. Natural barriers, such as mountain ranges, deserts and oceans, prevent the spread of many kinds of animal and plant. As a result, a species that evolves in one part of the world may not be able to reach another region.

Zoologists divide the world into six regions, according to the animals they contain. These are the Palaearctic, Ethiopian, Oriental, Australasian, Nearctic and Neotropical regions (see the map). The history of these regions goes back hundreds of millions of years.

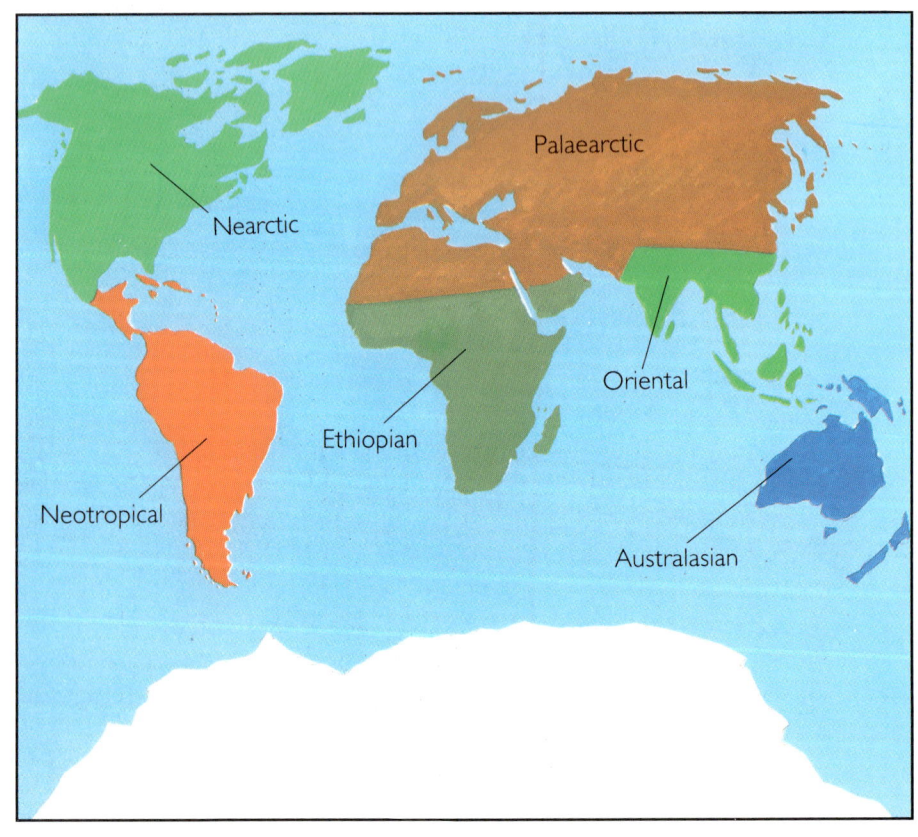

GEOGRAPHICAL DISTRIBUTION

Continents adrift

The world's continents have not always been where they are now. The Earth's crust is made up of a number of plates, which float on the molten rock below. Since the world first formed, movements of these plates have caused the continents to drift across the Earth's surface – and they are still drifting.

About 200 million years ago the continents were all joined together in one huge supercontinent, with the result that the land animals of that time, including the early dinosaurs and primitive mammals, were able to spread to most areas. Then the supercontinent began to break up and the parts have moved around ever since. At times some regions have been cut off from the rest of the world, allowing unique animal life to evolve in isolation. Australia, for example, owes its collection of marsupials to the fact that it has not been joined to any other land mass for some 60 million years. This made it possible for marsupials to evolve without competition from placental mammals.

South America developed a unique range of marsupial and placental mammals, too. Many of these, such as guinea pigs and llamas, still exist, despite South America becoming joined to North America about 7 million years ago.

The Palaearctic and Nearctic regions have very similar faunas because, about 1.5 million years ago, a land bridge existed across what is now the Bering Sea. Such animals as Brown bears, reindeer (caribou) and wolves are found in both regions, which are sometimes described as a single region, the Holarctic.

Because Australia was cut off from the rest of the world for many millions of years, a unique population of marsupials was free to evolve without competition from placental mammals.

ECOLOGY AND THE ENVIRONMENT

Polar Life

The coldest places on Earth are the Arctic and Antarctic regions, where the temperature regularly falls below -50°C during the winter. Nothing lives at such extreme temperatures, but a variety of animals survive in places where it is only slightly less cold.

The Arctic region consists of large areas of frozen sea at the centre of which is the North Pole.

Arctic life

The animal that ranges farthest north is the polar bear. During the winter it wanders across the ice, feeding on seals, especially ringed seals. However, the Arctic is a frozen ocean, not a landmass. During the summer, as the pack-ice breaks up, polar bears move south into the tundra.

The Arctic Ocean, like the Antarctic, is rich in plant and animal life. On the sea-bed, molluscs, echinoderms and crustaceans provide food for several kinds of fish, while nearer the surface plankton supports a food web that includes fish, squid and whales. Among the whales are toothed whales, such as the sperm whale, killer whale and narwhal, the males of which grow a long, pointed tusk whose purpose is a mystery. Baleen whales, such as the blue whale, are also present. Seals are common and the Arctic is also the home of the walrus, which uses its long tusks to dig for shellfish on the sea-bed.

ARCTIC AND ANTARCTIC

The Arctic consists of an ocean surrounded by land, but the Antarctic is a landmass, and a very mountainous one, surrounded by water. Because the ocean is milder than the land, the Antarctic is much colder than the Arctic. The land is covered with a permanent ice cap which, in some places, is nearly 2km (1 mile) thick. It is therefore much harder for life to survive there. The Arctic has nearly 1,000 species of flowering plants; the Antarctic has only two or three.

POLAR LIFE 125

Antarctic life

The Antarctic continent is probably the world's most unfriendly environment. Yet even here a few tiny animals – insects, nematode worms and protozoans – manage to exist. The land is icebound and almost barren, but the seas that surround the continent are a rich source of nutrients which support a large number of planktonic animals and plants, which in turn support a number of larger creatures that live around the Antarctic coast. The waters teem with fish, squid and crustaceans, especially the shrimp-like creature known as krill. These animals provide food for penguins, seals and other larger animals.

Penguins are found only in the southern hemisphere. Some live on islands and coasts of the southern oceans, and some species breed on sub-Antarctic islands. Two species manage to breed on the Antarctic mainland itself. Adélie penguins breed on the beaches in September and October, during the Antarctic spring. Emperor penguins breed during the long dark winter, and their nursery colonies may be up to 100km (60 miles) from the edge of the ice. Four true seals are found in the Antarctic. Crabeater seals and Weddell seals live along the coast; Ross seals and leopard seals are found on the pack-ice. Leopard seals are ferocious and will even attack the cubs of other seals.

The Antarctic is the most southerly continent. It surrounds the South Pole and contains about 90 per cent of the world's ice.

Arctic tern
The Arctic tern breeds in the Arctic then flies south to spend the winter in Antarctic seas.

emperor penguin

leopard seal

rockhopper penguin

ECOLOGY AND THE ENVIRONMENT

Tundra and Mountains

Tundra is the name given to the type of vegetation found in the most northern parts of Europe, Asia and North America, around the edge of the Arctic. Similar conditions are often found on mountains, where the height and biting winds together produce very low temperatures. Living in such cold places is not easy. Body heat is easily lost to the outside and food is often scarce during the coldest season. The plants and animals that live in the tundra and on mountains have special adaptations that enable them to survive.

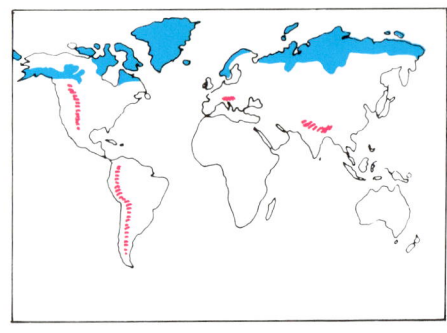

Above: *The world's tundra and mountains.*

Surviving the cold

Many animals have a thick layer of fat, or blubber, under the skin. This acts as an insulating layer to prevent the animals losing too much heat from their bodies. Large land animals generally have a thick covering of dense fur. Small animals tend to avoid the most harsh conditions. Some tunnel under the snow, where it is relatively warm and they are sheltered from the biting wind. Others hibernate during the coldest season. Their body functions slow down and many of them survive on a store of fat built up during the autumn. Many animals have white coats, which provide camouflage in snow and also help to reduce heat loss, because white objects give out less heat than dark ones.

Plants, too, have special adaptations. Tundra and mountain plants are nearly all small, and grow close to the ground. Many of them form cushions or mats to help keep out the cold, and some are covered in tiny white hairs. Plants in cold regions have to flower and produce seed in a very short time, as the summer is usually over very quickly. Some start early, by producing flowers underneath the snow. They emerge from the snow in full flower some time before it finally melts.

In northern regions mountain plants are mostly low-growing species. In tropical parts of the world, however, some mountain plants are very large and rather strange.

saxifrage

giant lobelia

giant senecio

edelweiss

lichens and mosses

Arctic poppy

dwarf willow

Animals of cold regions

Among the larger animals of the tundra are herbivores such as reindeer and musk oxen. They are preyed upon by wolves and sometimes grizzly bears. Smaller carnivores include foxes and weasels, which hunt such animals as Arctic hares, lemmings, shrews and ground squirrels. The tundra also provides food for a number of birds. Summer visitors include ducks, geese, waders and insect-eating birds. Resident birds include the ptarmigan, redpoll, snowy owl and peregrine falcon.

A similar range of animals is found in mountain areas, although the species vary in different zoogeographical regions. Mountain sheep and goats are common, as are ground squirrels and birds of prey. Carnivores include several cats, such as European and Canadian lynxes and the mountain lion, or cougar, of North America.

ECOLOGY AND THE ENVIRONMENT

Coniferous Forest

Most of the world's coniferous forest lies in a broad band south of the Arctic region. Here, rainfall is fairly low and the water that is available to plants is often frozen. In addition, the soils that were left behind as the ice retreated at the end of the last Ice Age are very poor. A few broad-leaved trees, such as birch, aspen and willow, survive in these conditions. But most of the trees are conifers, particularly spruces, pines, larches and firs.

Nothing much else grows in these dark forests. The densely packed leaves prevent light from reaching the forest floor, and decaying leaves make the soil too acid for most plants. However, fungi are common and plants such as bilberry and cowberry grow in the clearings.

Above: The world's coniferous forest. Below: Insects and seeds in a coniferous forest provide food for small animals and birds. These provide food for larger predators, such as bears, hawks and owls.

Forest mammals

Despite their dark, forbidding appearance, coniferous forests do support a great variety of wildlife. Plant-eating animals feed on leaves, seeds and bark. Where there are herbivores there are carnivores that prey on them.

The largest herbivore of the forest is the elk (known as the moose in North America). It feeds largely on low-growing plants and the leaves of deciduous trees. In the autumn caribou also move into the forest to avoid the harsh winter conditions in the tundra. Smaller mammals include a variety of rodents, such as squirrels, chipmunks and lemmings, which eat mostly seeds and tender shoots. In America there is even a marsupial, the Virginia opossum, which has succeeded in spreading this far north. Tree porcupines are also found in North America.

Carnivorous mammals include the wolf, brown bear, wolverine and mink. In America these are joined by the black bear, while in the forests of northern Europe and Asia the northern lynx preys on hares.

black bear

goshawk

capercaillie

red squirrel

CONIFEROUS FOREST

Lichens and shrubby plants also provide food for elk and, in winter, reindeer, which move in to avoid the harsh conditions in the tundra.

Forest birds

During the summer the northern forests provide food for vast numbers of insects. In turn, insects are a source of food for birds, such as warblers, that migrate north in spring. Other birds, such as tits and woodpeckers, feed on insects during the summer and survive on seeds and berries during the winter.

Many birds live almost entirely on seeds. The crossbill uses its curiously shaped beak for picking conifer seeds out of their cones. Other seed-eaters include grosbeaks and jays. Waxwings eat both seeds and berries, and game birds, such as the capercaillie and spruce grouse, eat a variety of plant material. Predatory birds include owls and hawks.

ECOLOGY AND THE ENVIRONMENT

Deciduous Woodland

The large leaves of broad-leaved trees enable them to carry out photosynthesis and growth much more efficiently than conifers. However, large delicate leaves are easily damaged by frost and lose large amounts of water. In temperate regions, where in winter temperatures regularly fall below zero, broad-leaved trees shed their leaves in the autumn in order to survive. They are known as deciduous trees.

Deciduous woodland is the natural vegetation of much of the northern hemisphere. In Europe, very little of this natural woodland remains, as it has been cut down to provide timber or make room for farmland. Most of the deciduous woodland that exists in Europe today has been planted by humans. However, in North America and Asia large areas of natural forest remain.

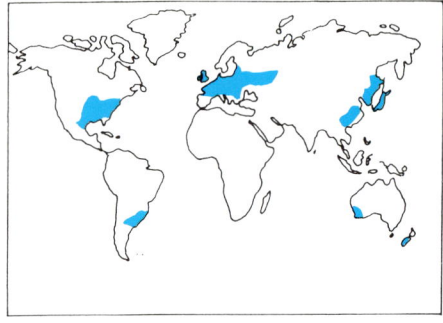

Above: *The world's deciduous woodland.*

Plants and plant-eaters

A deciduous woodland or forest is a rich environment. The leaves of the plants provide food for a host of animals, and there is not one but several layers of vegetation. The bottom layer consists of plants that grow close to the ground, such as mosses, ferns and other small plants. Above this is a layer of green-stemmed flowering plants that tolerate or even prefer living in shade. They often flower early in the year, before the light is reduced by the leaves of the trees. Above this is a layer of shrubs and young trees, and the uppermost layer is the canopy formed by the branches and leaves of the mature trees.

The leaves of broad-leaved plants are much easier to eat than the needles of conifers, so they attract many small plant-eating animals such as snails, caterpillars and sap-sucking insects. Other plant-eating animals include mice, voles, hedgehogs, rabbits and squirrels. Larger herbivores include several kinds of deer and the wild boar.

Some of the large number of animals that inhabit woodland in North America. The bobcat is one of the largest predators.

DECIDUOUS WOODLAND   131

Predators and birds

The top predator used to be the wolf, but this too has practically disappeared from deciduous woodland, along with the European lynx and the mountain lion of North America. In Europe the top predator is now the red fox. In America there are more predators, including red and grey foxes, the bobcat, the raccoon and the skunk.

Birds are also present in large numbers. Many of them spend all year in the same place. European residents include the blackbird, jay, chaffinch, wren, and several kinds of woodpecker, finch and tit. In summer they are joined by insect-eating birds, such as warblers and flycatchers. Woodland birds of prey include the sparrowhawk, buzzard and a few species of owl. American forests contain a similar range of birds, including the brightly coloured tanagers and the blue jay.

In Europe, since the disappearance of the wolf, the largest woodland predators are the red fox and the badger. They prey on a number of mice, voles and birds.

ECOLOGY AND THE ENVIRONMENT

Grasslands

Grasslands occur in places where the rainfall is more seasonal than in areas of deciduous woodland. Rain falls only at certain times of the year; at other times the ground may be baked dry or covered by snow. The only plants that can survive such conditions are grasses and a few small herbaceous plants. Trees need a good supply of water throughout the summer, as they constantly lose water through their leaves. They therefore find it difficult to survive periods of drought.

Grasslands are also maintained by grazing animals, which nibble off most of the tree shoots that do grow. In the dry season, there may also be occasional grass fires. The grass grows again as soon as the rains return, but tree shoots and other small plants are killed.

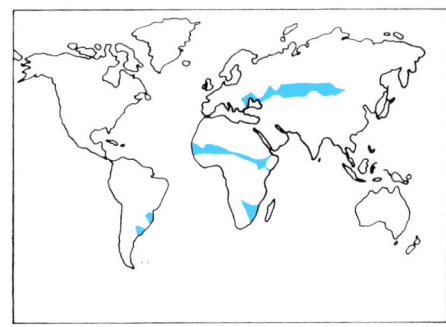

Above: *The world's grasslands.*

Temperate grasslands

The temperate grasslands of the world include the prairies of North America, the steppes of Asia, the pampas of South America and the veld of South Africa. Each of these regions has its own distinctive grazers, such as the bison and pronghorn (now uncommon) of North America, the saiga antelope of Asia and the pampas deer and guanaco (a relative of the llama) of South America. North American species include jack rabbits, cottontails and prairie dogs, which are not dogs but ground squirrels that live in huge colonies. They are preyed upon by coyotes and mountain lions. The South American pampas contains a unique range of rodents, such as the pampas guinea pig, the viscacha and the tuco-tuco, together with several kinds of armadillo. Predators include the maned wolf, the southern fox and the pampas cat.

Left: *The steppes of Asia, like other grasslands, are the home of a number of animals that graze grass or browse the leaves of other small green plants. These include the Mongolian gazelle, the saiga antelope and a number of ground squirrels, such as susliks and marmots.*

GRASSLANDS 133

Tropical grassland
The best-known tropical grassland is the African savannah. In this region rain falls during four months of the year only, but the grasses that grow support enormous herds of grazing animals, such as wildebeest, zebra, hartebeest and gazelles. In more wooded areas of savannah such animals as springbok, kudu, white rhinoceroses, giraffe and elephant are found. Savannah predators include several big cats, such as the lion, cheetah and leopard. Among the smaller predators are jackals and hyenas, together with the wild dog, serval, civet and banded mongoose. Savannah birds include the world's largest living bird, the flightless ostrich. Among other birds are the oxpeckers, marabou storks, weaver birds and huge flocks of queleas. The secretary bird stalks about in search of reptiles, and vultures feed on dead carcasses.

The African savannah is famous for its abundance of wildlife. Huge herds of grazing animals are common.

ECOLOGY AND THE ENVIRONMENT

Deserts

Deserts are places where very little rain falls. They are usually (though not always) also very hot. Yet a number of animals and plants have managed to adapt to these inhospitable conditions.

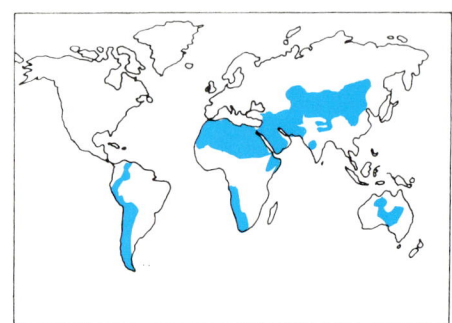

Above: *The world's deserts.*

Deserts of the world

Some deserts occur in the middle of large areas of land, because moisture-carrying winds from the sea have shed their rain before they reach the area. Sometimes mountains or forests cause the prevailing winds to lose their rain before they reach the desert.

All the world's large land masses have deserts. In North America, desert lands are found to the west of the Rocky Mountains, in Nevada and Arizona. In South America, east of the Andes, desert covers a large area stretching from Bolivia in the north to Tierra del Fuego in the south.

The deserts of central Asia are very cold in winter, as they are swept by icy winds from the Arctic. To the west and south are the deserts of the Middle East, which are almost joined to the world's largest desert, the Sahara desert of northern Africa. Farther south is the Namib desert of southern Africa. Much of central Australia is also desert.

Desert plants are designed to gather and conserve precious water. Cacti store water in their stems and defend themselves with spines. Pebble plants have fleshy leaves disguised as stones. The leaves of the strange Welwitschia absorb dew.

DESERTS 135

Desert animals have to cope with heat and lack of water. Camels are well-known for their ability to go for long periods without drinking. Most smaller animals venture out only at night.

Bactrian camels
sand grouse
rattlesnake
fennec fox
burrowing owl
jerboa
sand skink

Desert life

Water is essential to living organisms, and the main problem for desert plants and animals is finding and keeping water. Some plants avoid the periods of drought completely; their seeds germinate only after rain and they flower and produce new seeds within just a few weeks. Other plants store water in fleshy leaves, stems or roots. The cacti of North America are well-known succulents. Tough skins and spines help to ward off plant-eating animals.

Some desert animals manage to avoid drought. In the United States and Australia there are toads that spend most of their lives in closed underground burrows, emerging only after rain in order to reproduce. Other animals live more normal lives on the surface of the ground. They mostly rely on their food to provide the water they need.

Keeping cool is another problem. Some animals venture out only at night, but this is not practical for large desert animals, such as addax, eland and camels. These animals rarely sweat, as sweating involves losing valuable water. Instead they allow their bodies to heat up and only sweat if absolutely necessary.

Some animals have special ways of keeping cool. Desert foxes have large ears that act as heat radiators (they also help the animals to detect their prey). Lizards hold their bodies off the ground and often stand in such a position that only a small surface area faces the Sun.

ECOLOGY AND THE ENVIRONMENT

Tropical Rainforest

Of all the world's biomes, tropical rainforest is the richest of all in plant and animal life. Rainforest grows where there is plenty of rain and the temperature is high throughout the year. In the wettest regions plants grow continuously, and there is always something in flower or producing fruit. This constant supply of food provides a paradise for animals, of which there are an enormous variety and huge numbers – ten times as many as there are in deciduous forests.

Rainforests grow only in tropical and subtropical regions. In most of Central America and a large part of South America, rainforest is the natural vegetation. Rainforests are also found in the western part of central Africa, in most of south-east Asia and near the northern and eastern coasts of Australia.

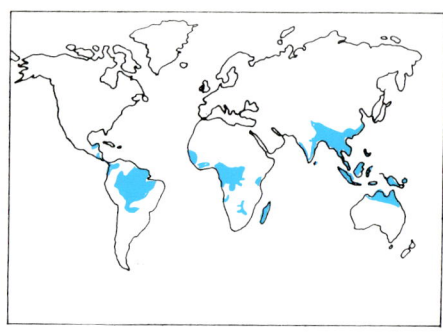

Above: *The world's tropical rainforests.*

Rainforest layers

As in deciduous forests, there are several layers of vegetation in a rainforest. The ground layer contains a variety of mosses and ferns. There are also many kinds of fungi, which rapidly break down dead plant material and make it available to growing plants.

Above this layer is a shrub layer that includes tree ferns and climbing plants known as lianas. Next comes a wide layer formed by the crowns of young trees, and above this is the thick canopy formed by the crowns of mature trees. A few trees stand out above the canopy and are described as the emergent layer.

Forest animals

The whole forest teems with life. Insects abound and this is the home of many of the world's most beautiful butterflies. The moist atmosphere of the forest makes it a comfortable environment for amphibians, and reptiles find it a rich source of food.

Left: *The layers of a tropical rainforest. Each layer provides homes for a different range of animals, and because the plant life is so luxuriant at all times of the year, it supports a huge range of animals. There are possibly millions of species that scientists have yet to discover.*

The canopy, which receives most of the sunlight, is home to a host of birds. In the Amazon forests of South America, toucans, parrots, parakeets and macaws feed on fruit, and a similar range of birds are found in other forests.

Rainforests are also home to many kinds of monkey and ape. In the Amazon forests there are capuchins, titis, spider monkeys, tamarins and marmosets. African forests are home to the guenons, the colobus monkey, the drill, the chimpanzee and the gorilla. Asian primates include the langurs, macaques and gibbons, together with the strange proboscis monkey and the orang-utan.

The rainforest supports many other mammals: in South America, tree porcupines, sloths, coatis, rodents such as agoutis, and forest predators like the jaguar and the ocelot; in Africa, hooved mammals, such as the okapi, bongo and the tiny water chevrotain; in south-east Asia, the tiger and several kinds of rare, one-horned rhinoceros.

TROPICAL RAINFOREST 137

[Illustration labels: mangabey, guenon, crowned hawk eagle, touraco, potto, silver-cheeked hornbill, scalytail, okapi, butterfly, golden cat]

DISAPPEARING FORESTS

The world's rainforests are being cut down to provide timber and to make room for farmland. They are disappearing at the rate of over 21 hectares (52 acres) every minute. If this rate continues, there will be no rainforest left by the year 2035.

Destruction of the rainforests will cause the extinction of thousands of plants and animals, many of which could probably be of great use to us. At the same time the planet will lose the most productive of all its biomes – for good. The rainforests will not grow again. Clearing large areas of forest makes it impossible for plants to spread rapidly enough from untouched areas and provide sufficient ground cover to prevent soil erosion.

Rainforest soil is poor, as most of the nutrients in the growing forest are contained in the plants themselves. The land can therefore be farmed for only a few years, after which it is left exposed to the wind and rain. The soil is quickly washed away.

Removal of the rainforests will also affect the world's climates. Without these large areas of greenery to use up carbon dioxide in photosynthesis, the greenhouse effect may be increased.

Left: *The animals of the African rainforests are often similar to those found in South America. However, these two regions have been separated for millions of years and contain completely different species.*

Life in Freshwater

Life on Earth began in the seas about 3,500 million years ago. But it was not until about 400 million years ago that organisms began to spread into freshwater habitats as well. It seems likely that freshwater algae appeared at about this time, although they left no fossil evidence. The first known vascular plants (plants with tissue that conducts water) appeared some time during the Devonian period. Plants were soon followed by animals, and by the end of the Devonian period there were freshwater molluscs, a variety of small arthropods and several kinds of fish.

Freshwater animals

A few animal groups have never managed to colonize freshwater environments. There are, for example, no freshwater echinoderms or brachiopods. But most of the other groups have freshwater members. There are a number of protozoans, and a few freshwater sponges, coelenterates, moss animals and flatworms. Freshwater molluscs, such as snails and clams, are common, as are annelid worms, such as leeches and tubifex worms. Freshwater crustaceans include crayfish, water fleas and freshwater shrimps.

Among the most common inhabitants of freshwater lakes, rivers and streams are insect larvae, such as those of mosquitos, midges, gnats, caddis flies and hoverflies. Underwater nymphs include those of dragonflies, damselflies and stoneflies. Some insects, such as water beetles and water scorpions, spend all their lives underwater.

A number of vertebrate animals also inhabit freshwater environments. The most numerous are, of course, the fishes, of which there are many

The freshwater river systems of the Amazon Basin are the home of many kinds of fish, including several species that use electricity to locate or kill their prey.

LIFE IN FRESHWATER 139

different kinds. Some feed on plant material, some on small invertebrates and others are among the top predators of freshwater ecosystems. Other freshwater vertebrates include the amphibians, all of which live in freshwater for at least part of their lives. Some reptiles, particularly members of the crocodile family, have also returned to freshwater. There are also many birds and mammals that live their lives in and around freshwater environments.

Ecosystems

With so many different inhabitants, a freshwater lake, river or stream is very often a completely self-contained ecosystem. However, as with all ecosystems, the inhabitants vary widely in different parts of the world. A European river may be home to such fishes as salmon, trout, roach, bream, chub, eel and pike. The Amazon river in South America is the home of the hatchet fish that catch insects in the air, the electric eel, the arawana and the huge arapaima, among others (including many species that have not yet been classified). African freshwater fish include a variety of cichlids, the primitive bichir and the African lungfish, which survives periods of drought by sealing itself into a mud burrow.

In temperate regions, freshwater streams and ponds support a range of fish and amphibians. Insects, particularly insect larvae, are very common.

ECOLOGY AND THE ENVIRONMENT

Oceans

> The world's oceans are regarded as one biome because, although very large (they cover over two thirds of the Earth's surface), they form one type of environment. However, within this biome there are many different habitats, which result from differences in depth, pressure and temperature in various parts of the oceans.

Plankton followers

Most of the organisms that live in the sea are found near the surface, where there is enough light for plants to grow. The richest ecosystems are near the coasts, particularly in warm tropical waters where coral reefs form. Here small plants are the food for a host of worms, sponges, molluscs and echinoderms, as well as the coral polyps themselves. Fish of all types and sizes also find plenty of food.

In deeper waters the plant life consists mostly of microscopic plants known as phytoplankton. These plants drift with the ocean current, together with the tiny animals that feed on them. These small animals in turn are eaten by other, slightly larger creatures; together they are known as zooplankton. The food chain continues up the scale with animals such as jellyfish and small crustaceans. They in turn are the food of larger animals, such as fish, squid and sea mammals. Near coasts that have a continental shelf extending out into the ocean, the sea-bed may be inhabited by echinoderms and brachiopods, some of which can be found at considerable depths.

Ocean zones

The ocean is divided into layers, or zones. The upper layer is known as the epipelagic zone. It ends at a depth of about 500m (1,600ft), which is as far as light can penetrate. Below is the bathypelagic zone, which extends down to the abyssal zone, the region of water immediately above the sea-bed. In some places, deep trenches in the sea-bed provide an additional zone, known as the hadal zone.

Because there is no light, there is no plant life in the bathypelagic zone. It is inhabited mostly by squid and crustaceans, together with a number of specialized deep-sea fish. They feed on material that descends from the epipelagic zone above, and on other deep-sea animals. Many of them carry their own lights, which help members of the same species recognize one another, and sometimes act as lures to catch prey.

Some of the bathypelagic fish are very strange creatures. Food is scarce and they have become adapted to making the most of what prey comes their way. Viperfish, lantern fish, bristlemouths and angler fish have large mouths and fearsome teeth. The deepest waters are inhabited by rat tails, gulper eels and swallowers. Tripod fish rest on the muddy bottom, perching on the long, stilt-like rays on their fins.

Left: A coral reef is a rich source of food and thus teems with sea life. Shoals of brightly coloured fish are common.

OCEANS 141

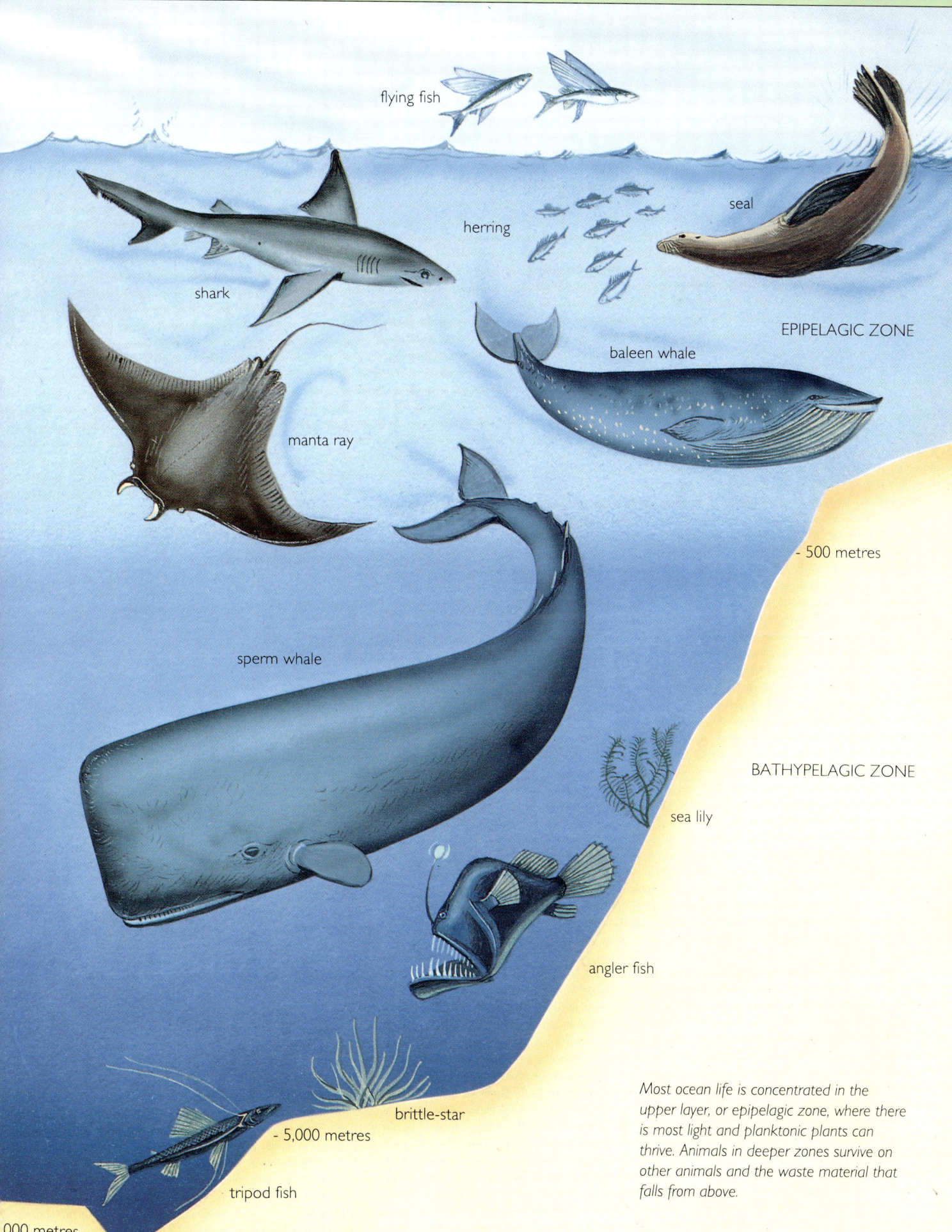

Most ocean life is concentrated in the upper layer, or epipelagic zone, where there is most light and planktonic plants can thrive. Animals in deeper zones survive on other animals and the waste material that falls from above.

ECOLOGY AND THE ENVIRONMENT

Islands

Islands can provide us with 'living laboratories', where the ways in which ecology and evolution work can be studied. When a new island is formed, scientists can monitor the species that colonize it and the speed at which they do so. Of course, new islands are not created very often, but the explosion of volcanic Krakatoa (Indonesia) in 1883 destroyed every living organism on the island and life had to begin again. Another volcanic eruption off the coast of Iceland in 1963 created the new island of Surtsey.

Early colonists

The first organisms to become established are usually lichens and mosses. Larger plants have to wait until pockets of soil have formed from eroded rock and remains of plants. Gradually, more and more plants become established, until eventually most of the ground is covered. Meanwhile, animals start to form breeding colonies. Mites and insects, particularly flies, are among the first to arrive. Plant-eating insects and birds quickly become established, and they are soon followed by predatory species. Animals that cannot fly, such as reptiles and mammals, naturally take a long time to become established, and often only a few species succeed in reaching the island.

Right: Where island animals have evolved in complete isolation for perhaps millions of years, they are often very distinctive. Islands or groups of islands, such as the Galapagos, Hawaii, the Seychelles, Mauritius and Aldabra are 'living laboratories' where nature can experiment without interference from mainland species.

ISLANDS 143

Evolution in isolation

Island animals and plants often provide us with dramatic examples of how species evolve. Islands far from large continents may be invaded by organisms that become isolated from the mainland populations. As they adapt to local conditions, they slowly evolve into completely new species.

The Galapagos Islands, for example, contain a variety of unique animals and plants, which must have descended from the same ancestors as the animals and plants of mainland South America. Among the unique Galapagos species are the huge land iguana and the marine iguana, the world's only sea-going lizard. These islands are also the home of several kinds of giant tortoise (a similar, yet different tortoise has evolved on Aldabra Island in the Indian Ocean), and of 15 species of finch (Darwin's finches), as well as the red crab, the Galapagos flightless cormorant, and other creatures found nowhere else.

Other islands have also produced unique species. Hawaii has 14 different kinds of honeycreeper; Christmas Island has its land crabs. The pig-like babirusa of Celebes, the Komodo dragon and the Seychelles magpie robin are other examples.

Flightless birds, such as the dodo of Mauritius, evolved on a number of islands where there were no natural predators. Unfortunately, these isolated environments are very vulnerable to interference by humans. On some islands, plants introduced from elsewhere have spread rapidly and swamped the native species. Animals introduced by humans, such as goats, rats and cats, have also caused the disappearance of many island plants and animals, especially flightless birds. The dodo was hunted to extinction.

Above: *Island plants can be just as unusual as island animals. Argyroxiphium and Dubautia species are confined to Hawaii, while Scalesia species are found only in the Galapagos Islands.*

Flightless birds are particularly vulnerable when hunted by humans or other introduced predators. The dodo, solitaire and Laysan rail are all now extinct. The barred-wing rail has been rediscovered, but it is unlikely to survive.

Life on the Seashore

A seashore forms an unusual and interesting ecosystem. Here, habitats gradually change from areas of land to regions that are covered in sea water for most or all of the time. These habitats are the home of many organisms that are not found anywhere else.

The upper end of a seashore may consist of cliffs or sand dunes. Cliffs are usually being eroded away by the sea – slowly or rapidly, depending on the material of which they are made. Sand dunes may be being built up or washed away. Farther down the shore there is generally a flatter region of mud, sand, gravel, pebbles or rock. Somewhere in this region is the high-tide mark.

Seashore plants

Above the normal high-tide mark, the land is seldom, if ever, covered by water. However, this region receives a lot of salty spray, particularly in rough weather. The plants that live here must therefore be able to tolerate such salty conditions. High above the high-tide mark plants such as sea lavender, scurvygrass (a member of the cabbage family, so named because sailors used to eat it as a cure for the disease of scurvy) and salt-marsh rush may be found. Sand dunes are often covered with sea couch or marram grass, whose underground stems help to bind the dunes together. In salt marshes, cord grass, which can tolerate being covered by sea water, helps to bind the mud. Other plants tolerant of salt found in these marshes include glasswort, sea aster and seablite.

Seashore animals

A number of small animals live above the high-tide mark, and many birds nest on cliffs or in sand dunes. On sandy shores, near the high-tide mark, there are usually small crustaceans – sand hoppers and beach fleas – which are scavengers, feeding on the material washed up by the waves.

Below the high-tide mark may be small habitats such as rocks, rock pools, patches of seaweed and areas of sand or mud. Animals found on rocks include limpets, mussels and barnacles. Small holes indicate the presence of piddocks – small, rock-boring, bivalve molluscs. Rock pools are favoured by many animals, such as hermit crabs, prawns, shrimps and sea anemones. Occasionally larger animals, such as edible crabs and sea urchins, are also found in rock pools. Among seaweed and under stones small crabs, winkles, topshells, chitons and sea squirts may be found.

Other animals bury themselves in sand or mud. On sandy shores cockles, razor shells, gapers and lugworms are usually present. Heart urchins may be found near the low-tide mark. Animals that live in mud include ragworms, peacock worms, daisy anemones, carpet shells and slipper limpets. Common shore crabs also favour muddy shores.

razor shells

Venus shells

dogfish egg purses

lugworms

mussels

sea anemone

ECOLOGY AND THE ENVIRONMENT

Wildlife in Towns and Gardens

Wild animals are not found only in wild places. Many species take advantage of the food that is available in environments that human beings have created for themselves.

Country environments

Farmland is probably the most widespread environment made by humans. And because the animals that have adapted to life in farmland are so familiar, we have come to regard them as part of the natural scene. Animals that once would have inhabited the edges of woodlands, such as fieldmice and hedgehogs, are now commonly found in hedgerows. Insects, rodents and birds feed on planted crops.

A number of animals invade our gardens, attracted by the plants that grow there. Insects such as froghoppers, aphids, ladybirds, soldier beetles and capsids are common visitors to gardens. A country garden can attract many kinds of butterfly if the right kinds of food plant are grown. Many caterpillars like to feed on nettles, so it is worth leaving a patch of these to grow. Adult butterflies like the flowers of colourful plants such as buddleias, petunias, aubrietia and honesty.

Similarly, birds such as blackbirds, robins, thrushes, finches and tits are often seen in country gardens. They can be encouraged by providing nest boxes and, in winter, food on a bird-table safe from cats.

Certain garden plants, such as the buddleia shown here, are very attractive to butterflies. Butterflies are also helped if gardeners can provide the food plants that their caterpillars need.

WILDLIFE IN TOWNS AND GARDENS

Town animals

Urban, or town, environments also have their populations of wild animals. Our homes, for example, are often invaded by small animals, including birds, mice, rats, bats, toads, millipedes, woodlice, spiders and mites. To these can be added a host of insects, such as flies, silverfish, cockroaches, thrips, clothes moths, booklice, wood-boring beetles and weevils. In tropical countries homes are frequently invaded by more exotic kinds of insects such as mantises, together with scorpions, lizards and even snakes.

Outside, a number of animals have adapted to life in towns, and many live there permanently. Pigeons are a common sight in many European cities, as are house sparrows. In summer they are often joined by migratory birds, such as swifts and house martins. Kestrels sometimes nest on tall buildings, and in warmer climates storks can often be seen nesting on roofs. Among the mammals that have taken up residence in our cities, the strangest is perhaps the fox. Yet many foxes have adapted to a life of preying on small urban mammals and raiding dustbins and other sources of leftover human food. A number of cities now have large, permanent fox populations.

Foxes are opportunists and despite their instinctive fear of humans have adapted well to living in towns.

Below: A bird-table supplied with food during the winter months attracts many birds and helps ensure their survival.

Above: In southern Europe white storks often nest on buildings. They are believed to be symbols of fertility and good luck.

ECOLOGY AND THE ENVIRONMENT

References

Alpine plants Plants that live in the alpine zone of a mountain, above the tree line (where trees will not grow) and below the region permanently covered by snow.

Arctogaea One of the three zoogeographical realms into which zoologists divide the world. It is basically the northern area of the world: Nearctic, Palaearctic, Oriental and Ethiopian regions.

Australasian region The zoogeographical region that includes Australia, New Zealand and the islands west of Wallace's line.

Biome A major community of plants and animals, characterized by a particular type of climate and vegetation.

Cactus A desert plant that stores water in a swollen stem: its leaves are reduced to spines or prickles. Cacti are native to North America, although some species, such as the prickly pear, have been introduced elsewhere.

Community A collection of plants and animals living in the same place.

Coniferous forest A biome where the temperature is low, the soil is rather poor and the available water is at times frozen.

Consumer An organism that consumes food materials produced by others. The primary consumers of an ecosystem are the plant-eating animals. They are preyed upon by secondary consumers, which in turn may be eaten by tertiary (third) consumers. The ultimate consumers are the decomposers – those organisms, such as bacteria and fungi, that break down dead plant and animal matter.

Continental shelf The sloping sea-bed bordering the continents, where the water is shallow.

Deciduous forest A biome of temperate climates with moderate rainfall, where the dominant plants are deciduous trees.

Deciduous tree A tree that sheds all its leaves in the autumn to protect itself from frost and wind.

Desert A biome of hot dry climates where rainfall is very low, and the plants are specially adapted to deal with extreme drought.

Ecology The study of plants and animals in their environment.

Ecosystem A self-contained plant and animal community that forms part of a larger biome.

Environment The conditions in which an organism or community of organisms exist.

Ethiopian region Zoogeographical region that consists of Africa south of the Sahara desert.

Fauna All the animals of a particular region.

Flora All the plants of a particular region.

Habitat The local living area of an animal or plant.

Holarctic region The zoogeographical region that includes all of North America, Europe and northern Asia.

Ice Age A period when the climate was colder and ice sheets covered large areas of land. The last Ice Age ended 25,000 years ago.

Liana A tropical climbing plant with a woody stem.

Nearctic region Zoogeographical region that consists largely of North America.

Neogaea One of the three zoogeographical realms, the same as the Neotropical region.

Neotropical region The zoogeographical region that consists of South America and most of Central America.

Notogaea The zoogeographical realm of Australasia. See **Arctogaea**.

Oriental region The zoogeographical region that includes India, south-east Asia and the islands east of Wallace's line.

Pack-ice An area in the polar oceans where ice floes are driven together by winds and currents.

Palaearctic region The zoogeographical region that includes Europe, northern Asia and the northern part of Africa.

Pangaea The name given to the supercontinent that existed 200 million years ago.

Savannah A type of tropical grassland found in Africa.

Succulent A plant that stores water in its stem or leaves.

Temperate grassland A biome of temperate regions where the rainfall is seasonal. It includes the North American prairies, the South American pampas, the steppes of Asia and the South African veld.

Tropical grassland A biome of hot, dry regions where the rainfall is seasonal. Tropical grasslands include the African savannah, the Brazilian campos, the chaco of Argentina and Paraguay, and parts of Australia.

Tropical rainforest A biome of hot climates where the rainfall is high.

Tundra A biome found around the Arctic circle, where organisms are subjected to very low temperatures throughout the year and much of the available water is frozen.

Wallace's line An imaginary line that runs east of Borneo and Bali along the Macassar Strait, which separates these islands from the islands of Celebes and Lombok. This stretch of water appears to have acted as a barrier to animals in the past, as the animals that are found on the eastern islands are quite different from the animals found on the western islands. This fact was first pointed out by the English naturalist, Alfred Wallace, in 1860.

Zoogeographical region A region of the world characterized by the presence of certain animals and the absence of others.

Zoogeography The study of the geographical distribution of animals.

Wildlife in the Future

Nature and Human Beings

Living things have existed on Earth for about 3,500 million years. Modern humans have existed for only about 1 million years. But during this short period of time, humans have learned how to dominate all other forms of life, and have brought about great changes in the world's environments.

Taming nature
Early humans were just one more species among many in the animal kingdom. They lived much like other creatures, gathering plants and hunting animals for food as necessary. They led a nomadic existence, wandering from place to place in order to find food. Then, about 12,000 years ago, humans discovered that certain useful animals could be tamed and kept together in herds. Sheep and goats were probably the first animals to be tamed. Herds of these animals travelled with the nomads, providing a constant supply of milk, meat and skins.

About 10,000 years ago an even more important change occurred. People began to grow crops. Until then they had simply gathered the seeds of wild grasses. Now, however, a new variety of grass appeared. It had plump grains but, unlike other grasses, it was not very efficient at scattering its own seeds. In order to ensure a supply of this grass, people had to sow it deliberately. The grass became known as wheat, and its appearance marked the beginning of the farming revolution.

Farming practices developed in many parts of the world. Other animals, such as cattle and chickens, were domesticated. Other plants were grown for food, including rice in the Far East and maize in the Americas.

Below: The farming practices that have evolved in Britain over thousands of years have led to today's patchwork of fields.

Above: Modern breeds of domestic animals are the result of thousands of years of selective breeding by farmers.

NATURE AND HUMAN BEINGS

Changing environments

Farming has changed the face of the world. All across Europe forests have been cut down to make room for fields. In North America and northern Asia natural grasslands have given way to farmland, and today it is the world's tropical rainforests that are being cleared to provide yet more land for growing food.

At the same time the world's population is increasing, often in areas where growing food is most difficult. Overgrazing of sparse vegetation is causing more and more land to become desert-like. Erosion of exposed topsoils by wind and water has caused many areas to become barren; exposed rainforest soils that have exhausted their ability to grow crops are very prone to erosion. Elsewhere, excessive irrigation has allowed too much salt to collect in the soil, which has become useless as a result. Even in temperate regions today's farming methods, in which chemical fertilizers and pesticides play an important part, are adding to the world's pollution problems. Modern, high-intensive farming is now not just changing the landscape; it is destroying environments.

Large-scale destruction of rainforest removes essential nutrients from the system and often leads to soil erosion.

Acid rain, which forms from the gases produced by burning coal and oil, damages lakes and trees.

Ploughing up heathland to create more room for growing crops is leading to the disappearance of many unique species.

WILDLIFE IN THE FUTURE

Pollution

Environmental changes are also being caused by other factors. The world's industries generate many kinds of waste chemicals, which are polluting the air, the sea and the land. For example, gases such as carbon monoxide, ozone and several oxides of nitrogen are released into the air. Heavy metals, such as lead, cadmium and mercury, can be found in the air, in water and in soils. A range of organic chemicals, such as PCBs (polychlorinated biphenyls), benzene and formaldehyde, also find their way into the environment. Many of these chemicals are poisons. Others cause rainwater to become acid, and some gases, particularly carbon dioxide, are believed to be causing a process known as the greenhouse effect. They are thought to be helping to warm the Earth by absorbing some of the heat that would otherwise escape into space. Some scientists believe that this greenhouse effect will warm up the atmosphere by 4.5°C during the next 60 years. The result would be major changes in climate in all parts of the world.

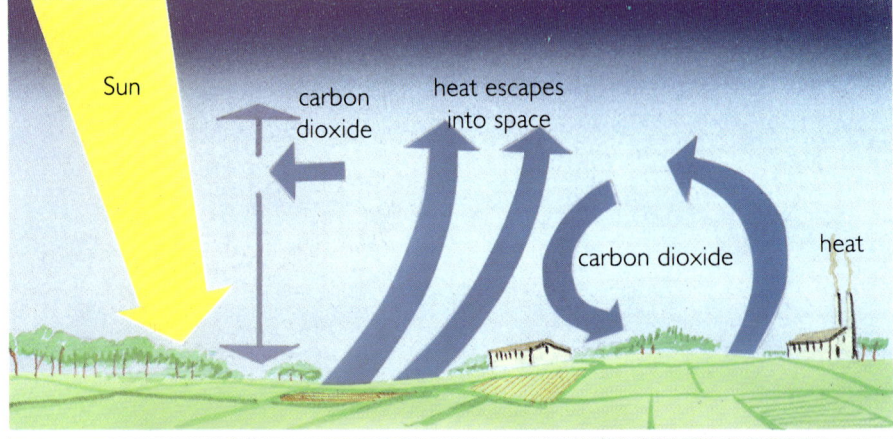
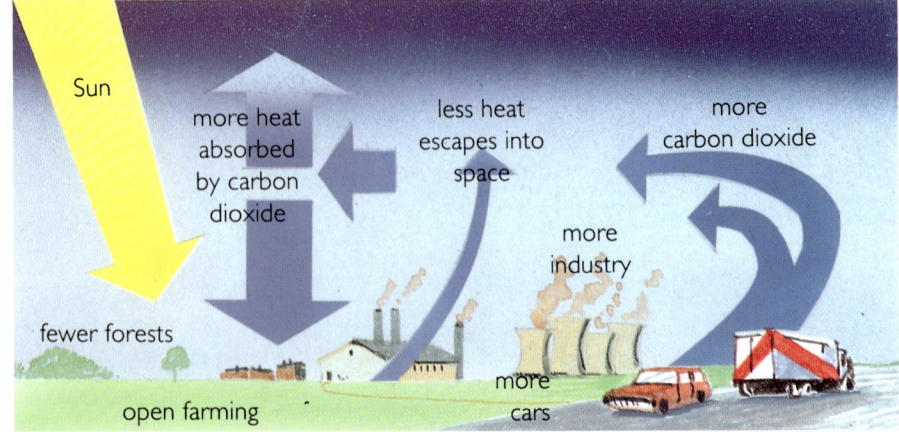

Above: The greenhouse effect has helped to keep the Earth warm for hundreds of millions of years. However, by increasing the amount of carbon dioxide in the atmosphere we may cause it to become warmer and thus alter the climate.

Below: Coral is easily killed and is very sensitive to pollution. When a polluted reef dies, the other inhabitants either die or leave and the reef becomes a crumbling, dead skeleton with little or no chance of recovery.

NATURE AND HUMAN BEINGS

Animals and plants in danger
All these things affect not only ourselves but every other living thing on this planet. Many plant and animal species are now extinct or endangered due to the activities of humans.

The destruction of wild habitats is one of the main causes of animals and plants becoming scarce. It is thought to be at least part of the cause in over 70 per cent of cases, and it is probable that, as the rainforests disappear, the world is losing many species that have never been discovered.

Habitat destruction is often aggravated by other human activities. In some places, where native animals and plants have evolved without the presence of predators or competing animals, they have been unable to cope with animals introduced by humans. Cats, dogs, goats and rats have been responsible for the disappearance of many species, particularly on islands.

Some animals have been over-hunted. For hundreds of years people have hunted not only for food but also for sport and for ornaments such as skins and horns. Many animals have already been hunted to extinction. Others, including many kinds of whale, deer, otter and sea turtle, have been brought to the point at which they are greatly endangered. Even today, in spite of the fact that rhinoceroses and elephants are protected by international laws and agreements, poachers are still killing them for their horns and tusks.

Ivory comes from the tusks of elephants (above) and has been prized for making ornaments for hundreds of years. The high value of ivory has meant that people could make a great deal of money by selling elephant tusks, and in spite of attempts to conserve elephants in reserves, poachers killed many (below). Trade in ivory has now been banned by international agreement.

Wildlife in the Future

Conservation

Why should we bother to protect wildlife? After all, no animal appears to be concerned about the survival of other species. And most of the animals and plants in the world do not, at first glance, seem to be essential to our survival.

In 1972 the Arabian oryx became extinct in the wild. However, during the 1960s some of these animals had been captured and taken to Phoenix Zoo in Arizona, USA, and in 1982 it became possible to release a large number back into the wild, in Oman.

Useful species

There are several very good reasons why we should be concerned with the survival of other living things. The survival of the species we use for food is clearly vital, but their survival alone will not be enough. We rely on today's environments to provide these species with the right conditions in which to grow, and these environments can only be maintained by the proper balance of an enormous number of other animals and plants.

We also need a huge variety of animals and plants to provide us with the resources that will be needed in the future. The species that we use today may alter or they may be attacked by disease. Only by keeping a wide range of similar species can we hope to overcome such problems. At the same time, there are probably many, as yet undiscovered, kinds of animal and plant that could be of use to us, particularly in rainforests.

These are all good practical reasons in favour of the conservation of wildlife. There is another reason, which some people would say is just as important, and perhaps more important. We do not own the world; we are just in charge of it for a short time.

If we cause the extinction of too many animals and plants, we will turn the world into a barren and boring place for future generations. We human beings do not have the right to cause the disappearance of any other species, unless it threatens our own survival.

CONSERVATION

Conservation in action

Fortunately, much is being done to try to conserve wildlife by people and organizations throughout the world. First there are international organizations, such as the International Union for the Conservation of Nature and Natural Resources (IUCN) and the World Wide Fund for Nature (WWF). Among other projects, they try to protect individual species and to reintroduce species to habitats where they have become extinct. Some people carry out biological research, which is vital in order to understand animals and plants and how they relate to one another. Other organizations are at work in individual countries, districts, and even in villages or schools. Anyone can help to save wildlife by the simplest acts, such as clearing ponds or putting out nest boxes for bats.

There have been some notable successes. The tiger, for example, is no longer in danger, and the Arabian oryx has been successfully reintroduced into the wild. However, although individual species are important, conservationists now recognize that we need to concentrate on protecting the world's remaining natural environments. If we can save the environments, we will save the species they house.

Greenpeace is an international organization whose aim is to publicize a variety of environmental issues, particularly those concerned with the sea, such as whaling and dumping of nuclear waste.

Over the years many ponds have been filled in with rubbish. But by clearing this out, such ponds can be made habitable again, thus increasing the number of places available for amphibians to breed.

References

Acid rain Rain containing small amounts of sulphuric and nitric acids. These acids get into the atmosphere as the result of chemical reactions produced by burning fossil fuels. Acid rain is known to pollute freshwater lakes and is probably a major factor in the death of trees.

Chipko A conservation movement aimed at protecting trees from being felled. It began in the Himalayan region of India in 1973 and has since spread to other north Indian hill states.

CITES (Convention on Trade in Endangered Species) An international agreement that has been signed by over 90 countries. The governments of the signing countries undertake to control trade in certain species, including materials derived from them, such as skins and ivory.

Desertification The disappearance of plant life from an area of land, resulting in the land having a desert-like appearance. The plant life may disappear as the result of a change in climate, in which case desertification is more or less permanent. When desertification is produced by overgrazing alone, it may sometimes be reversed by removing the grazing animals and allowing plants to recolonize the area naturally.

Endangered species A species of animal or plant that is unlikely to survive unless the reasons for its decline are checked.

Erosion The wearing away of rock or soil by the action of wind, water or both.

Extinct species A species of animal or plant that has disappeared. Some species are described as being extinct in a particular region, while still existing elsewhere. Others are described as being extinct in the wild, although there may be some individuals living in captivity. Truly extinct species no longer exist at all.

Fertilizer A material spread over the ground in order to promote the growth of plants. Natural fertilizers include farmyard manure and guano (a form of concentrated bird droppings). Artificial fertilizers are chemicals made from oil products.

Friends of the Earth An organization whose purpose is to act as a pressure group by mounting public campaigns on environmental issues.

Greenhouse effect The way in which carbon dioxide and other gases in the atmosphere act like the glass of a greenhouse to retain heat. Heat from the Sun warms the surface of the planet. Most of the heat that is radiated out again escapes back into space. However, carbon dioxide gas in the atmosphere absorbs some of the radiated heat and prevents it from escaping. In the past 200 years, since the start of the Industrial Revolution, the amount of carbon dioxide in the atmosphere has slowly increased as a result of burning fossil fuels. At the same time the atmosphere has warmed up. Many scientists believe that the temperature of the atmosphere will continue to increase, perhaps by as much as 4.5°C.

Greenpeace An organization whose purpose is to campaign against the destruction of the environment and wildlife, particularly in the world's oceans and seas.

IUCN (International Union for the Conservation of Nature and Natural Resources) An international organization, founded in 1948, that is concerned with the scientific study of the environment. The IUCN produces the *Red Data Books*, which list all the species of plants and animals whose numbers are declining, and is also involved in such areas as education, biological research, conservation and environmental planning.

Overgrazing Allowing too many animals to graze an area of land, with the result that the plants there have no opportunity to regrow. Overgrazing leads to desertification and soil erosion.

Pesticide A chemical designed to kill an organism, such as an insect or a fungus.

Pollution The release into the environment of a substance or material that is harmful or which cannot easily be broken down by natural processes.

RSNC (Royal Society for Nature Conservation) The parent organization of the 48 local wildlife trusts in Britain. Together these trusts form the largest voluntary organization concerned with wildlife conservation in Britain. Local societies offer everyone the chance to get involved in wildlife walks, habitat management and fund-raising events.

RSPB (Royal Society for the Protection of Birds) An organization concerned with all aspects of the study, conservation and welfare of birds in Britain, including both residents and migratory visitors.

Soil erosion The removal of exposed topsoil by wind or water. This usually occurs as the result of removing the natural plant cover. Clearing tropical rainforest often results in the soil, no longer held by roots, being washed away by the heavy rainfall.

WATCH The young person's section of the RSNC.

WWF (World Wide Fund for Nature; formerly the World Wildlife Fund) An international organization founded in 1961 as a fund-raising body linked to the IUCN. Over the years many conservation projects have been financed by the WWF. The organization is still known as the World Wildlife Fund in Australia, Canada and the USA.

Index

Page references to illustrations are shown in *italic* type.

A
aardvarks 60, *60*
adaptation 68
adaptive radiation 34
Africa
    apes/monkeys 56–7
    freshwater fish 139
    rainforest 136, 137
    savannah 133, *133*
    see also tropical regions
albatrosses 46, *46*, 104, 116
    wings *104*
algae 9, *12*, 12–13, 16, 70–1, *70*, *71*, 84, 114, 138
    blue-green 9, 11
    freshwater 138
    green (*Chlorophyta*) 70
    marine (seaweed) 71, *71*
alligators 44, 45
Allosaurus 92, *93*, 93
Alpine plants 148
Amazon 121, *121*, 136, *138*, 139
amber, insects in 87
ammonites 87, *87*, 92, 93, 96
amoebas 11, *11*, 102
amphibians 42–3, 44, 91, 106, 139
    see also frogs; newts; toads
anacondas 45, *45*
ancient life *see* prehistoric
angler fish 109, 140, *141*
annelid worms 21, 24, 115, 138
Antarctic 128
    see also Arctic
anteaters 52, *52*, 60, *60*
antelopes 63, *106*, 132
    prehistoric life 95
anthers 79, 80
antibiotics 15, 16
ants 26, 29, *29*
    and whistling thorns 113, *113*
apes 57, 95
aphids 27, 146
arachnids 24, 34, 115
    see also scorpions; spiders
Archaeopteryx (first bird) 88–9, 93
archosaurs 92, 96
Arctic 124
    birds 116, *125*
    compared with Antarctic 124
    fox 64
    marine life 124
    preserved animals 87
    see also Antarctic; tundra
Aristotle's lantern 33, *34*
armadillos 60, *106*, 132
arthropods 24–5, 34, 106
    prehistoric 87, 138
arum, wild 81, *81*
Asia 130, *132*, 136
aspens 128
asses, wild 62, *62*
associations between living things 118
    see also symbiotic relationships
attack/defence 108–11
Australasia/Australia 52–3, 122, 123, 136, 148
    marsupials 53, 123, *123*
    monotremes 52

B
baboons 56
backbones 36
    animals with (vertebrates) 16, 35–68
        evolution of 36, 90
        primitive surviving 37
    animals without (invertebrates) 17–34
        prehistoric 90
bacteria 9, *10*, 11, 14, 99, 115, 117
    bacilli *10*

cellulose-breaking 100
and cheese-making 15
defined 16
see also viruses
badgers 65, 131, *131*
balance, sense of/stability 106, 118
balance of nature 120
baleen *see under* whales
bandicoots 53
barnacles 25, 144
bass *105*
bats 55, *55*, 81, *107*
    and echolocation 107
bears 64, 65, *65*, 95
    black 128, *128*
    brown 123, 128
    grizzly 127
beavers 58, *58*
bees 26, 29, 81, 111, 117, *117*
beetles 26, 28, *28*, *105*, *111*, 146
belemnites 87, 96
beluga 66
bilberries 128
bilharzia 20
binocular vision 57
biomes/ecosystems 120–1, 148
    ocean 140
birch 114, 128
    fruit/seeds 82, *82*
bird-eating spiders 31
birds 46–9, 81, 127, 144
    beaks 47, *47*–8
    breeding of 49, *49*
    of cold regions 127
    conservation 146, *147*
    evolution 46, 92, 93, 96
    feet/legs 47, 106
    food 47–8
    forest/woodland 129, 131, 136
    insect-eating 48, 131
    migration 116, *116*, 117
    of paradise 49
    of prey 46, 47, 127–9, 131, *132*
        see also eagles; kestrels; owls; peregrines
    wading 46, 48, 127
        beaks 47
    wings/flight 47, 104, *104*, *105*
bison 120, 132
bivalve molluscs 23, 102, 144
blackbirds 48, 131, 146
blackcap 131
black widow *31*
bladderwort 79
bladderwrack 71, *71*
blindworms 42
blood suckers 21, 27, 30, 58, 138
bluethroat *129*
bluff/camouflage, animals using 109, *109*, 111, 118
boas 45
bobcat *130*, 131
body temperature, regulating 135
bowfins 40, *40*
brachiopods 21, 34, 87, *90*, 140
Brachiosaurus 92
bracken 74, *74*
bramble fruit 83
breathing *see* respiration
brittle-stars *32*, 33, *141*
broad-leaved trees *see* trees, deciduous
Brontosaurus 93
broomrapes 115
bryophytes 72–3
bryozoans 112
buddleias 146, *146*
bugs 26
buoyancy, fish 38, 40
burdock 83
bushbabies 56, *56*
bustard, great 132
buttercups 79
butterflies 26, 27, 111, 116, *116*, 137
    bluff/camouflage 109, *109*, 111
    common blue *28*

food plants 146, *146*
hairstreak *111*
migration 116, *116*
peacock 109
swallowtail *28*
butterworts 79
buzzards 104, 131

C
cacti 81, *134*, 135, 148
caecilians 42
caimans 45
California 77
Cambrian period 89, 90
camels 63, 95, 135
    Bactrian *135*
camouflage 109, 111 118
capercaillie *128*, 129
capuchins 56, 136
capybara 58
carapace 68
carbon dioxide 9, 98, 99, 136, 152
    see also photosynthesis
Carboniferous period 89, 91
caribou (reindeer) 95, 123, 127, *128*, 129
carnivores (meat-eaters) 64–5, 100, 127, 128
    food chains and 101
    plants 79
    posture 106
carnosaurs 92, 96
carpels 79
carpet shells 144
carrion flowers 81
cartilage 38, 68
castes, insect 29
caterpillars 26, 100, 130
catfish 41
catkins 80, *80*
cats 51, 64, 132, *137*
    mountain 127
    see also lions; tigers
cattle 63, 95
    musk oxen 127, *127*
cedars 76, *76*
cells, animal/plant 10–11, 16
    colonies 12–13
    nuclei 10, *10*, 16
    phloem 98
    with special tasks 13
    structure 10, *10*
cellulose 10, *16*, 70
    digestion of 100
Cenozoic era 94–5
centipedes 24, *24*
cephalopods 23
Cetacea see whales
chameleons 45, 108, *108*
cheese-making 15
cheetah *50*, 64, 133
chewing the cud 63
chimpanzee 57, *57*, 136
chipmunks 128, *129*
Chiroptera (bats) 55, *55*, 81, *107*, 107
chitin 34
chitons (coat-of-mail shells) 24, 34, 144
Chlamydomonas 12, *12*, 70
chlorophyll/chloroplasts 10, 11, 70, 98
    see also photosynthesis
choanocytes (collar cells) 13
chordate animals 36, 68
chrysophytes 71
cilia 11, 102, 118
    see also flagella
civets 65, 133
Cladophora (algae) 70
cleansing animals 112
cliffs, life on 144
clubmosses 75, *75*, 91
cnidarians 18–19
coal 86, 91, 96
    fossils in 87
coatis 65, 136
cobra *110*
cocci bacteria *10*

coccolithophores (plant-animals) 71
cockles 23, 144, *144*
cockroaches 26, 27, 100
coelacanths 40, *40*
coelenterates (corals etc) 18–19, 115, 138
Coelophysis (dinosaur) 93
cold regions 124–5, 126–9
    surviving in 76, 95, 126
collar cells 13
colonization of islands 142
colugos (flying lemurs) 60
comb star 32
Commiphora 134
condors *127*
condylarths (*Andrewsarchus*) 94, *94*, 96
cone shells 22, 110
conifers *see under* trees
conservation 154–5
    in gardens 146
    organizations 155
continental drift 122
continental shelves 140, 148
cooling of climate 95
copepods 25, *25*
corals 18–19
    reefs 140, *140*, 152
cord grass 144
cormorants 47, *142*, 143
cougar/puma *see* lion, mountain
courtship rituals 49
cowberries 128
cowries 22, *22*
coyote 64, *64*, 132
crabs 25, 144, *145*
    edible 144
    hermit 112, *112*, 144
    king 24, 25, *25*, 34
    land 143
    mangrove 142
    red 142, 143
    robber *142*
    shore 144
crab spiders 31, *31*
crayfish 25, 138
creodonts 94, 96
Cretaceous period 89, 92–3
crocodiles 44, 44, 45, 108
crops, sown 146, 150
crossbills 48, *48*, 129, *129*
cross-pollination 79, 81
    see also pollination
crows 46, 48
crustaceans 24–25, 140
    in Antarctic 125
    freshwater 138
    of high-tide zone 144
    parasitic 115
cuckoo 115, *115*, 116
    breeding habits 49
curlew *145*
cuttlefish 23, *23*
cycads 77
cypresses 76
cytoplasm 10, 16

D
daffodils 78
daisies 79
damselfly *139*
dandelions 82, *82*
Darwin, Charles 96
Darwin's finches 48, 143
deciduous *see under* trees
decomposers 99
deer 63, *63*, 130, *131*, 132
    reindeer (caribou) 95, 123, 127, *128*, 129
defence, attack and 108–11
Deinonychus (dinosaur) 93
Dermoptera (flying lemurs) 60
deserts 120, 121, 134–5, 148
    water conservation 135
destruction of habitats 137, 151, *151*, 153
    see also conservation; poisons;

158 INDEX

pollution
devil's coach horse 27
Devonian period 89, 91, 138
diatoms 71, *71*
dicotyledons 78, *79*
digestion, feeding and 100
dinosaurs 44, 92, *92*, 93, *93*, 96
    body temperatures 93
    end of the 93
Diplodocus 92, *92*
diseases, cause of 11, 20
divers 46
DNA (deoxyribonucleic acid) 9, 10, 16
dodders 115
dodo 143, *143*
dogfish 39, *39*
dog-rose fruit *83*
dogs 64, 133
    hunting *133*
    prairie 132
dolphins 66, *66*, 67, 105, 117
domestic animals and wildlife 143, 150, *150*, 153
dormice 58, 99, *131*
Douglas firs 76
dragonflies 26, *28*, *139*
drainage of soil 21
drills 136
    mandrills 56, *56*
Dryosaurus (dinosaur) 93, *93*
ducks 46, 48, 127
    pintail *48*
dung beetles 26, *26*
Dutch elm disease 15

E
eagles 46, *47*, 137
earthworms 21, *21*
    movement 103, *103*
earwigs 26
echidnas (anteaters) 52, *52*
echinoderms (spiny-skinned animals) 32–3, *90*, 140
echolocation 55, 66, 107
ecology and the environment 119–155
ecosystems 148
    and biomes 120–1
    freshwater 139
    and habitats 120
edelweiss *126*
edentates (*Edentata*) 60, *60*
eggs 68
eels/elvers 139, 140
    gulper 140
    migration 41, 117, *117*
    movement 103, *103*
    see also electric
eelworms 20
eland 112, *135*
electric
    eels 110, *110*, *138*, 139
    rays 39, *39*
elephants (*Proboscidea*) 61, *61*, 133
    ivory trade 153, *153*
    prehistoric 87, 94, 95, *95*
elks 128, 129
embryos 68, 84
    mammal *51*
endangered species 153
endoplasmic reticulum 10, *10*
energy 8, 101, 118
    food and 98–101
enzymes 16, 34, 100
Eocene epoch 88, 89, 94
Eohippus (horse ancestor) 88
epiphytes (ferns) 74
Ethiopian region 122, 148
Eudorina (simple plant) 12, *12*
euglenoids (plant-animals) 71, *71*
Europe
    birds/mammals *131*, 131
    freshwater fish 139
evergreens 76
    see also trees, coniferous

evolution 86, 88–95, 143
    adaptive radiation 34
    theory of, evidence for 88–89
    see also Darwin
excretion 8, 16
explosive pods 82
extinct animals/plants 88, 137, 143, *143*, 153
    see also prehistoric

F
falcon *see* peregrine falcon
fanworms 21, *102*
farming/farmland 146, 150–1
fat, in mammals 50
feet, false 102
fennec 64, *135*
ferns 74–5, 130
    tree 74, *75*, 87, 136
fertilization 84
    flowering plants 82
fieldmice 146
filamentous algae 70, *70*
filter feeding 67, 102
finches 46, *47*, 48, 127, 131, *131*, 146
    Darwin's/Galapagos 48, 143
fins, fish 105
fires, grassland 132
firs 76, *76*, 128
fish
    Amazon *138*, *139*
    bony 40–1
    camouflage/defences 41, 109
    deep sea 140
    freshwater *138–9*, 139
    lice 25
    migration 117
        see also eels; salmon
    prehistoric 90–1, 138
    primitive 40
    swimming method 105
five-sided animals 32
flagella/flagellates 11, 71, *71*, 118
    see also cilia
flatfish 41, 109
flatworms 20, 115, 138
fleas 26, 27
    beach 144
fledgelings 49
flies 26–8, *27*
flight 28, 104
    see also flying animals
flowering plants 78–83, 84
    prehistoric 94
flukes 20; 21
flycatchers 48, 131
flying animals 68
    see also bats; birds; insects
'flying animals'
    fish 41, *141*
    frogs 43
    lemurs (colugos) 60
food/feeding
    chains/pyramids/webs 99, *99*, 101, *101*, 118, 124, 140, 148
    and digestion 100
    and energy 8, 98–101
foraminiferans (index fossils) 11, 87
forests/woodlands *see* trees
fossils/fossilization 86–7, 90–5
    and evolution 88–9
    formation process 86, 86–7, 96
    'living fossils' 34, 40, 77
foxes 64, 127, 131, 132, 147, *147*
    Arctic 101, *127*
    desert 135
    flying 55
foxgloves *81*
    freshwater life 138–9, *139*
frogs 42, *42*, 43, *43*
    arrow-poison *110*, 111
    tree *111*
fruit *see* seeds
fruit bat *55*

fungi 14–15, *14*, *15*, 114, 128, 136
    as decomposers 99
    living together with plants 114, 118
    parasitic 115
fur 50

G
Galapagos Islands 44, 142–3
    Darwin's finches 48, 143
game birds 46, 129
gametes/gametophytes 73, 74, 75, 84
gapers 23, 144
gardens/towns, wildlife of 146
garpikes 40, *40*
gastropods 22, *22*
gavials 45
gazelles *132*, 133
geckos 45, *45*
geese 116, 127
gemsbok *122*
'General Sherman' 77
genes 16
genetics 10
genets 65, *122*
geographical distribution 122–3
geology/Geological Time Scale 89, 90–5, 96
    dating rocks 87
    see also fossils; prehistory
gibbons 57, *57*, 136
gills *see* respiration
giraffes 63, 95, 133
Globigerina ooze 11
golgi body 10
gorillas 57, *57*, 136
goshawks *128*
graptolites 87, 96
grasses 78, *78*, 83
    reproduction 80, *80*
grasshoppers 26, 27, *28*, 100
    rear legs 106
grasslands 120, 121, 132–3, 148
    temperate 132, 148
    tropical 133, 148
    see also pampas; prairies; savannah; steppes; veld
grazing animals 95, 132, 133
greenhouse effect 137, 152, *152*
grouse 129, *135*
guenon monkeys 56, 136, *137*
guinea pigs 58, 123, *132*
gulls 46, 48, *145*
    beaks *47*
gulpers 40
gymnosperms 76–7, *76*, *77*

H
habitats 68, 148
    destruction of 137, 151, *151*, 153
    ecosystems and 120
    see also conservation; pollution
hagfish 37, 38
hares 59, *59*, 128
    Arctic *127*
hart's tongue fern 74, *75*
Hawaii 142, 143
hawks 101, 128, 129
hawthorn/haws *83*, 115
hay fever 80
hazel 80, *80*, 83
hearing 107, 118
hedgehogs 54, *54*, 130, 146
herbivores 94, 128, 130
    parasites of 112
hermit crabs 112, *112*, 144
herons 47, *47*
herring *141*
hibernation 68
high tide zone 144
hippopotamuses 63, 122, *122*
'hitch-hiking' animals 112
Holarctic region 123, 148
Holocene epoch 89, 95
Homo sapiens see human beings

honey creepers 142, *143*
honey fungus 15
hooved mammals 62–3, *63*, 94, 136
    posture 106
hornbills *137*
horses (*Equus*) 62, *62*
    evolution of 88, 94
horsetails 75, *75*, 91
housefly, head of *27*
house martins 147
houses, animals invading 147
hoverflies 26, *26*, 110, 111
human beings (*Homo sapiens*) 57, 95
    ancestors of 95, 96
    parasites of 20
    and wildlife 150–5
humming-birds *47*, *121*
hydras 18, *18*, 19
hyenas *64*, 133
hyraxes 61, *61*

I
ibex *127*
ice ages 87, 95, 148
Iceland 142
ichthyosaurs 92, 93, 96
Ichthyostega 91
iguanas 45, *106*, 142, 143
index fossils 87, 96
    see also ammonites
Indricotherium 94, *94*
innkeeper worm 112
insects 24, 26–9, 115, 129, 136
    body, parts of 27
    castes 29
    flight 28, 104
    with larvae (*Endopterygota*) 26
    legs 27, 106
    mouthparts 27
    with nymphs (*Exopterygota*) 26
    pollination by 81, *81*
    social 29
    winged/wingless 26
introduced animals 143
invertebrates *see* backbones, animals without
irises 78, *78*
islands 142–3, 152
isopods 25
ivory trade 153, *153*

J
jackals 64, 133
jaguar 64, 136
jaws 39
jays 129, *129*, *130*, 131
jellyfish 18–19, *19*, 110, 140
jerboas (desert rats) 58, *135*
jet propulsion 23, 105
Joshua trees *134*
Jurassic period 89, 92–3

K
kangaroos 53, *53*
kelp (oarweed) 71, *71*
kestrel *104*, 147
kingfishers 46, *47*
koala 53, *123*
Komodo dragon *142*, 143
kookaburra 48, *48*, *123*
Krakatoa 142
krill 67, 125
kudu 133

L
lacertids *see* lizards
lacewings 26
ladybirds *27*, 146
lamp shells 21
lampreys 37, *37*, 38, 115
lancelets 36, *36*, 37, 102
langurs 56
larches 76, *76*, 114, 128
largest animals/plants *see* whales;

INDEX

redwoods; wellingtonias
larvae 26, 138
leafy seadragon *109*
leeches 21, 138
legs/feet 106
lemmings 58, 101, 127, *127*, 128
lemurs 56, *56*
leopard 64, *127*
lianas 136, 148
lice 25, 26
lichens 114, *114*, *126*, 129
light, response to *see* vision
lights, fish carrying 41, 140
limpets 22, *22*, 144
ling *41*
lion 64, *100*, 109, 133
    mountain (cougars/pumas) 127, 131, 132
liver flukes 20, 21
liverworts 72, *72-3*
living things, characteristics 8-9
lizards (lacertids) 44, 45, *45*, 92, *123*, 135
    see also iguanas
llama 63, *63*, *123*, 132
lobefins 40, *40*
lobelias *126*
lobsters 25, *25*
lugworms 21, *21*, 144
lungfish 40, *40*, 139
lungs *see* respiration
lynx 127, 128, 131

M

macaques 56, 136
macaws *121*, 136
mackerel *41*
magnetism, navigation by 117
maidenhair tree 77, *77*
mallard wing *105*
mammals 50-9, 81, 128
    body heat control 50
    defined 50
    egg-laying 52, 53
    first 92
    insect-eating 54
    legs 106
    migration 116
    pouched (marsupials) 53, 81, *123*, 123
    prehistoric 92, 94-5, 96
    sea 140
mammoths 95, *95*
    preserved 87
mandrills 56, *56*
mangabey *137*
mantises 26, 27, *27*, 109
marabou stork 133, *133*
marine *see* sea
marmots 58, 132
marram grass 144, *145*
marsupials (pouched mammals) 53, 81, *123*, 123
martens 65, *131*
Mauritius 142, *143*
mayflies 26, *31*, *139*
meat-eaters *see* carnivores
medusas 18
meercats 65
Megalosaurus (dinosaur) 92
membranes 16
mesosaurs 92, 96
mesozoans 13
Mesozoic era 92-3
metamorphosis (change of form) 26
    see also frogs; toads
meteorites 9
mice 58, 130, 131, 146
    harvest 58
migration 116-17, 118
mildew 15
milk 51, 53
millipedes 24, *24*
mimicry 118
mink 65, 128

Miocene epoch 88, 89, 95
mistletoe 83, 115, *115*
mites 30, *30*, 112
mitochondria 9, *9*, 10, 16
molecules, organic 9
moles 54, *54*
    marsupial 53
molluscs (*Mollusca*) 22-3, 34, 115, 138, 140
    bivalves 23, 102, 144
    movement 103
mongooses 65, 133, *133*
monkeys 56, 56-7, 120, 136
monocotyledons 78, *78*
monotremes 52, 53
moose 128
moss animals 34, 138
mosses 72-3, *72*, *73*, *126*, 130, 136
    generation alternation 73
moths, 26, *27*, 28, 107, *107*, 109, 110, 111, *111*
moulds 14
moults, insect 26
mountainous regions/tundra 120, *126*, 126-7
movement, animal 8, 102-3
Mucor (pin mould) 14
mud-dwellers 23, 144
mussels 23, *23*, 144, *144*
mustelids 65
mycelium 14, 15
myriapods 24

N

narwhal 66, 124, *124*
natural selection 88
nautiloids *90*
nautilus 23, 34
navigational skills 117
Neanderthal man 95, 96
Nearctic region *122*, 123, 148
nectar 81, 84
nematode worms 20, 125
neon tetra *138*
Neopilina 23, 34
Neotropical region *122*, 123, 148
nervous systems 16
nests, birds' 49
New World 68
newts 42, *42*, 139
nitrogen 79
North America (Nearctic region)
    birds *130*, 131
    butterflies 116
    deserts 134
    forests 130
    grasslands 132
    mammals *130*, 131, 132
notochords 36, 40
numbat 53, *123*
nymphs 138

O

oceans *see* seas
ocelots 64, *64*, 136
octopus 23, *23*, 110
okapis 136, *137*
Old World 68
    see also Africa; Asia; Europe
Oligocene epoch 88, 89, 94
opossums 53, *53*, 128
opuntia 134
orang-utans 57, *57*, 136
orca 67
orchid 78, *78*, 82
Ordovician period 89, 90
Oriental region *122*, 148
origin of life 9
oryx *154*, 155
ostrich 46, *48*, 133
otters 65, *138*
ovaries, flower 82, 84
oviparous/ovoviviparous animals 68
owls 46, 128, *129*, 131

    burrowing *135*
    great horned *129*
    snowy 101, *127*
    tawny *107*
oxen, musk 127, *127*
oxpecker 112, *112*, 133
oxygen 8, 9, 22, 29, 40, 51, 98
    see also photosynthesis; respiration
oystercatcher *49*
oysters 23, *23*

P

paca *138*
Palaearctic region *122*, 123, 148
Palaeocene epoch 89, 94
palaeontology *see* fossils; geology
Palaeozoic era 90-1
palisade cells *98*
palm trees 78, *78*
pampas (grassland) 132, 148
pandas 65
Pandorina 12, *12*
Pangaea 148
pangolins (scalytails) 60, *60*, 137
Paramecium 11, 102, *102*, 103
parasites 16, 20, 114, 115, 118
    barnacles 25
    fungi 14, 15
    plants 118
    sheep liver flukes 21
    worms 20
parasitoids 118
parrots 46, 48, 136
'partnerships' 112-3
Passeriformes 46
pebble plants *134*
pelicans 46, *47*
pencil fish *138*
penguins 46, 47, 105, 125
    Adélie 125
    emperor 125, *125*
    rockhopper *125*
    swimming skills 105
Penicillium/penicillin 15
penny bun *15*
peregrine falcon *46*, 47, 127, *127*
Permian period 87, 89, 91, 92
pheasants 104
phloem cells *98*
Pholidota (anteaters) 60
photosynthesis 9, 10, 11, 16, 70, 71, 98, *98*, 130
piddock 23, 144
pigs/wild boars 20, 63, 130
pig-deer 63
pigeons 46, 117, *117*, 147
pike *100*, 139
pill bugs 25
pin mould (*Mucor*) 14, *14*
pinnae/pinnules 74
pines 76, *76*, 77, 114, 128
pipits 48, 116
piranha *138*
placentas 51, *51*
    placental animals 68
plankton/zooplankton 68, 125, 141
    followers of 117, 140
plants
    adapted to cold 95
    animal-like 71
    animals eating *see* herbivores
    definition of 70
    first land 98
    food production in *see* photosynthesis
    living with fungi 114
    types/parts of 84
Plasmodium 11
platypus 52, *52*
Pleistocene epoch 88, 89, 95
plesiosaurs 93, 96
Pleuracanthus 91
Pleurococcus 70, *70*
Pliocene epoch 88, 89, 95

plover, golden 116
poisons 30, 110, 118
polar bears 124, *124*
polar regions *see* Arctic; Antarctic
pollination 79, 80-1, 82
    by animals 81, 113
    of conifers 76
    of flowers 79
pollution, environmental 151, 152
polyps 18-19
ponds *155*
poppies 82, *82*, 126
population swings, animal 100
porcupines 58, *121*, 128, *129*, 136
Portuguese man o' war 19, *19*
possums *see* opossums
postures, feet/legs 106
pottos 137
prairies (grasslands) 120, 132, 148
prairie dogs 58, *59*, 120
Pre-Cambrian period 89, 90
predators 131, 133
    see also birds of prey; carnivores
prehistoric life 75, 90-5, 138
    see also coal; fossils
prey, catching/subduing (predation) 108, 110
    see also predators
primates 56-7, 94
    see also apes; chimpanzees; gorillas; humans; monkeys
primrose 80, *80*
Proboscidea see elephants
proboscis worm *20*
pronghorns *120*, 132
prosimians 56
protecting wildlife *see* conservation
proteins 16
Protista (fungi) 14
protozoans (single-celled organisms) 9, 11, *11*, 100, 102, 115, 125, 138
    and digestion of wood 100
    parasitic 115
ptarmigan 127, *127*
Pteranodon 93, *93*
pteridophytes 75
pterodactyls 93, *93*
pterosaurs 92, 93
puffballs 14, *15*
puma *see* lion, mountain
pupae 26
pythons 45

Q

Quaternary period 89, 95
    see also Holocene; Pleistocene
queen insects 29
quelea 133
quillworts 75, *75*

R

rabbits 59, *130*, 132
raccoons 64, 65, *130*, 131
radiolarians 11, 16
Rafflesia 81
ragworms 21, *21*, 144
ragwort 79
rails 143, *143*
rain 132, 133
rainforests 120, 121, 136-7, 148, 150, *151*
    Amazon 121, *121*
    destruction of 137
    layers making up 136
rats 58
    desert 58, *135*
rattlesnake *135*
raven *127*
rays 39, *39*, 105, 110, 141
razor shells 23, 144, *144*
redstart *131*
redwoods 77
regeneration 20
reindeer 95, 123, 127, 129

INDEX

reproduction 8, 70, 84
   algae 70
   birds 49, 115
   conifers 76–7
   ferns 74–5
   flatworms 20
   flowering plants 78–83
   frogs/toads 43
   fungi 14
   insects 26–9
   liverworts/mosses 73
   mammals 51
   marsupials 53
   polyps/coelenterates 18–19
   reptiles 44–5, 46, 50
   prehistoric 91, 92–3, 96
respiration/breathing 8, 16
   frogs 43
   insects 29
   invertebrates 29
rhinoceroses 62, *62*, 133, 136
   prehistoric 87, 94, 95
rhizomes 74
Rhizomnium punctatum 73
RNA (Ribonucleic acid) 16
rock types 96
   seashore rock pools 144
   see also fossils
rodents 58, 81, 94, 128
roses, wild *79*
rosy tetra *138*
rotifers 34
roundworms 20, 115
ruminants 63
running/walking 106
rust (fungus) 14

S
Sacculina 25
saguaros *134*
salamanders 42
salmon 41, 117, *117*, 139
   migration 116, 117
sand dunes 144
sand hoppers 25
sandstone, desert 86
Sargasso Sea 41, 71, 117
Sargassum (seaweed) 71
sargassum fish 109
savannah (grasslands) 116, 133, 148
saxifrage *126*
Scalesia 143
scallops 23, 105, *105*
scalytails (pangolins) 60, *60*, 137
scorpions 30, *30*, 110
scrub, tropical 121
scurvygrass 144
seas 140–1, *141*
   migration in the 117
   origin of life/early life in the 90–94
sea anemones *18*, 18–19, 110, 112, *112*, 144
sea butterflies 105
sea couch 144
sea cows (*Sirenia*) 66
sea cucumber *33*, 33
sea firs 18, 19
sea horses *41*
sea lamprey 37
sea lavender 144, *145*
sea lettuce (*Ulva*) 70
sea lilies 33, 102, *141*
sea lions 65
seals 65, 125, *125*, *141*
sea molluscs 22
sea mouse *21*
sea scorpions 90
seashore, animals/plants of the 144–145
sea snails 22
sea spiders 24
sea squirts (tunicates) 36, *36*, 37, *37*, 102, 144
sea urchins 32, 33, *33*, 144
seaweeds 71, *71*

sea worms, 21, 102
secretary bird 47, 133
sedimentary rocks 86
   see also fossils
seed-eaters 129
seeds/fruits, dispersal 76–7, 82–3, 84
self-pollination 79
   precautions against 80
senecio, giant *126*
senses of living things 8, 107
   'extra' 107
serval 64, 133
Seychelles 142, 143
shade-tolerant plants 130
shaggy ink cap 15
sharks 38, 38–9, 51, 117, *141*
   blue *38*, 117
   teeth *38*
sheep 63, 127
   parasites of 20, 21
shelducks 145
shells, animals with 22–3
   brachiopods 34
   earliest 90
   fossilization *86*
ship worms 23
shrews 54, 56, *122*, 127, *130*
shrimps 25, 138, 144
shrubs 84, 129, 130, 136
Silurian period 89, 90, 91
single-celled organisms *see* protozoans
skates 39
skeletons 38, 40, 68
   animals with outer 24–34
skinks 45, *135*
skunks 65, 131
sloths 60, *60*, 136
slugs 22
smell/taste 107
snails 22, 130
   water snails 21, 22, *22*
snakes 44, 45, 68, 109, 110
   coral, true/false 111, *111*
   green tree *45*
   movement of 45, 103
soil, earthworms and 21
solitaire 143
South America 53, 58, 123, 134
   pampas (grasslands) 132
   rainforest 136, 137
   see also Amazon
sparrows 46, 147
sparrowhawks 104, 131
spawn 68
spiders 24, 30–1, *30*, 31, 34, 109, 110
   black widows 31
   catching prey *30*, 31
   garden *30*, 31
   spitting 108
   trapdoor 30, 108, *108*
spiny-skinned animals (echinoderms) 32–3, 90, 140
Spirogyra 70, *70*
sponges 13, *13*, 90, 102, 138, 140
spores/sporophytes 14, 73, 74, *74*, 75, 84
sporozoans 11
spruces 76, 114, 128
squids 23, *23*, 110, 124, 125, 140
   swimming method 105
squirrels 58, *83*, *83*, 128, 130, 132
   ground 127
stamens 79, *80*, 84
starfish 32, *32*
starlings 46, 48
starry houndshark 39
Stegosaurus 92, *92*
Stentor 11, 102
steppes (grasslands) 132, *132*, 148
stick insects 26, *109*
sticklebacks 139
stigmas 79, *80*, *80*, 84
stoats 65, *131*
stone flies 26
storks *122*, 133, *133*, 147, *147*

stromalites 9, *9*
sturgeons 40, *40*
Styracosaurus 92
succulents 148
   see also cacti
sugars, plant 98
sunbirds 81
sunfish *40*
sunlight, energy from 98
sun-stars 91
survival of the fittest 88
susliks 132
swallows 46, 48, 104, 116
swamp forests 91
swifts 46, *46*, 48, 104, 147
   wings 105
sycamore seeds 82, *82*
symbiotic relationships 15, 113, 114
   see also associations

T
tadpoles 43, *43*
tamarins 56, 136
taming nature 150
   see also crops; destruction; domestic animals; farming; human beings
tanagers *130*, 131
tapeworms 20, *20*
tapirs 62, *62*
tar pits 87, 96
Tasmanian devils 53, *53*
teeth *38*, 51, 60
teleosts 41
termites 26, 29
   digestive system 100
terns 116, 117
Tertiary period 89, 94–5
   see also Eocene; Miocene; Oligocene; Palaeocene; Pliocene
thecodonts 96
thistles *79*, 82, *82*
thong weed 71
thrift 145
thrips 26
thrushes 46, 48, 144
ticks 30
tiger 64, *64*, 109, 136, 155
tiger barbs *41*
tillodonts 94, 96
tits 48, 129, 131, 146
toads 42–3, *42*, 43, 110, 135, *139*
toadstools 14, *15*
toothworts 115
topshells 22, 144
tortoises 44, 68, 143
   giant *44*, 142
toucans *121*, 136
touch, sense of 107, 118
touracos 137
towns/gardens, animals/birds in 146–7
trees
   coniferous 76–7, 118, 120, 121, 128–9
   prehistoric 91
   see also pines
   deciduous 120, 121, 130–1, 148
   forests/woodlands 74,114,128–131
   oldest/largest 77
   water requirements 132
   see also rainforests
Triassic period 89, 92
trilobites 87, 90, *90*, 91, 96
tripod fish 140, *141*
tropical regions 41, 148
   see also Africa; rainforests
tuatara 44
Tubulidentata (aardvarks) 60, *60*
tundra 120, 121, *126*, 126–7, 148
   and mountains *126*, 126–7
tunicates *see* sea squirts
turbot *41*
turtles 44, *44*, 92, 105
   migration 117

tusk shells 23, 34
Tyrannosaurus rex 92

U
ungulates *see* hooved mammals

V
vacuoles 10
vampire bats 55
veld (grasslands) 132, 148
Venus flytrap 79, *79*
vertebrates *see* backbones, animals with
viperfish 140
viruses 115
   see also bacteria
viscacha 132
vision/response to light 57, 64, 107, 118
viverrids 65
viviparous animals 68
volcanic explosions 142
voles 58, 130, 131
Volvox 12, *12*
vultures 47, 133

W
walking/running 106
walrus 124, *124*
warblers 46, 48, 116, 129, 131
   blackcaps *131*
warning coloration 41, 110, 111, 118
warthog 63, *63*, 133
wasps 26, 29, 111, 115
water beetles 105, 138, *139*
water boatman *139*
water buffaloes 63
water fleas 25, 138
water lilies, giant *138*
water spider 31, *31*
water-storing plants 134
   see also succulents
waxwing 129
weasels 65, *65*, 127
weaver birds 49, *49*, 133
webs, spiders' 30, 31
wellingtonia 77
Welwitschia plant 77, *134*
wentletrap 22
whales 66–7, *67*, 94, 116, 124
   swimming method 105
   toothed 66, *67*
   whalebone (baleen) 67, *67*, 117, *141*
whale sharks 38
wheat 150
whelks 22
whistling thorns and ants 113, *113*
wildebeest *122*, 133
willows 80, 115, 128
   dwarf *126*
wind dispersal of seeds 82
wind pollination 80
winged fruits 82
wings, birds' 47, 104, *104*, 105
wolf spiders 31
wolverines 65, 128
wolves 64, *106*, 123, 127, 128, 131, 132
wombat 53, *123*
wombs (uteri) 51, *51*
woodlands/forest *see* trees
woodlice 25
woodpeckers 46, 48, 129, 131, *131*
worms 20–22, *20*, 21, 24, 141, 144
   see also annelid worms; earthworms

Y
yeasts 15, 16
yews 77, *77*
young, mammals' care of 51
yucca flowers/moths 113, *113*

Z
zebras 62, 133
zoogeographical regions 122, 122–3, 148
zooplankton 68